The Quest
for God & the
Good Life

The Quest for God & the Good Life

LONERGAN'S THEOLOGICAL ANTHROPOLOGY

Mark T. Miller

The Catholic University of America Press
Washington, D.C.

Library of Congress Cataloging-in-Publication Data

Miller, Mark T.

The quest for God and the good life : Lonergan's anthropology / Mark T.
Miller.

pages cm

Includes bibliographical references and index.

ISBN 978-0-8132-2139-7 (pbk. : alk. paper)

1. Theological anthropology—Catholic Church.   2. Catholic Church—
Doctrines.   3. Lonergan, Bernard J. F.   I. Title.

BT701.3M56 2013

233—dc23

2012045869

CONTENTS

ACKNOWLEDGMENTS

Like all good things for which one person takes credit, this book has been a team effort. When I reflect on the many people without whom I could not have completed this work, I am tempted to thank the communion of saints, living and dead, united with God. Due to our interconnectedness, only gratitude so expansive would do justice to the great breadth of assistance I have received.

Still, there are those whose depth of help and influence merits at least a special mention: Rev. Raymond Kemp, Otto Hentz, SJ, James Walsh, SJ, Fred and Sue Lawrence, M. Shawn Copeland, Charles Hefling, Stephen Brown, Louis Roy, OP, Patrick Byrne, Joseph Flanagan, SJ, Sr. Lorraine Forster, Gasper LoBiondo, SJ, Grant Kaplan, Jeremy Wilkins, Rene Sanchez, Christian Krokus, Joseph Mudd, Chris Jacobs-Vandergeer, Kevin Vander Schel, Suzanne Hevelone, Chris Lee, Kerry Cronin, Bob Doran, SJ, Gilles Mongeau, SJ, Peter Bisson, SJ, Robin Koning, SJ, Rev. John Foster, Joseph Everson, MM, Msgr. Richard Liddy, Monica Olsson, the Oblates of St. Francis de Sales, the Woodstock fellows, my friends and colleagues at the University of San Francisco (particularly my colleagues in the department and the students in two Lonergan seminars who commented on a draft of this work), the Bradley Foundation and the Fund for Theological Education (for funded fellowships), the University of Toronto Press (for allowing the reproduction of a chart in chapter 4), CUA Press editors James Kruggel, Theresa Walker, and Aldene Fredenburg, my siblings, aunts, uncles, cousins, nephews, my wise, loving parents, and my patient, dedicated wife, Eveline.

INTRODUCTION

My favorite chapter of Bernard Lonergan's *Method in Theology* begins with this wonderful line: "The facts of good and evil, of progress and decline, raise questions about the character of our universe."[1]

This book, like Lonergan's own works, is written for those who care about such questions. It is written for those who have observed our world and celebrate what is good in it while lamenting what is not so good. It is written for those who love the world enough to be willing to work for its welfare, those willing to build themselves up in order to promote progress and reverse decline. More particularly, and perhaps more importantly, it is written for those who know that in order to make good choices, ones that will do more good than harm, this work must be directed by understanding—the kind of understanding that comes from serious contemplation of the deepest, most universal questions raised by the problems of human living: such questions as, Why is there so much violence and suffering in the world? Why do we hurt ourselves and each other? Why do we continue to do what we know is wrong? How can we stop this? How can we heal the damage? How can we start to live our lives in a way that promotes not mere survival, but full flourishing for everyone and everything? Are such lives possible? If so, what would make them possible? What truly makes life, or anything, "good"? Who decides? How can we know?

Answering such questions is not easy. In fact, it may be that no one knows, or has ever known, the answers to such questions. Certainly this little book will not answer them, not completely or

---

1. Bernard Lonergan, *Method in Theology* (Toronto: University of Toronto Press, 1994), 101.

perfectly. But I believe it is important that we try to answer them. For no matter what our answers are—even if we answer that there is no answer—we all live by our answers. And while there may be no perfect answers to these questions, I believe we can make progress. We can learn. We can grow. We can improve our lives and the lives of each other. Finally, I believe that even if we do so at different times, to different degrees, and from different contexts, we all care about our world, and we all ask ourselves these questions.

I came to these questions in part through the work of my parents. My father directed Catholic Charities, and my mother was an elementary school teacher. They brought their work home, hosting foreign refugees, foster children, and others. And they brought my siblings and me to their work, to volunteer at adoption agencies, homeless shelters, and more. Personal friendships and conflicts with my siblings or schoolmates drove me continually to wonder about the best way to live and the right way to know. Community issues such as the push to build a nuclear waste dump in Nevada, national debates about cutting various social services, and international events from the People Power Revolution in the Philippines to the famines in Africa were just as challenging.

In the early 1990s, when I was finishing high school and applying to college, my love for the world, my desire to help make it better, and my interest in life's deeper questions led me to study international relations. It was the broadest major I could imagine, the one that promised to teach me the most about the world. It would encompass history, economics, languages, culture, political science, philosophy, religion, and (since I would be attending a Catholic university) theology.

The overarching questions of our international relations program were about conflict: How was it caused? How could it be stopped? How could it be prevented? Conflict filled the pages of our textbooks, our newspapers, and our lives. Despite this, we students grew up thinking the world was mostly at peace. Was not World War I "the war to end all wars"? Were not biases like racism and sexism overcome in the Civil Rights movements of the 1960s? Slowly, through experience and study, we came to realize that while there has been progress, conflict and bias still pervade our world.

This fact was writ large and made inescapable by the horror of the Rwandan genocide in the spring of 1994, my sophomore year in college. I was taking four courses that promised to offer some insight into the Rwandan situation: one on contemporary foreign governments, another about how our current international borders had been formed, and two on the history of Africa. But my fifth class provided the greatest understanding of bias and conflict in general and of the Rwandan genocide in particular. It was a theology course called "Struggle and Transcendence."

Taught not by a doctor of theology, but by an experienced pastor, the Reverend Raymond B. Kemp, the course was named after the African American struggle and Bernard Lonergan's transcendental method. More than any thinker I had encountered in any discipline, Lonergan seemed to offer the most helpful set of tools for addressing and improving the human condition. Others I had read seemed to value various pieces of human reality: the individual or society, permanence or change, objectivity or subjectivity, the heart or the mind, science or revelation, experience or authority, love or power. Lonergan, on the other hand, seemed to value the whole. Incredibly, to me at least, he was also able to take the further step of relating the many pieces of this whole into a flexible, dynamic order.

I was struck in particular by how Lonergan made unrestricted love, the love that only God can give, both the fulfillment of natural human desire and the foundation for genuine human living. At times I found Lonergan's work so exciting that I could not sit still. I would read a page or two and then have to get up and walk around, usually in search of some friend with whom I could share what I had just learned.

In the years after taking Fr. Kemp's class, while studying and teaching at various places in the U.S., Germany, and the Philippines, I was sad to learn that while Lonergan is highly admired among theologically educated Catholics, his work is often viewed as frustratingly inaccessible. Those who teach Lonergan and those who wish to learn from him still discuss how best to approach his thought.

This book is a modest attempt to meet the need for a clear and basic, yet broad and solid introduction to Lonergan's thought.[2] Its approach will be theological, and its focus will be on humanity. Thus this book is about Lonergan's theological anthropology—in other words, his reflection on the human condition in light of humanity's relationship to God. It does not attempt in any way to be a comprehensive summary of Lonergan's formidable body of work on philosophy and theology. Such an undertaking would require perhaps a volume each on his cognitive theory, metaphysics, ethics, Trinitarian theology, Christology, pneumatology, ecclesiology, and soteriology. Its goal is humble—simply to provide an introduction to Lonergan's anthropology from a theological perspective.

We (the reader and I, in conversation) shall approach his theological anthropology through three main categories: progress, decline, and redemption. These three general categories account for human achievement, human failure, and divine assistance. They constitute Lonergan's translation of the traditional categories of nature, sin, and grace into a broader, historical context that better accounts for changes over time.

Lonergan calls progress, decline, and redemption together a "tripolar dialectic of history."[3] It was an early fruit of his studies, arising from the urgent questions about human living that he and others faced in the late 1930s during a global economic depression that followed one world war and led up to another. In this context Lonergan strove to figure out the underlying causes of such catastrophic events and what human beings might do, with God's help, to prevent them from happening again.[4]

2. As an introduction it is intended as a gateway to studying Lonergan's own writings, not as a replacement for them. Consequently there will be many footnotes directing the reader to further reading in Lonergan's texts or to works by other scholars of his thought. Several footnotes will explain his thought directly, and some will consider minor controversies among his interpreters.

3. Lonergan, *Insight: A Study of Human Understanding*, edited by Frederick Crowe and Robert Doran (Toronto: University of Toronto Press, 1992), 749. Lonergan mentions how he shifted from a dualist or bipolar way of thinking about good and evil when he distinguished between the created goodness of nature and the supernatural goodness of grace. Thus to the goodness of progress and the evils of decline he added redemption to make for a tripolar dialectic. He does not comment on the oddity of a dialectic with more than two principles. However, previously in *Insight*, on page 242, he discusses many different definitions of dialectic. For Plato it is philosophical dialogue contrasted with eristic (argumentative) or specious (superficial) reasoning. For Aristotle it is a process of reviewing opinions to discover the truth. Only in Hegel and Marx is it an opposition of two poles to produce a third. Lonergan's own definition is "a concrete unfolding of linked but opposed principles of change."

4. See Michael Shute, *The Origins of Lonergan's Notion of the Dialectic of History* (Lantham, Md.:

At the time, liberalism and Marxism were the world's most influential social theories. Lonergan thought that underlying the two economic systems were competing philosophies of history: the former attributed progress to individual competition, and the latter credited it to class struggle. Lonergan acknowledged some good in both systems; however, he believed that they were inadequate for fostering long-term peace and justice, since they failed to acknowledge the negative influence on history of the sinful egoism of individuals[5] or groups,[6] as well as the positive influence of divine grace.[7]

Lonergan sought a comprehensive philosophy of history that would do justice to these elements in order to ground an authentic "Christian praxis" and to promote progress on a global level.[8] In 1937 or 1938 he had a breakthrough when he adopted an analogy from Newton's analysis of the motion of planets.[9] The advantage of Newton's analysis was that it explained the complex movement of a concrete, dynamic process.[10] And human history, no less than the motions of the planets, is a complex, concrete, and dynamic process.

University Press of America, 1993), and William A. Mathews, *Lonergan's Quest: A Study of Desire in the Authoring of Insight* (Toronto: University of Toronto Press, 2005).

5. Liberalism, according to Lonergan, is right to aim for progress, but it places too much faith in individual egoism, since it holds that unfettered, competitive self-interest can produce automatic progress. Lonergan warns that in a capitalist context, "enlightened self-interest easily comes to mean really profitable self-interest"; Lonergan, "Questionnaire on Philosophy: Response," in *Philosophical and Theological Papers, 1965–1980* (Toronto: University of Toronto Press, 2004), 368; cf. *Insight*, 260, 710–11; Shute, *Origins*, 6–7).

6. Marxism, Lonergan thought, correctly criticized the oppression of the working class, but it was flawed in its belief that the group egoism of a revolutionary proletariat and the resulting violent class conflict would accelerate progress and produce an ideal classless and stateless society; see *Insight*, 260, 265–66; Lonergan, "Questionnaire: Response," 366–70.

7. As early as 1933 or 1934 Lonergan wrote, "[T]he hope of the future lies in a philosophic presentation of the supernatural concept of social order" in an unpublished essay called "The Philosophy of History," 117, as quoted by Shute, *Origins*, 59, ft. 70.

8. "Questionnaire: Response," 370. Lonergan follows Aristotle in contrasting *praxis* and *poesis*, doing and making, conduct and product. Praxis is a kind of practice that includes deliberation, choice, and conduct that falls "under the guidance of the practical wisdom that Aristotle named *phronesis* and Aquinas named *prudentia*." In this Lonergan would include much of the praxis of liberation theology, particularly its nonviolent efforts; Lonergan, "Theology and Praxis," in *A Third Collection: Papers by Bernard J. F. Lonergan, S.J.* (New York: Paulist Press, 1985), 184.

9. Lonergan, "Insight Revisited," in *A Second Collection: Papers by Bernard J. F. Lonergan, S.J.*, edited by William Ryan and Bernard Tyrrell (Toronto: University of Toronto Press, 1996), 271.

10. For Lonergan, what is concrete is real or actual. But it is not necessarily physical. A mother's love for her child, for example, is concrete in the sense that Lonergan uses the term. Love in

Newton explained the actual, irregular ellipses of each planet's motion by abstracting three distinct forces. He conceived of each of these forces as moving in straight lines, or "vectors." The three Newtonian vectors are: (1) the forward momentum or inertia of moving bodies, (2) the pull of gravity between the sun and each planet, and (3) the pull of gravity among planets. Together these vectors result in the irregular ellipses in which the planets actually move. Since the three vectors accounted for the differences in planetary motion, they are also called "differentials."[11] Individually, none of the three vectors or differentials corresponds to the actual, elliptical movement of the planets. But together, in a unified theory, they explain the concrete motion of the planets in a way that is reasonably accurate and empirically verifiable.

Since human history too is a complex motion, Lonergan appropriated Newton's vector or differential analysis to study it. As mentioned above, Lonergan's philosophy of history is comprised of three vectors or differentials: progress, decline, and redemption. Each differential is an abstraction of a particular aspect of the complex reality that is human history. Taken individually none of them provides an accurate account of human history in its entirety, because human history is never in a pure state of nature, a pure state of sin, or a pure state of grace. But taken together as a dynamic whole, progress, decline, and redemption provide a full and highly verifiable framework for understanding and explaining human history—in other words, for a theological anthropology that accounts for changes over time.[12]

Progress is the first vector, and it is driven by natural forces. Nature, for Lonergan, is everything that is not God—everything that God has created. It is an intricate, interdependent order. And it is dynamic in that existing things set the conditions for the pos-

---

general may be abstract, but this particular mother's love for her child is concrete, since it is real or actual.

11. Lonergan discusses the role of differentials in a mathematical context in *Insight*, 42, 62–64. In Lonergan, *Topics in Education* (Toronto: University of Toronto Press, 1993), 27, he writes simply, "What makes the difference in the human good at different times we call a differential."

12. For more background information on Lonergan's development of the dialectic of history, see Shute, *Origins*; Richard M. Liddy, *Transforming Light: Intellectual Conversion in the Early Lonergan* (Collegeville, Minn.: The Liturgical Press, 1993), 84–87; and Mathews, *Lonergan's Quest*, 88–92.

sibility of new, higher, more complicated things to emerge. Human beings are a relatively new, higher, more complicated development. We are part of creation and are still subject to natural laws. But more than any other part of creation, we can discover the workings of nature and with this knowledge affect the direction in which nature unfolds.

We have this ability due to our tremendous capacities to experience, to question, to understand, to judge, to decide, and to act. And while some theories hold that human nature is inherently sinful, evil, and selfish, Lonergan believes that human nature is good and directed toward the other—not necessarily in all of its actions, but in its fundamental orientation. The cause of this orientation is a good, natural desire for sense stimulation, understanding, factual knowledge, moral responsibility, and love. This desire is one, because ultimately it is a desire for God. All authentic human activities involve a fidelity to this good, natural desire. Lonergan situates human individuals more or less operating in accord with their good, natural desire within human communities and human history. Authentic individual operation and authentic social cooperation drive progress, the topic of the first part of this book.

The second part examines the fact that while human individuals, communities, and histories can be authentic in their activities, they can also be inauthentic. Such inauthenticity is sin. It causes and is caused by various biases, which are distortions of human beings' good, natural desire. Sin and bias have negative consequences on human individuals, on human societies, and on the world as a whole. Over time such consequences accumulate and become progressively worse. Sin, in other words, causes decline.

But thankfully, the concrete human situation is a product not simply of nature and sin, of progress and decline, but also of God's grace, which brings redemption. To human persons and a world marked by sin, God has given us supernatural gifts, most notably an unrestricted, redeeming love. This love bears fruit in a conversion that heals us from the damaging effects of sin and elevates us to the supernatural virtues of faith, hope, and charity. Although it is intensely personal, redemption is not merely an individual affair. It takes place in and through a graced community, the church, the Body of Christ. Its goal is the total salvation of all humankind throughout history. This is the subject of our third and final part.

Thus to introduce Lonergan's theological anthropology we shall consider the traditional categories of nature, sin, and grace in Lonergan's own terms of progress, decline, and redemption. Within each chapter we shall proceed from the basic to the complex, from deeply traditional notions to Lonergan's more original contributions, from general metaphysical principles to historical operations by individual persons in their communities and across space and time.

Because an understanding of nature is fundamental to Catholic theology in general and Lonergan's work in particular, nature, or progress, will provide the beginning and the bulk of our reflection. Building on this part is a part each on sin and grace. While parts 2 and 3 are smaller than part 1, I do not mean to indicate that their topics are less important. But as mentioned earlier, our focus is on Lonergan's anthropology from a theological standpoint. We leave to other works the detailed exposition of other elements of Catholic thought.

Part 1   # Progress

NATURE AS GOOD

1 | The Natural World

Deeply troubled by the Great Depression, two world wars, and modernity's challenges to religion, Bernard Lonergan attempted to do for our age what Thomas Aquinas did for his—that is, to integrate the best of secular and sacred teaching in order to further the ongoing Catholic tradition of using both faith and reason to promote the common good and to participate in God's work of redemption. Echoing centuries of the Catholic tradition's esteem for secular and sacred, or natural and supernatural, forms of learning, Lonergan affirms that "God becomes known to us in two ways: as the ground and end of the material universe; and as the one who speaks to us through Scripture and Tradition. The first manner might found a natural religion. The second adds revealed religion."[1]

For Lonergan an important purpose of God's self-communication, whether revealed through the material universe, scripture, or tradition, is to transform "the aims and purposes, the direction and development of human lives, human societies, human cultures, human history."[2] In light of this purpose, Lonergan views the task of theology as twofold: "to reflect on revelation" and "to mediate God's meaning into the whole of human affairs."[3] This is no easy task—first, because of the tremendous difficulty of coming

1. Lonergan, "Theology in Its New Context," in *A Second Collection*, 61.
2. Lonergan, "Theology in Its New Context," 62.
3. Lonergan, "Theology in Its New Context," 62.

to understand revelation, even in part, and second, because human affairs take place within a multitude of changing cultures that also must be understood by theologians if they are to help mediate God's message through them.

Since divine revelation is primarily stable and human affairs are highly alterable, theologians must be comfortable with both continuity and change. Lonergan explains that while theology must grow and develop in response to changes in the world, "the novelty resides not in a new revelation or a new faith, but in a new cultural context."[4] Given the current cultural context, Lonergan warns and encourages faithful theologians that their work of reflection on and mediation of God's word "is not a small task, but because it is not [small]—in a culture in which God is ignored and there are even theologians to proclaim that God is dead—it is all the more urgent."[5]

The drafting of secular culture for service in promoting Christian revelation is at least as old as Paul's speech at the Areopagus in Athens.[6] But Lonergan's primary role model was Thomas Aquinas, who adopted the best of then-contemporary secular learning, particularly the philosophy of Aristotle, in order to illuminate revealed teachings and teach them to the rest of society.[7] Thomas's influence on Lonergan can hardly be overstated. In fact, Lonergan wrote that he spent over ten years "reaching up to the mind of Aquinas" and then tried "to import his compelling genius to the problems of this later day."[8]

Lonergan took seriously Pope Leo XIII's call in the encyclical *Aeterni Patris* to revive and continue the work of Thomas Aquinas as a part of the larger project of "*novis augere et perficere.*"[9] In following the pope's call, Lonergan studied not only Thomas's and Aristotle's writings, but also modern advances in the natural sci-

---

4. Lonergan, "Theology in Its New Context," 58.

5. Lonergan, "Theology in Its New Context," 62.

6. Acts 17:22–34.

7. Thomas discusses the use of other sciences for advancing theological understanding of revealed mysteries in his *Summa Theologiae* I, q. 1, a. 1.

8. Lonergan, *Insight*, 769–70.

9. "To strengthen and complete the old by aid of the new"; Pope Leo XIII, *Aeterni Patris* 24. The translation is from the Vatican website. Lonergan cites this phrase and the pope's call in *Insight*, 768; cf. Lonergan, "Aquinas Today: Tradition and Innovation," in *A Third Collection*, 35.

ences, economics, history, and psychology. Because of the richness of Lonergan's sources, his theological anthropology is complex. Let us begin with the fundamental category of nature as considered in two contexts: the classical worldview of Thomas and Aristotle and the historical worldview of more contemporary scholars, both of which are often misinterpreted.

Two Views on Nature: Classical and Historical

First, let us distinguish between something that is "classic*al*" and something that is "classic*ist*." The first term is positive, and the second is negative. The second takes a positive element from the first and exaggerates it to the exclusion of other goods. Similarly, to be called "rational" is usually thought to be positive. But to be called "rationalist" is often considered negative, since rationalism exaggerates the value of reason to the exclusion of all other forms of knowing, such as experience or faith. Speaking of faith, to be "faithful" or to have "fidelity" is good, while to value faith to the exclusion of other ways of knowing is to be "fideist," which, for Catholic theology, at least, is not thought to be ideal.[10]

To return to the subject at hand, something is labeled "classical" in the positive sense if it is fundamental, common, and lasting. As Lonergan writes, "The classics ground a tradition. They create the milieu in which they are studied and interpreted. They produce in the reader through the cultural tradition the mentality, the *Vorverstandnis,* from which they will be read, studied, interpreted."[11] As mentioned, Aristotle and Thomas are the authors of some of Lonergan's favorite classics. Their works are classical not only in the sense that they are studied in a way that is fundamental, common, and lasting, but in that the content of these works focuses on what is fundamental, common, and lasting in human society and in the world in general.

An important part of this content is Aristotle's definition of science as true and certain knowledge of things through their univer-

---

10. For a good explanation of the complementarity between faith and reason, see Thomas Aquinas, *Summa contra Gentiles* I, 6–8.
11. Lonergan, *Method*, 161–62.

sal, necessary causes.[12] Things that are universal are the same no matter the time, location, culture, or any other condition. Things that are necessary must be or have to be. In contrast to what is universal and necessary is what is contingent; thus contingent things are not the same always and everywhere. They vary depending on particular circumstances.

It is important to note that for Aristotle, only math and divine things are entirely universal and necessary, so all other disciplines may be called sciences "by courtesy, since they are occupied with matters in which contingency plays a part."[13] Aristotle acknowledges this in his *Nicomachean Ethics*.[14] Thomas Aquinas agrees, and he would add that the existing world order, the one that God chose in infinite wisdom and love, is governed by both necessary and contingent causes.[15]

"Classicism" as a negative way of thinking took something positive in classical thought—namely, the focus on what is fundamental, common, and lasting—and overemphasized it. Against Aristotle's own judgment, classicists applied Aristotle's strict definition of science to all forms of knowing. So instead of sometimes seeking causes that were universal and necessary and sometimes seeking contingent ones, thinkers of all kinds, including philosophers and theologians, began to seek universal and necessary causes, patterns, and laws. Anything else, anything that varied according to time, place, or other conditions, became viewed not as science or any other type of true, objective knowledge, but merely as opinion.

Perhaps the clearest and most influential example of classicism's obsession with absolute, universal, necessary laws is exemplified in

---

12. Aristotle, *Posterior Analytics* I.2.71b 9–16. Lonergan refers to Aristotle's definition in multiple places, such as "Aquinas Today," 41–44; *Insight*, 326, 435; *Method*, 16, 304; and Lonergan, *Topics in Education*, 146–54.

13. W. David Ross, Aristotle's *Prior and Posterior Analytics* (Oxford: Clarendon Press, 1949), 14, cf. 51; Lonergan quotes this in *Method*, 3.

14. "When the subject and the basis of a discussion consist of matters that hold good only as a general rule, but not always, the conclusions reached must be of the same order.... For a well-schooled man is one who searches for that degree of precision in each kind of study that the nature of the subject at hand admits: it is obviously just as foolish to accept arguments of probability from a mathematician as to demand strict demonstrations from an orator"; Aristotle, *Nicomachean Ethics*, translated by Martin Oswald (Upper Saddle, N.J.: Prentice Hall, 1999), I.3.1094b24.

15. Aquinas, *Summa Theologiae* I, q. 22, a. 4.

Immanuel Kant's "categorical imperative."[16] Kant wrote during the period of history most associated with the classicist movement, the Enlightenment, when people "glorified in the achievements of Newton ... and moved towards a materialist, mechanistic determinist interpretation no less of man than of nature."[17] During this period philosophers and theologians reinterpreted classical scholars like Aristotle and Thomas in light of classicist assumptions, leading to what Lonergan calls "decadent" scholasticism.[18]

As part of his effort to follow Pope Leo XIII's call "to strengthen and complete the old by aid of the new," Lonergan's theological anthropology attempts to recover reason from the rationalists as well as the classics of Aristotle and Thomas from the decadence of modern misinterpretations. "Progress" is Lonergan's attempt to recover the classical, abstract, and often static concept of nature and to strengthen it with the insights of more recent advances in natural and human sciences, particularly those of history.[19]

As a transposition of the classical view of nature into a historical framework, Lonergan's notion of progress is by no means a total repudiation or complete elimination of the classical view. It is more a transcendence of that view. "Transcendence" is an absolutely central term in Lonergan's work. Basically, it means "going beyond." One thing can go beyond another in such a way that the first has nothing to do with the second. However, for Lonergan transcendence indicates that a second thing goes beyond a first by lifting the first into a greater and richer context that preserves and fulfills the first's proper features.[20]

16. What is categorical is found in or applies to all categories. It is universal and necessary. So a categorical imperative is a command that must be applied to all categories of human life. Kant developed this idea in his *Groundwork for the Metaphysics of Morals*, trans. James W. Ellington (Indianapolis: Hackett Publishing, 1993).

17. Lonergan, "Theology in Its New Context," 57. More will follow on mechanistic determinism.

18. *Insight*, 278, 624; *Method*, 80.

19. Lonergan once said that his whole work had been to introduce history in particular into theology; see Lonergan, *Curiosity at the Center of One's Life: Statements and Questions of R. Eric O'Connor*, edited by J. Martin O'Hara (Montreal: Thomas More Institute, 1984), 427; see also Frederick E. Crowe, "All My Work Has Been Introducing History into Catholic Theology," in *Lonergan Workshop* 10 (1994): 49–81.

20. This view of transcendence is closely related to the term "sublation" as used by Karl Rahner, the German Jesuit theologian and contemporary of Lonergan; see *Method*, 241; see also Lonergan, "Horizons," in *Philosophical and Theological Papers, 1965–1980*, 23. This was a lecture given at the Thomas More Institute, Montreal, in 1968. During a question-and-answer period that

Thus Lonergan's account of the human person transcends classical thought in that it includes and respects classical definitions of human nature as well as more contemporary ideas about humanity as historical. Human history forms the larger context for the study of human nature, but both are valuable, as Lonergan said at a 1977 address to the American Catholic Philosophical Association: "A contemporary ontology would distinguish between two components in the concrete human reality: on the one hand, a constant human nature; on the other hand, a variable human history. Nature is given man at birth. Historicity is what man makes of man."[21] Both are valid. And both are necessary for a complete understanding of human beings.

Lonergan highly regards Aristotle's classical view of human nature as the *zôon logikon*[22] and the *zôon politikon*,[23] the "logical" or "rational animal" and the "political" or "social animal." As rational and social animals, humans are complex: like all of being, human beings are governed by metaphysical laws; like all of being that is in motion, human beings are governed by physical laws; like all of being in self-motion, or living being, human beings are subject to biological laws; like all sensitive beings in self-motion, or animals, human beings are subject to zoological laws.[24] However, human beings are unique, according to Aristotle's view of human nature, inasmuch as we are rational (we discover the intelligible order of the universe, create social principles in harmony with this order, and live according to them)[25] and social (the good life is lived in community with friends).[26] As rational and social, humans attain their end—that is, happiness, primarily through friendship

---

followed, Lonergan contrasts transcendence in cognitive theory and theories of relationships with an immanence that knows only appearances and leads to relativism and atomistic individualism.

21. Lonergan, "Natural Right and Historical Mindedness," in *A Third Collection*, 170. Lonergan's thought on history was influenced by his reading of Christopher Dawson's *The Age of the Gods* in the early 1930s, and Arnold Toynbee's *A Study of History* in 1940–41; see Richard M. Liddy, *Transforming Light: Intellectual Conversion in the Early Lonergan* (Collegeville, Minn.: The Liturgical Press, 1993), 84; and Mathews, *Lonergan's Quest*, 50–51, 110–11. "Ontology" is the study of being or existence in general.

22. Aristotle, *De Anima* III; *Topics in Education*, 80.

23. Aristotle, *The Politics* I.2.1253a3; Aristotle, *Nicomachean Ethics* I.7.1097b11; *Insight*, 211.

24. Aristotle, *De Anima* II.

25. Aristotle, *Nicomachean Ethics* I.7.1098a4.

26. Aristotle, *Nicomachean Ethics* I and IX.

and *arête*, which is usually translated as "virtue" or "excellence."[27]

Lonergan's view of the human person is to some degree based on these elements of Aristotle's classical conception of human nature: a complex being governed by rules affecting beings in general and, more specifically, an animal that is rational, social, and capable of attaining happiness through virtue and friendship. This forms much of the basis for Lonergan's anthropology insofar as he considers human persons according to their nature or substance. But Lonergan acknowledges that there are limits to this type of thought. To speak of human nature or substance tells only the most basic generalities about an actual, particular person. When Lonergan wishes to emphasize the conscious awareness by which individuals transform themselves and the world, he contrasts the human as "substance" with the human as "subject":

Of the human substance it is true that human nature is always the same; a man is a man whether he is awake or asleep, young or old, sane or crazy, sober or drunk, a genius or a moron, a saint or a sinner. From the viewpoint of substance, those differences are merely accidental. But they are not accidental to the subject, for the subject is not an abstraction; he is a concrete reality, all of him, a being in the luminosity of being.... The being of a subject is becoming.[28]

Consequently, Lonergan believes that any adequate account of humanity, any anthropology that wishes to study humanity in its concreteness, must consider the human being as it "becomes" or develops over time. Such an anthropology must have a substantial historical component. The remainder of this chapter and next few chapters will examine the historical aspects of nature in general and of human nature in particular. They will attempt to explain how human beings work within a global order to grow, to develop, to transcend—in other words, how progress, the first part of Lonergan's theological anthropology, progresses. The rest of this chap-

27. Aristotle, *Nicomachean Ethics* I. In addition to virtue and friendship, Aristotle names other requirements for happiness, including health, some measure of respect from one's peers, a moderate amount of material goods, and friends (including family) who themselves are virtuous, healthy, respected, and enjoy a moderate amount of material goods.

28. Lonergan, "Existenz and Aggiornamento," in *Collection: Papers by Bernard J. F. Lonergan, S.J.*, edited by Frederick Crowe (New York: Herder and Herder, 1967), 241; cf. *Topics in Education*, 79–82; and Lonergan, "Self-Transcendence: Intellectual, Moral, Religious," in *Philosophical and Theological Papers, 1965–1980*, 314.

ter will focus on a fundamental principle of nature that Lonergan calls "emergent probability." Chapter 2 will discuss how through insight and the self-correcting process of learning human beings come to discover the truth. Chapter 3 will examine how learning the truth is part of a larger method of self-transcendence. Chapter 4, the final chapter of this part, situates the operations of self-transcendence within a community cooperating across time and space, hopefully in a way that brings progress.

To provide another perspective on how the next chapters will unfold, a quick note on progress might be helpful here. Lonergan defined it as "a cyclic and cumulative process in which concrete situations give rise to insights, insights to new courses of action, new courses of action to changed situations, and changed situations to still further insights."[29] The following section of this chapter, on emergent probability, will explain what Lonergan means by "concrete situations" and "a cyclical and cumulative process." It will present the global or cosmological context for our later considerations of what is strictly human or anthropological. Chapter 2 focuses on how "concrete situations give rise to insights." Chapter 3, on transcendental method, relates insight to experience, knowledge, choice, and "action." Chapter 4, on the cooperating human community, will discuss how the "concrete situations," the "cyclical and cumulative process," the "rise of insights," and the "courses of action" are all related in a nexus that is social, cultural, and historical.

Emergent Probability: A Dynamic World Order

Human beings are part of a whole. This whole is sometimes called a "world." The world sets the basic conditions and norms for the possibility of human progress.[30] Thus a study of human nature and history, of human being and becoming, must be situated in the larger, more fundamental context of the world's nature and history, its being and becoming. In other words, an anthropology is situated within a cosmology.

---

29. Lonergan, "Questionnaire: Response," in *Philosophical and Theological Papers, 1965–1980*, 366; emphasis added.

30. Humans also have the ability to transform the world, as later chapters will discuss.

Lonergan identifies two ways of doing cosmology: "It may be placed in universal propositions, self-evident truths, naturally known certitudes. On the other hand, it may be placed in nature itself, in nature not as abstractly conceived, but as concretely operating. It is, I believe, the second alternative that has to be envisaged if we are to determine norms in historicity."[31] In this section we seek to answer such questions as: How does the world operate concretely? What are its norms? How do these operations and norms ground human progress?

Determinism, Indeterminism, and Emergent Probability

"Emergent probability" is Lonergan's term for the operation of a world process that sets many of the norms for human life and for human progress. To gain a clearer view of emergent probability, it is helpful to contrast it with an opposed worldview: "mechanistic determinism." Mechanistic determinism is a mistaken, but still common, theory that conceives of the world as a closed, controlled system. Everything important in the world has existed since its beginning, and the relations of all things are predetermined from the beginning of the world. These relations are expressed in unchanging, universal, and necessary laws.

As such, this worldview is a part of the classicist mindset. In a minor part, this view has its roots in Aristotle, who distinguished between necessary and contingent laws and believed that the necessary movements of the heavens caused contingent movements on the earth. It was advanced by Galileo's distinction between secondary causes, which are mere appearance and known by the senses, and primary qualities, which are objective and known mathematically. Descartes, Hobbes, Locke, Berkeley, and Hume argued that abstract classical rules were concrete and thus completed the mechanistic worldview.[32]

Such a worldview is compatible with a kind of theism, particularly the deism popular in the seventeenth and eighteenth centuries and embraced by America's founding fathers. The deistic im-

---

31. "Natural Right and Historical Mindedness," 172.
32. *Insight*, 138, 151–54; see *Method*, 280.

age of God is that of a removed watchmaker who made a machine, set it to operate according to a constant set of laws, and then let it go on moving according to those laws. For the creation process, deism imagines that God conceived of various parts of creation and then put them together. Lonergan compares this to thinking that the individual forms of things or "Plato's ideas are in the divine mind pretty much as the animals were in Noah's ark."[33] Such a notion conceives of individual finite natures as prior to whole world orders. The relationships among finite things are determined by their individual natures. Since individual natures are absolute, unchanging, and necessary, so too are the various relationships among finite things. Thus the world order that encompasses these relationships is unchanging, absolute, and necessary.

In contrast, Lonergan's worldview of emergent probability affirms that the whole world order is prior to individual finite natures. "God sees in his essence, first of all, the series of all possible world-orders each complete down to its least historical detail," and, in knowing world orders, God knows finite natures.[34] By placing the priority (not in the chronological sense) on world orders, Lonergan is able to understand the world as dynamic. The finite natures of individual things do not fix the relationships of things and thus do not require a static world order. A dynamic world order with its own intrinsic intelligibility provides for the emergence of new things. What is that world order?

In some ways it is similar to Charles Darwin's theory of evolution. Since Darwin (1809–82), natural science has understood that the world is not populated by a fixed, unchanging assembly of plant and animal species. New types or species of plants and animals emerge, and existing ones become extinct. Furthermore, their emergence and extinction are not based on necessity, but on *probability*. The probability for new life-forms to emerge or not to emerge, to survive or to become extinct, depends on a host of underlying factors in the natural environment. These underlying factors do not exist in the same amounts in different places and at

33. Lonergan, "The Natural Desire to See God," in *Collection: Papers by Bernard J. F. Lonergan*, 88.

34. "The Natural Desire to See God," 88.

different times. Thus the probabilities for a plant's or an animal's emergence and survival are not universal, but localized.[35]

Darwin's discoveries and several successive advances, notably by Sigmund Freud in psychology and Albert Einstein in physics, have contributed to a general discrediting of mechanistic determinism. Consequently, despite the persistent temptation, contemporary thinkers may no longer imagine the world as a watch with all its parts related and governed by unchanging, universal, and necessary laws.[36]

While mechanistic determinism does not do justice to the actual world order, there is a temptation to move from its extreme position and easy certainties to the opposite extreme, which we might call "relativistic indeterminism." According to this latter view there is no comprehensive worldview; there is no world order; there are no intelligible relationships, necessary or contingent. Or at least, if they do exist, there is no way for anyone to know them with any accuracy or certainty.[37] In other words, the one thing that seems true and certain in relativistic indeterminism is that there is no truth or certainty.

This theory arose in part due to the discoveries of modern science, but in large part it is a reaction against modernity, particularly the cultural imperialism that accompanied the classicist obsession with universality and necessity. This reaction has sparked a movement that champions particularity and contingency. The movement is often referred to as "postmodernity," and can be seen in philosophy, literature, and various fine arts.[38]

In many ways the postmodern concern for particularity and contingency is a positive corrective of the excesses of classicism. But as reactionary movements tend to do, postmodernity can lead to un-

---

35. *Insight*, 154–55.
36. *Insight*, 448–49. Freud discovered that psychological disease has properly psychological causes. Einstein's quantum mechanics "removed from science the relevance of any image of particles, or waves, or continuous process"; cf. *Method*, 280, where Lonergan discusses such changes in math, economics, and physics.
37. *Insight*, 157–61.
38. Examples of postmodern products abound. My favorites from philosophy and literature are by Nietzsche and Sartre. Much of their thought is prefigured in the works of modern and premodern thinkers like Dostoyevski, Machiavelli, and Plato (see, for example, the character Thracymachus in Plato's *Republic* I).

healthy extremes. A person can become so focused on change and particularity that nothing seems to be shared across time, place, or person. The denial of objective truth and goodness can make an individual pessimistic or even nihilistic. And there are social consequences, such as the refusal to acknowledge any possibility of empathy for another. Ultimately there are tremendous practical dangers that could come from the negation of any type of universality. For example, denying any form of common human nature shatters the grounds for condemning such actions as rape or genocide. If every culture and even each individual person is completely different, then who am I to criticize anything that anyone else does?

Lonergan's emergent probability seeks a higher ground that retains the good of both classical modern thought and indeterminate postmodern views while getting rid of some of their excesses. Emergent probability is a theoretical framework that attempts to do justice to the actual world order in which things persist and things change, in which some things are universal or general and some are particular or localized. Thus Lonergan does not wish to discover exclusively how things with eternally fixed natures are related by necessary, universal, and unchanging laws. Nor does he abandon the quest for understanding the essences and real relations of things. Rather, Lonergan's goal is an ongoing discovery of the intelligible relationships governing the world order as it concretely exists, an order in which new things have various probabilities of emerging.

And so we come to a basic definition of emergent probability: It is a theoretical framework for understanding a natural world order in which new things arise or "emerge," and this emergence does not *have* to happen, as it is not necessary, but only contingent or "probable." This natural world order of emergent probability is governed by both classical and statistical laws.

Classical and Statistical Law

Lonergan acknowledges that not everything in nature follows a perfect pattern. Some things are systematically intelligible and some are not. Consequently, emergent probability is not a completely rigid system, nor is it the total abandonment of systematic understanding. It is an open, heuristic structure for anticipating a world order that is intelligible and dynamic, orderly, but also on the move.[39] Because of this, Lonergan's emergent probability makes use of both "classical" laws (that identify systematic relationships) and "statistical" laws (that look at actual occurrences or events and seek ideal frequencies, or probabilities, from which actual frequencies may diverge, but only non-systematically).[40] Both classical and statistical laws seek to explain world processes, to be empirically verifiable, and to be practically applicable.

For example, in medicine, classical researchers analyze how pulmonary or digestive systems function in general, while statistical researchers determine normative or ideal frequencies at which these systems function in actual populations. Doctors use both sets of information to diagnose and treat patients.[41]

But it is not only specialists like doctors who use a combination of classical and statistical laws. We all do. Let us take a simple example: As kids we are taught to look both ways when crossing the street. More or less, we still follow this advice as we get older. Why? Because if we do not look, we might get hit by a car or a truck, and this might kill us. We know this because we know through such classical laws that vehicles travel on roads, that when vehicles strike human flesh and bones they cause damage, and that certain types of damage cause death. But is important to note that a person who does not look will not *necessarily* get hit, nor will a person who does get hit necessarily get killed. Still, it would be foolish not to look, particularly given certain circumstances, such when crossing a busy road, going against the light, and/or wearing headphones. Such circumstances increase the chances that one might get hit, especially if one forgets to look both ways. And other circumstances make it more likely that if one does get hit, then one will get killed (the size and speed of the vehicle, for instance). We know that various conditions, or "ifs," in-

39. A "heuristic structure" is a flexible theoretical model or framework that helps one to make sense of one's experience.

40. *Insight*, chap. 2–4, particularly 126–39.

41. This example comes from Joseph Flanagan, *Quest for Self-Knowledge: An Essay in Lonergan's Philosophy* (Toronto: University of Toronto Press, 1997), 99.

crease the likelihood or the probability that we might get hurt. And while we may not know the exact statistics, we are wise to look both ways when crossing the street.

Our wisdom comes from knowing that (1) some things will cause death, which we know through classical laws, and (2) various conditions increase the probability that these things will occur, which we know through statistical laws. Through their knowledge of classical and statistical laws, doctors working to heal their patients as well as pedestrians crossing the road seek to promote the emergence and survival of desirable schemes of recurrence.

Schemes of Recurrence: Emergence and Survival

Emergent probability is an expansion and generalization, or transcendence, of the Darwinian evolutionary worldview. Darwin focused on the probabilities for the emergence and survival of successive species of plants and animals given various underlying environmental factors. Lonergan's emergent probability more broadly considers the probabilities for the emergence and survival of any successive thing or groups of things given various underlying other things and groups of things.[42] These underlying things and groups of things may be plants or animals, but they need not be. Lonergan tends to refer to them as "operations" and "events." These terms emphasize the dynamism of each thing, and they allow for a more complete account of reality that includes nonphysical realities. Operations and events can be grouped into what Lonergan calls "schemes of recurrence" or "recurrent schemes." A recurrent scheme is simply a series or a pattern of interdependent, regularly recurring things. Simply put, a recurrent scheme is a cycle. When one event arises, it may lead to another event, which may lead to a third, a fourth, a fifth and so on, until the cycle of events returns back to the first event and the whole process or "scheme" repeats or "recurs." The number of events in a recurrent scheme is not important. What is important is that the events occur, that they are linked interdependently in a circular manner, and that they recur.

---

42. *Insight*, 156–57. Another difference, as I see it, is that Darwin gives struggle and competition a more fundamental role than does Lonergan.

Such schemes of recurrence are the common building blocks of our universe. They are operative, for example, in the recurrent perturbed ellipses of the planets in our solar system, in water's circulation around the earth, in the nitrogen cycle necessary for earthly life, in animal digestive rhythms, and in human economic patterns of production and consumption.[43]

The emergence and survival of various schemes of recurrence do not occur by necessity. Rather, there are different probabilities for different events to emerge; there is the further probability that these events will group together into recurrent schemes; and there is the continual question of how long and how well a scheme will survive. Many diverse factors need to occur in the right amount and in the right order for the events of any scheme of recurrence to emerge and to survive. Given such uncertainties, there is an almost miraculous character to much of our universe. Take, for example, the rarity if not the uniqueness of planets habitable to any form of life, let alone plants, animals, or people.

From the limited perspective of a human lifetime, many types of events are rare. But on a universal level, when given very large numbers, distributed across very large areas, over a very long period of time, even events with very low probabilities for emergence and survival are virtually certain to emerge and survive. As Lonergan mentions, a scheme of recurrence with just a one-in-a-million chance of occurring will occur a million times if given "a million million" simultaneous or successive opportunities for emergence.[44] Given the magnitude of our universe, in both time and space, this is not so unlikely. And its result is a mind-blowing diversity, or at least the probability for the emergence of such diversity. This wondrous diversity of successive schemes of recurrence is organized into a dynamic, interdependent hierarchy.

A Dynamic, Interdependent Hierarchy: Transcendence, Sublation, and Vertical Finality

The previous section discussed how in a world governed by emergent probability, things or events are related to each other in-

43. *Insight*, 141.   44. *Insight*, 146

terdependently and dynamically in various schemes of recurrence. In this section we shall see how schemes of recurrence themselves are related in an interdependent and dynamic way.

Some schemes of recurrence arise earlier than others. Often these earlier schemes set the conditions of the possibility for the emergence of later schemes.[45] In other words, just as some events are dependent on the prior existence of other events, some recurrent schemes of events are dependent on the existence of other schemes. In the previous section the motion of the planets, of water, of nitrogen, of digestion, and of the human economy represented examples of recurrent schemes of events. The order in which they were presented reveals an order of their dependence. Planetary motions set the conditions for chemical cycles, such as of water and nitrogen, which set the conditions for biological functions, such as digestion, which set the conditions for human economic activities as well as other aspects of human life.

The earlier, more fundamental schemes Lonergan calls "lower," and the later schemes that depend on and build on the lower he calls "higher."[46] These higher schemes are not merely later, but also higher, because in some ways they add qualitatively different relationships, functions, and events that are not possible on the lower levels. In some ways these higher schemes encompass and go beyond or "transcend" the lower schemes.[47] So, for example, the human schemes of intelligence, emotion, and love include and go beyond "lower" biological and chemical operations.

Furthermore, while higher schemes are dependent on lower ones for their emergence and survival, in some ways lower schemes depend on the higher. A higher scheme goes beyond or transcends the lower, and in doing so, the higher lifts up or "sublates" the lower into a new context (the higher scheme itself), in which the lower

---

45. It is important perhaps to note that while Lonergan and Karl Rahner share the use of the phrase "conditions of the possibility," Rahner tends to use it in the sense of "a priori" or prescinding from the particularities of concrete reality, and Lonergan tends to use it to identify the concrete conditions required for the emergence of particular events or things. For more on the relationship between Rahner and Lonergan, see Otto Muck, *The Transcendental Method* (New York: Herder and Herder, 1968).

46. *Insight*, 148.

47. See note 20 for a discussion of transcendence as used by Lonergan.

scheme is able to find a flourishing and a fulfillment that it could not have attained on its own.[48]

There is, in short, a mutual relationship of dependence between higher and lower schemes of recurrence. The higher schemes could not exist if the lower ones did not already exist. Without material, plant, and animal schemes of recurrence, human schemes of commerce, culture, love, etc., could not emerge. On the other hand, higher schemes emerge as a more systematic patterning of lower schemes in ways that promote more sophisticated relationships and more fulfilling operations. In animals and plants, chemicals come alive.

At times people may wonder which levels are more important—the higher, more advanced levels, or the lower, more fundamental levels? For Lonergan they are equally important, but differently so. Consequently, he speaks of the lower as more "essential" and the higher as more "excellent."[49]

These interdependent levels of recurrent schemes, with some schemes higher than others, form a united whole as an interdependent, dynamic hierarchy. Because the schemes in a series are related as progressively ascending, the whole is a hierarchy. Because lower schemes ground the higher ones and higher schemes order the lower, every single part on every single level is interdependent. Because there is change or motion both within individual schemes and among groups of schemes, the hierarchy is dynamic.

What all of this means is that the world order of emergent probability is one of a dynamic, interrelated hierarchy of recurrent schemes. The dynamic relations among levels of schemes result primarily from what Lonergan calls "vertical finality."

"Finality" denotes a thing's orientation to a goal, purpose, or end. The scholastic theology of Lonergan's early education included two notions of finality: "ultimate" or "absolute" and "proportional" or "proximate." For Christians, God is the ultimate, absolute end of all things in creation.[50] In other words, the ultimate

48. In understanding sublation, Lonergan relies to a degree on Hegel; see *Insight*, 446–47.
49. Lonergan, "Finality, Love, Marriage," in *Collection*, 17, 22.
50. Following Thomas Aquinas, Lonergan affirms that "man and, as well, all creatures according to their mode naturally love God above all things. And, of course, this love of God above

finality of all created beings is directed toward God. Proportional or proximate finality is the orientation toward a more immediate goal, particularly a goal that is proper to a thing's or a group of things' inherent or essential capacities or potentialities. For example, an apple tree's ultimate end, like that of all things, is to serve the glory of God. Its proximate end, the one particular to its own essence, is to produce apples and eventually more apple trees.

A spatial metaphor might help us to understand the different types of finality. So one might imagine an interdependent, dynamic hierarchy as a stack of things and their ends. Each level of the stack contains a thing and an end. This end, located on a thing's own horizontal level, is its proportionate, proximate, or "horizontal" end. The orientation of the thing to its proximate end could be imagined as a horizontal arrow pointing from the thing to its proportionate end. God as the ultimate, absolute end is perhaps best imagined as located above the entire stack of things and their proximate ends. The absolute finality of all things to God might be imagined as a long, vertical arrow starting at the bottom of the stack and stretching through all levels until it reaches God at the top, far above the rest of the stack.

Between the many little horizontal arrows representing horizontal finality and the one large vertical arrow representing ultimate finality, one might imagine many short diagonal lines pointing from one level to the next higher one.[51] These diagonal lines indicate vertical finality, which is the orientation of everything in one horizontal level, both a thing and its goals, toward higher fulfillment as part of a higher level.

To continue the example given about an apple tree, we might say that in addition to the apple tree's ultimate goal of serving God and its horizontal goal of producing apples and apple trees, it has a vertical finality that includes providing sustenance and shelter to birds and other animals (higher level, sensitive life-forms). To

---

all is only a particular case of the general theorem that absolutely all finality is to God"; "Finality, Love, Marriage," 25, citing Thomas's *Summa Theologiae* I-II, q. 109, a. 3 c.; *Questiones quodlibetales* I, a. 8 c. & ad 3m.

51. Lonergan depicts a similar scheme in "Finality, Love, Marriage," 42. Absent there is a representation of ultimate finality toward God.

complicate things further, however, we must remember that each level is not constituted simply by one thing, one goal, and one orientation that connect them to each other. Rather, each level is comprised of a recurrent scheme. So the biological schemes involving plant life are based on lower physical and chemical schemes of recurrence. And they in turn support higher animal, psychological, and spiritual schemes. Vertical finality is Lonergan's term for the orientation of things in a lower scheme of recurrence toward a type of fulfillment on a higher, more excellent level.

Lonergan's most common example of vertical finality involves oxygen. Its ultimate end, like that of all things, is God. Its horizontal, or essential, end is "to perform the offices of oxygen as oxygen, but its more excellent [vertical] end is its contribution to the maintenance of human life and this end attains not in isolation nor *per se* but in combination with other elements and within the human biological process."[52] In other words, on its own, in isolation, oxygen does not live, and it does not need to live. For living is not something demanded by the particular essence of oxygen. Oxygen is oxygen whether or not it is part of a living organism. But in some sense, oxygen is oriented toward life. And it gains some fulfillment as part of the recurrent schemes of biology. This orientation toward life, toward biological fulfillment, is its vertical finality.

Classical science is very adept at considering the world as a whole oriented in all of its parts universally to God. Classical science is also adept at analyzing a particular thing's particular essence. Thus, according to Lonergan, one needs classical science to know ultimate and horizontal finality. But vertical finality is not known by discovering what is universal to the whole or what is particular to a particular thing's essence. It is discovered through contemporary natural science's method of observing and seeking to understand the various actual relationships of things in various sets of conditions. The relationships of things in various conditions operate not merely according to classical law, but also according to statistical laws. Lonergan explains succinctly the three types of finality, how they are related, and how they are known:

52. "Finality, Love, Marriage," 22.

Absolute finality is to God in his intrinsic goodness: it is universal; it is unique; it is hypothetically necessary, for if there is anything to respond to motive or to proceed to term, then its response or tendency can be accounted for ultimately only by the one self-sufficient good. Horizontal finality results from abstract essence; it holds even when the object is in isolation; it is to a motive or term that is proportionate to essence. But vertical finality is in the concrete; in point of fact, it is not from the isolated instance but from the conjoined plurality and it is in the field not of natural but of statistical law, not of the abstract *per se* but of the concrete *per accidens*. Still, though accidental to the isolated object or the abstract essence, vertical finality is of the very idea of our hierarchic universe, of the ordination of things devised and exploited by the divine Artisan. For the cosmos is not an aggregate of isolated objects hierarchically arranged on isolated levels, but a dynamic whole in which ... one level of being or activity subserves another.[53]

A cosmology that takes advantage of both scholastic and contemporary science accounts for the tremendous complexity of a world order in which things relate to God and to each other, through their essences and their accidents, in ways that sometimes are universal and necessary and sometimes are contingent and probable. It considers all three types of finality and thus is better able to explain the way new, higher, and more excellent things or schemes of recurrence can arise out of older, lower, more essential ones. In other words, it is able to explain a world order of emergent probability.

Lonergan summarizes emergent probability as "the successive realization in accord with successive schedules of probability of a conditioned series of schemes of recurrence."[54] The world order it envisions is a dynamic world process, characterized by (1) "successive world situations," (2) an "initial world situation" valued only for the possibilities it contains and the probabilities for realizing these possibilities, (3) an openness to new possibilities emerging according to various probabilities (rather than determinism's absolute necessity or indeterminism's merely random chance), (4) increasingly systematic, harmonious relations, (5) the possibility of "enormous differentiation," especially given large numbers, large spaces, and a long time, (6) the possibility of breakdown, since survival is only probable, (7) the possibility of "blind alleys," or a

53. "Finality, Love, Marriage," 21–22.
54. *Insight*, 148–49.

stunted development, since material that might be used in higher schemes can get bound in earlier schemes, (8) later schemes having narrower distribution, (9) long periods of time being required for less probable later schemes to emerge, (10) larger initial absolute numbers required to offset dead ends and breakdowns, and (11) generic intelligibility, since it anticipates classical and statistical laws but leaves the "determinate content" of particular laws to natural science.[55]

In sum, emergent probability is Lonergan's cosmology, or his theory for explaining the order of the universe. It is an account of the ordering of the cosmos as a result of the divine wisdom that makes world order prior to individual things. It understands the cosmos as fertile and dynamic, as providing the conditions for the possibility of its elements to combine in unpredictable, but intelligible ways that are creative of new levels of interdependent recurrent schemes.[56] It is a complex, ongoingly creative world order, one far more befitting a supremely wise creator than either a world set to mechanistic determinism or one abandoned to chaotic relativism.

Reflection Questions for Chapter 1

- Bernard of Chartres said famously that he could see far because he was a dwarf standing on the shoulders of giants. With this Bernard hoped to pay tribute to the generations who went before him. Like Bernard, all of us are who we are because of the people who lived before us. Our existence is not necessary. It is due to our own choices and effort, but also due to the choices and effort of our ancestors. Moreover, human existence in general is sort of a dwarf standing on the shoulders of giants, since our existence depends on vast populations of animals, insects, and plants, innumerable chemical processes and planetary motions, as well as light from the sun and other stars.

55. *Insight*, 149–50.
56. From the old, new things arise. From the elements of lower levels, there is an emergence of new sets of intelligible relationships, new wholes drawn from previously non-systematically related elements. But this is not creation in the strict, theological sense of *ex nihilo*, or from nothing; see Lonergan, "Healing and Creating in History," in *A Third Collection*, 102.

- Take some time to think about your own talents and achievements. What is it about yourself that you like? Then call to mind how who you are and what you have done rests on the talents and achievements of others: your parents, your teachers, your coaches, your friends and relatives. For example, did your grandparents immigrate so they and future generations could have better lives? Have your parents worked hard to provide for you? Has someone you've never even met inspired you?
- Think too about the earth, how it has nourished you with its fruits. Think of how the sun has warmed you by day and the stars delighted you by night. Have you ever stood in awe of a sunset? Have you ever picked a ripe strawberry? Have you ever been comforted by a pet? How can we best pay tribute to our ancestors and to this glorious creation? What about our thinking should we change? What about our feelings and our actions should we change? What should we continue?

2 | Insight and the Self-Correcting Process of Learning

The previous chapter considered Lonergan's understanding of the cosmos as a self-transcending, hierarchical order governed by emergent probability. Human beings are part of this cosmos. We have emerged from the creative world process of emergent probability. As a relatively late, higher-level emergence, humanity is a complex entity subject to both classical and statistical laws on multiple levels of being: physical, chemical, biological, and more uniquely human levels. With the advent of humanity two significant new things arrive in creation: (1) a creature's ability to discover and work with classical and statistical laws, and thus to guide and accelerate emergent probability, and (2) the possibility of a creature's rejection of the created order through sin.

Without humanity and its ability to understand and direct world processes, there would be some type of progress in the world, but this progress would be more limited than the kind that can be achieved by human ingenuity. On the other hand, without humanity, there would be no decline, at least not the devastation brought about by sin.[1]

---

1. Things would atrophy and die; for Lonergan, "decline" is a technical term indicating the negative consequences of human sin. Without human sin, there would be neither decline nor any redemption from sin and decline, at least not in Lonergan's use of these terms. Later chapters will focus on these topics.

The remainder of this part of the book will discuss humanity's unique role in creation and progress, a role it plays through insight, a broader transcendental method, and a still broader cooperating human community. Sin and decline will be studied in part 2.

Insight Itself

To a world organized hierarchically on physical, chemical, and biological levels, humanity adds levels of intelligence, reflectivity, responsibility, civilization, culture, and religion.[2] In Lonergan's view human intelligence is fundamental to all human endeavors. It gives humans the capacity to gain some understanding of or insight into anything they encounter. Built upon such insight is the human ability to guide and to accelerate world processes of emergent probability. Thus, when used correctly human intelligence is a primary engine of human progress.[3] Some of the most obvious examples of insight-driven progress come from scientific and technological advances in fields like medicine, communication, and aviation, but there are many others.

While human intelligence provides the impetus for developments within human history, human intelligence is itself a developing entity. We are intelligent more in our ideal, abstract potential than our actualized, concrete reality. Because of this, human beings are in the difficult position of needing to rely on our intelligence to guide our activity before our intelligence is fully formed.[4] We sometimes have to leap before we can get a thorough "look." And this can be dangerous, as illustrated by the tremendous social and environmental damage caused by unforeseen side effects of modern practices in areas like industry, agriculture, and military.

Nevertheless, great freedom and responsibility result from the use of the human intellect, both for the individual and for society.

---

2. Lonergan did not write much, if anything, about animal intelligence and the boundaries between it and human intelligence.

3. In *Insight*, Lonergan points to intelligence as the main source of progress, but *Method*, published almost fifteen years after *Insight*, gives a broader picture of human progress that includes other causes, such as the human response to value through feelings, the exercise of freedom in choice, and the effects of love, as will be shown in chapter 3 of this volume.

4. *Insight*, 711; Lonergan, "Finality, Love, Marriage," in *Collection*, 24–26.

Recurrent schemes of insight, communication, persuasion, agreement, and decision free human beings to a great degree from the binding significance of underlying planetary, chemical, and biological schemes.[5] Over multiple generations human beings have made discoveries and utilized them to improve their living standards. We have, for example, learned how to farm the land for wheat, to domesticate sheep for wool, to quarry granite for our homes, and to heat those homes with a variety of energy sources. With new intellectual discoveries come new social developments. These developments have made us less dependent on things like the weather or animal migration patterns and more likely to settle down, to store resources, and to spend our time in pursuits other than finding food and shelter.

If the developments of human intelligence are what drive human development in general, it might be beneficial to examine how intelligence works and how we may best harness it for the good of human society. Lonergan's largest and perhaps most famous work, *Insight: A Study of Human Understanding,* is—as its title indicates—a study of human insight, the primary product of human intelligence. Its purpose, as Lonergan explains in its preface and introduction, is "to thoroughly understand what it is to understand," to gain "insight into insight."[6] Highly abstract and theoretical, *Insight* is not simply an abstract, theoretical work. Its primary intention is practical and pedagogical. It is pedagogical because it aims "to assist the reader in effecting a personal appropriation of the concrete dynamic structure immanent and recurrently operative in his [or her] own cognitional activities."[7] Appropriating or grasping one's "own cognitional activities" is practical because these activities produce the understanding or misunderstanding that results in better or worse judgments, decisions, and actions, and thus in progress or decline. By heightening one's awareness of the processes by which one *can* generate insight and thus progress, one increases the likelihood of *successfully* generating insight and progress.[8] Insight is so central to progress that, Lonergan

5. *Insight,* 236.
7. *Insight,* 12.
6. *Insight,* 22, 8.
8. *Insight,* 6.

writes, "insight into insight brings to light the cumulative process of progress."[9] So just what is insight? What does it mean to understand?

Insight, or at least the intellectual part of coming to insight, begins with the conscious desire to understand. Human beings are not, however, always conscious. Lonergan contrasts human consciousness or subjectivity with human nature or substance. Fundamentally and at all times, the human person is a substance, or an instance of being, and in particular it is a substance or a being with a human nature. But despite always having a human nature or being a human substance, a human being is not always conscious and thus not always a human subject. "Subject" is simply Lonergan's term for a human being that has attained consciousness. When one is knocked out cold or lies in a dreamless sleep, one is alive and human, but one is only barely conscious, and thus not fully a subject as Lonergan defines it.

The beginnings of human subjectivity come in conscious dreams. Then, upon waking, our consciousness leaps to a new level. But even when waking, one is not immediately intelligent. Awakening takes time. First one may have a basic self-presence. Then one grows in a basic, sensitive awareness of her or his surroundings. Building on this sensitive awareness, one may take the first step into intelligent consciousness with questions that seek intelligible relationships or patterns among the various elements that make up one's surroundings: What is that noise? Who's there? What time is it? Can I go back to sleep? If one understands the parts as comprising an intelligible, familiar whole, one will recognize one's surroundings as normal and move on to other tasks, either going back to sleep or trying to wake up completely. But if any part of the environment is unfamiliar, even in just a single element, one will spontaneously ask further questions: What's going on? What is that? How did it get there? Before a person figures out what the unfamiliar element actually is, how it got there, why it got there, what it has to do with everything else, the person will experience an inner tension caused by a spontaneous human desire to under-

9. *Insight*, 8.

stand. Questions arise naturally as particular manifestations of this general, natural desire.

For Lonergan, the desire to understand is not limited to intellectuals or geniuses. It is not a culturally conditioned characteristic. Rather, it is a normal, natural aspect of human personhood and of the subject as conscious.[10] This natural human desire to understand is absolutely fundamental to Lonergan's philosophy and theology. He does not attempt to prove it, but rather invites his readers to attend to their own interiorities and verify this yearning within themselves.[11]

Insight is the proper fulfillment of this basic human desire. The arrival of insight releases the tension that accompanies the desire to know. One gains an insight, or one understands, when one grasps the relationship, the order, or the patterning of distinct elements into an intelligible whole. When things that seemed disjointed suddenly are connected, then one has had an insight. When things that for so long made no sense suddenly do, one has had insight; one understands. It is an "aha moment," a moment sometimes depicted in cartoons as a bright light bulb appearing over a character's head. Light, and the ability to see, which the presence of light makes possible, are featured in other common expressions, such as when we exclaim "I see!" to say we know or at least we think we know.

Despite such common expressions, understanding actually takes more than just turning on the light and taking a look, in the literal sense. For example, to understand this text or any text one cannot rely merely on seeing the text or running one's eyes over the page. Taking a good look, listening carefully, or using any of the five senses do not by themselves bring knowledge. Further steps need to be made. After sensing, the next step is taken by the mind. To understand a text, one needs intelligence to relate lines into letters, letters into words, words into sentences. Knowing begins with experience (either sense experience or the experience of one's interiority or inner experience),[12] but it is fully realized only

10. Lonergan, "Existenz and Aggiornamento," in *Collection*, 241; and *Insight*, 372–74.

11. The entire book *Insight* is an invitation to this personal exploration. Lonergan reveals his pedagogical method in the introduction (11–24).

12. Lonergan discusses both the data of sense and the data of consciousness; *Insight*, 95–97, 206–7, 260–61, 299–300).

in the further operations of authentic questioning, understanding, and judging.[13] Otherwise a two-year-old and a twenty-year-old sitting in a movie theater watching the same show and hearing the same sounds would come to the same understanding of the movie. This may sometimes be the case, but hopefully it is not a common occurrence.

To portray dramatically the characteristics of insight, Lonergan tells the famous story of ancient Greek scientist Archimedes leaping naked out of the Syracuse baths to run around town yelling, "Eureka!" King Hiero had charged Archimedes with discovering whether a crown was pure gold. Archimedes puzzled intently over the question until the answer struck him as he was entering the baths. The story brings to light five characteristics of insight. In the first place, insight, as mentioned above,

comes as a release to the tension of inquiry.... Deep within us all, emergent when the noise of other appetites is stilled, there is a drive to know, to understand, to see why, to discover the reason, to find the cause, to explain.... It [inquiry, the desire to know] can fill his [or her] waking thoughts, hide from him the world of ordinary affairs, invade the very fabric of his dreams. It can demand endless sacrifices that are made without regret though there is only the hope, never a promise of success. What better symbol could one find for this obscure, exigent, imperious drive, than a man, naked, running excitedly crying, "I've got it"?[14]

Second, insight comes suddenly, unexpectedly. "Archimedes' insight did not occur while he was in the mood and posture that a sculptor would select to portray 'The Thinker.' It came to him in a flash, on a trivial occasion, in a moment of relaxation."[15] Insight is reached "in the last analysis, not by learning rules, not by following precepts, not by studying any methodology. Discovery is a new beginning. It is the origin of new rules that supplement or even supplant the old. Genius is creative. It is genius precisely because it disregards established routines, because it originates the novelties that will be the routines of the future."[16]

Third, insight is a function more of inner conditions than of

---

13. Judgment, the final stage of knowing, will be discussed in chapter 3 of this volume.
14. *Insight*, 28–29.   15. *Insight*, 29.
16. *Insight*, 29.

outer circumstances. It is not the product of mere sensation. Many people can share an experience, but each can come to different interpretations of the same experience depending on the person's prior experience, intelligence, attentiveness, and inquisitiveness. Many people shared the town baths with Archimedes, but only he had the prior concerns and questions that led him to his discovery.

Fourth, insight pivots between the concrete/particular and the abstract/universal. Insights arise in particular, concrete situations as possible solutions to particular problems, but they tend to have "a significance greater than their origins and a relevance wider than their original applications."[17] One needs concrete images and other data from the senses to get insight, but insight is best expressed in abstract language, such as that of math and science. So Archimedes' insight provided a concrete solution to a concrete problem, but it has general implications that can only be expressed in "the abstract formulations of the principles of displacement and specific gravity."[18]

Fifth, though an insight is initially surprising, it becomes rudimentary. Before one solves a problem, the problem is difficult. "But once one has understood, one has crossed a divide. What a moment ago was an insoluble problem now becomes incredibly simple and obvious. Moreover, it tends to remain simple and obvious."[19] Once Archimedes had his insight he could explain it readily to the king. A similar process happens in diverse areas of human inquiry.

Insight Made Practical: Common Sense and Science

Such is insight, but how does insight drive progress? Early in the book *Insight,* Lonergan answers briefly and compactly:

[C]oncrete situations give rise to insights which issue into policies and courses of action. Action transforms the situation to give rise to further insights, better policies, more effective courses of action. It follows that if insight occurs, it keeps recurring; and at each recurrence knowledge develops, action increases its scope, and situations improve.[20]

17. *Insight,* 30.   18. *Insight,* 30.
19. *Insight,* 30.   20. *Insight,* 8.

"Concrete situations" are the real, everyday events and occasions that any person, anywhere, at any time might encounter. Concrete situations give rise to questions, concerns, problems, and opportunities. Each person encounters particular situations in particular ways and will have particular questions, concerns, problems, and opportunities. But there is a fair amount of overlap in these things, for even "our separate, unrevealed, hidden cores have a common circle of reference, the human community, and an ultimate point of reference, which is God, who is all in all."[21] In the task of everyday living, all people wonder: What's going on? What should I do? How I should live? How can we make things better? We may come to different, even competing ideas about how to live, but everyone comes to some ideas or insights about how to live, and we all act on those ideas. Moreover, our ideas and our actions change situations. New situations cause us to wonder anew: What's going on? What should I do? How should I live? How can we make things better?

The process by which life gives rise to questions, questions lead to answers, answers lead to new ways of living, new ways of living lead to new questions, and so forth, Lonergan calls the "self-correcting process of learning."[22] The process is not self-correcting in the sense that people are not involved. People are involved throughout. It is self-correcting in the sense that, due to our natural desire to know and to live well, we will pursue answers to questions and solutions to problems until we are satisfied with them. People often say that life is a process of trial and error. We try out one solution and, if it fails, we move on to another. Well, actually, before we move from one potential solution to another, other steps are involved. We have to figure out a new solution. To do this, we ask ourselves what else might work. Ideally we ask ourselves why the previous attempt failed. By our answers to such questions we come to work out our new solutions. So between trial and error are question and answer. Lonergan's self-correcting process of learn-

21. "Existenz and Aggiornamento," 240; Lonergan, "Self-Transcendence," in *Philosophical and Theological Papers, 1965–1980*, 314.

22. Lonergan, "Natural Right and Historical Mindedness," in *A Third Collection*; *Insight*, 197–98, 311–12, 314–16, 325, 328–29, 370, 729.

ing highlights the period of question and answer by which our failures and our discoveries lead to improved solutions and situations.

This process is at work in all fields, no matter what a person may do—from farming and construction to baseball and rap to brain surgery and rocket science. Thus Lonergan affirms that "one meets intelligence in every walk of life."[23] The pursuit and the implementation of insight are fundamental to human endeavors because they are essential to human nature.

In support of this Lonergan affirms that the "light and drive of intelligent inquiry" may be most visible in little children, particularly in their "secret wonder that, once the mystery of language has been unraveled, rushes forth in a cascade of questions. Far too soon the questions get out of hand, and weary adults are driven to ever more frequent use of the blanket 'My dear, you cannot understand that yet.' The child would understand everything at once."[24] As we get older we can preserve this natural, spontaneous wonder, the desire to know everything about everything. Often, however, we get jaded. We think we know it all—"Been there, done that," as the expression goes. Or we simply lose interest in various aspects of life. How often do we say or hear others say, "I couldn't care less"? We wall off the world into things that matter and things that we think do not. We pay less attention to our desire to know and more to our desires for other types of fulfillment. Still, though, in whatever area of life we are interested and engaged in, we ask questions and we get answers—at least we do to the degree that we wish to achieve things or to progress.

The self-correcting process of learning, with insight at its core, is the basis for not only an individual's progress, but also a community's. Human living is communal living. Through communal experimentation, discussion, and collaboration ideas are tested and refined. Society is not static, but an ongoing project spanning generations. Thus there is a communal, self-correcting process of learning, and it produces a common fund of insights that

23. *Insight*, 196.
24. *Insight*, 196–97.

have been tried and refined over time. Though this fund may be the product of thousands of years and millions of people, it remains ever incomplete, and thus ever subject to the self-correcting process of learning. In other words, on a social scale the natural human tendency toward spontaneous questioning, answering, testing, and collaborating leads to a dynamic, continually growing public store of knowledge. This public store or common fund Lonergan calls "common sense."[25]

Common sense is common, but it is not general in the way math or science is general or universal. Algebra and chemistry, for example, are not bound to a local community and a local culture to the degree that common sense is. This is not so much a flaw of common sense but an aspect of its purpose. Common sense specializes in answering the particular, practical questions that people face in their everyday, concrete living. Although particular situations are never exactly the same, there is a great degree of commonality in the daily routines followed by people in general. We all need to eat, to sleep, to shelter ourselves from the elements, to educate and entertain ourselves, and so forth. But there are many ways to fulfill these needs. Each group will have its own particular set of ways. Perhaps the most obvious examples of this are cultures that have formed within particular geographic areas. But groups can be brought together by many other distinguishing factors, such as shared occupation, musical preference, or some other social arrangement. Members within these groups share common ways of answering the practical questions of everyday life. They will thus share a common sense with each other, but the sense that is common to them will differ from that of other groups. For each group that faces particular experiences and goals, a new common sense will emerge. Individuals who operate in multiple communities will have to master multiple common senses. It would not be uncommon, for example, for a person to need to master one at home, one in the workplace, one at church, and one as a member of a nation.[26]

25. *Insight*, 197–98. Common sense is the main topic of chapters 6 and 7.
26. *Insight*, 203.

A common sense is simply a common fund of insights, a general storehouse of intellectual tools developed over time by a community. To make an existing common fund relevant and applicable to a new, particular problem, one normally will need to add at least one new insight into the current situation.[27] This is true because, as mentioned, each concrete situation will have some conditions similar to other situations encountered by the community, but it will also have some conditions that are unique.

Due to the fact that common sense must operate in this combination of similarity and uniqueness, or the general and the particular, it works through hints and pointers more than by absolute, necessary rules. Its immediate tools are proverbs and stories rather than scientific theories (which are practical, as we shall see later, but must be mediated to a community through its common sense). As a common fund that develops through trial and error over time, common sense is in some ways similar to the communal discourses of academic research. But it does not aspire to the rigorous systemization or the universality of academia. So its language is not particularly technical or formal.

In fact, in addition to stories and proverbs, common sense may convey meaning through the imprecise, but effective expressions of body language, gesture, pause, tone, and volume. "As the proverb has it, a wink is as good as a nod."[28] Because of this, common sense is tremendously resourceful in dealing with the vast and varied exigencies of human communication, a communication that is often not simply the communication of concepts, but *self*-communication. For such a weighty task common sense must be adaptable to situation and audience: "For common sense not merely says what it means; it says it to someone; it begins by exploring the other fellow's intelligence; it advances by determining what further insights have to be communicated to him [or her]; it undertakes the communication, not as an exercise in formal logic, but as a work of art."[29]

This is not to say that common sense is opposed to logic or that

27. *Insight*, 203.   28. *Insight*, 200.
29. *Insight*, 200.

it can do away with logic. Ideally it is logical in the sense of "intelligent and reasonable," but its logic is not formal and scientific in the sense of always and everywhere true or conforming to "a set of general rules valid in every instance within a defined range."[30] For Lonergan, the most significant way that common sense differs from strict logic and science is that while science seeks to understand things as they exist in relation *to each other,* common sense is content to know things as they are related *to us* or *to oneself.* Thus, for example, common sense describes the weather as "hot" or "cold," and science explains the weather by measuring one temperature in relation to other temperatures, such as 98° or 28° Fahrenheit.

An important consequence of the commonsense focus on things as they are related to oneself is a single-minded concern for the practical application or usefulness of knowledge. Scientists are often interested to some degree in the possible technological applications of their research, but they may also be motivated by what Lonergan calls "the pure desire to know"—a desire for knowledge for its own sake rather than for its usefulness.[31] Common sense, on the other hand, is "bounded by the interests and concerns of human living, by the successful performance of daily tasks, by the discovery of immediate solutions that will work. Indeed, the supreme canon of common sense is the restriction of further questions to the realm of the concrete and particular, the immediate and the practical."[32]

This focus on the concrete, particular, immediate, and practical is the strength of common sense—all people, including scientists, philosophers, and mystics, must use common sense to navigate their daily lives. However, this focus is also its weakness. Lonergan emphasizes that common sense is an indispensable aspect of knowing, but he also stresses that it is not the only aspect of knowing. There is more to life than what is immediately practical. If one overemphasizes the role of common sense, one will behave like a ten-year-old in math class, asking: Who cares? What difference does it make? When am I going to use this? "[A]nd if the answer is

30. *Insight,* 201.
31. See *Insight,* 372–74; Lonergan, "Openness and Religious Experience," in *Collection,* 198.
32. *Insight,* 201.

less vivid and less rapid than an advertisement," a person bound by common sense will not care about it.[33]

The problem is that while practicality is good, it is not the only criterion for the good, and while we may not recognize the usefulness of something, this does not mean it is not useful. Natural science and other academic disciplines are practical, but their practicality is indirect. They seek first of all to understand things in relation to themselves. It takes further insights by more common-sense approaches like business, politics, and social work to apply these advances to our lives. The many practical applications to math, chemistry, history, philosophy, and so forth are longer-term developments not immediately recognizable by common sense, which is why they are often derided as luxuries or "ivory tower" endeavors.[34]

Lonergan dramatizes the tendency of common sense to restrict one's interest to the immediately practical: "Rockets and space platforms are superfluous if you intend to remain on this earth."[35] Of course, ideally, given the natural, unrestricted desire to know, one would be interested in both the earth and the stars. Lonergan illustrates the value of both the commonsense focus on the earth and the scientific interest in the stars by mentioning the story of Greek philosopher Thales, who was laughed at by a milkmaid for falling into a well: "Thales was so intent upon the stars that he did not see the well into which he tumbled. The milkmaid was so indifferent to the stars that she could not overlook the well. Still, Thales could have seen the well, for he was not blind; and perhaps the milkmaid could have been interested in the stars, for she was human."[36]

Common Sense, Sensitivity, and Spontaneous Intersubjectivity

As a public fund of traditional insights into a community's daily concerns, common sense is indispensable for human progress.

---

33. *Insight*, 202.
34. More on the relation of common sense to other forms of knowing will follow in chapter 4 of this volume in the last section, "Realms of Meaning."
35. *Insight*, 202.   36. *Insight*, 96, 205.

Common sense intends, for better and for worse, to stay down-to-earth, because its specialty is to serve the community's everyday needs and desires. On a basic level there are needs for what Lonergan calls "particular goods." These are typically goods a person needs not once and for all, but repeatedly and regularly, such as food and shelter. In addition to such frequency, we desire not only the familiar, but also the novel. For example, one may have a favorite meal, but it would be virtually inconceivable for a person to be happy with the same food at every meal during one's entire lifetime. Moreover, not even a steady flow of a mixture of novel and familiar goods will keep a person satisfied, for the human person spontaneously and naturally desires the further fulfillment afforded by the opportunity to craft a dignified living, to become the kind of person she or he can be happy with and proud of. Such a craft is complicated, for on multiple levels, each person has individual "needs and wants, pleasures and pains, labor and leisure, enjoyment and privation."[37] Finally, there is a natural human need and desire for community, for falling in love.

As discussed in the previous section, common sense is a common fund that grows from the self-correcting process of learning performed by a community: concrete social situations lead to questions, questions lead to insights, and insights transform the social situation, causing new questions to arise and so forth. A significant element of the social situation is the community's needs and desires. Thus common sense develops largely in relation to a community's needs and desires. This does not mean that it is merely the servant of these needs and desires; rather, it exists in a creative tension with them. They have some tendency to conflict inasmuch as what we want is not always what common sense says is good for us. They have a cooperative relationship in that we learn what is good for us by paying attention to our desires, by fulfilling them, and by learning the various consequences of fulfilling them.

Thus although insight is a significant component of common sense and human progress, human beings are not simply cool and rational. There is more to our decision-making than a self-correcting

37. *Insight*, 237.

process of learning. Both individually and socially, people tend to make decisions relatively spontaneously. We typically identify the good not with an answer to a question, not with something we have judged to be good after a rigorous process of discernment, but with some immediate object of desire.[38]

Lonergan locates the source of such desire as well as of other spontaneous feelings in what he calls "sensitivity and spontaneous intersubjectivity."[39] They form a kind of precritical, prereflective level of human living. They are natural and personal, but they are not simply natural or purely individualistic, neither "animal impulse" nor "egoistic scheming."[40]

To some degree the individual's spontaneous desires, feelings, and preferences are natural, but to some degree they are habituated by society. As with common sense and science, the relation between common sense and "sensitivity and spontaneous intersubjectivity" is not necessarily one of competition. Ideally it is one of fruitful cooperation. On the one hand, common sense serves spontaneous needs and desires by seeking to fulfill them. On the other, common sense must also arbitrate among competing needs and desires. In both serving and arbitrating a community's needs and desires, common sense cooperates with natural drives to form an individual's or a community's aesthetic taste, its food preferences, physical habits, daily routines, and other standards and practices. So, for example, while people of all cultures spontaneously and naturally desire food and rest and all need to work, the members of one culture may prefer spicy food, afternoon naps, and late workdays, while another might prefer salty food, no naps, and an early end to the workday.

Thus our needs and desires are partly natural and partly cultivated. For Lonergan, whether natural or cultivated, our desires bind us together more than they drive us apart. In contrast to such modern political theorists like Thomas Hobbes, who believe that people are by nature individualistic and competitive, Lonergan af-

38. *Insight*, 237.
39. *Insight*, 237–39, 723. Lonergan recognizes multiple kinds of feelings, as shall be seen in chapter 3 of this volume.
40. *Insight*, 711.

firms that while we can be egotistical when seeking to fulfill our desires, there is a "spontaneous intersubjectivity" to our natural orientation. This spontaneous intersubjectivity underlies and accompanies our desires. It binds persons into strong communal feelings and relationships, even before the shared meanings and values of common sense have habituated people into their various cultural preferences:

> Prior to the "we" that results from the mutual love of an "I" and a "thou," there is the earlier "we" that precedes the distinction of subjects and survives its oblivion. This prior "we" is vital and functional. Just as one spontaneously raises one's arm to ward off a blow against one's head, so with the same spontaneity one reaches out to save another from falling. Perception, feeling, and bodily movement are involved, but the help given another is not deliberate but spontaneous. One adverts to it not before it occurs but while it is occurring. It is as if "we" were members of one another prior to our distinctions of each from the others.[41]

Such spontaneous, intersubjective bonds are most clearly visible in the family, but they also provide the basis for civilization, much more than the rational, self-interested calculation affirmed by social contract theorists like Hobbes. And these bonds remain even when a civilization assigns to its members other, nonspontaneous social relationships (such as formal relations between coach and athlete or teacher and student).

Although they can reinforce cultivated social bonds and common sense, sensitivity and spontaneous intersubjectivity may at times be in tension with commonsense reasoning. For example, after years of scientific research, health campaigns, and shifting public opinion, the common sense of a nation may increasingly disapprove of smoking. And a person of common sense may know that smoking is unhealthy and may want to avoid it, but he or she could still spontaneously smoke. Part of this spontaneous activity would be due to natural desires, and part would result from cultivated habits. Similarly common sense can tell one that regular exercise is healthy, but one may still prefer to watch TV and eat potato chips. Such oppositions between what a person or a society

41. *Method,* 57. One may recognize the language of Martin Buber; see also *Insight,* 237, and Lonergan, "Finality, Love, Marriage," in *Collection,* 24. To "advert" is to pay attention.

affirms to be good and what is spontaneously desired is problematic, because human beings naturally prefer to have their actions be in harmony with their spontaneous desires and with commonsense insight.[42]

Conflicts between spontaneous desires and insight can arise in large groups as much as in individual persons. Thus, in any given society, various subgroups can form, each with its own desires, feelings, and ideas that are more or less in harmony with society's good as a whole. In the best situations, a society's commonsense goals are good, and it maintains harmony among various subgroups by peaceful means:

It commands their esteem by its palpable benefits; it has explained its intricate demands in some approximate yet sufficient fashion; it has adapted to its own requirements the play of imagination, the resonance of sentiment, the strength of habit, the ease of familiarity, the impetus of enthusiasm, the power of agreement and consent. Then a man's interest is in happy coincidence with his work; his country is also his homeland; its ways are the obviously right ways; its glory and peril are his own.[43]

Even in such an ideal situation of harmony among the individual, the group, and the whole society, common sense will still remain in a kind of creative tension or dialectic with sensitivity and spontaneous intersubjectivity. Lonergan defines dialectic as "a concrete unfolding of linked but opposed principles of change."[44] In this case, the "change" is social progress. Its "principles" are common sense,[45] on the one hand, and sensitivity and spontaneous intersubjectivity on the other. The two principles are "linked" because common sense is an effort of human intelligence to order things practically, and intersubjective desires and fears form the practical drives that common sense seeks to govern.[46] They are

42. *Insight*, 241. Such a desire for internal harmony or integrity is part of the orientation of natural desire to what is good. More on this will be said in chapter 3 under the heading "Authenticity."

43. *Insight*, 241. The opposition of groups within society is discussed at greater length in chapter 6 of this volume in the section "Group Bias."

44. *Insight*, 242; see also the introduction of this volume, note 3.

45. In this case, common sense in a broad sense is meant. It would include the applied or practical aspects of natural and human sciences, such as technology, economics, and politics; *Insight*, 242–43.

46. This relationship is reminiscent of Plato's analogy for the human being in the dialogue *Phaedrus*. There Plato likens a person to a chariot with horses and driver. The driver is intellect or

"opposed" because as common sense advances in insight and in the technological, economic, and political ways of organizing a society, its members' sensitivities and spontaneous intersubjectivities either lag behind in habituation or speed ahead with desires and fears that common sense cannot yet meet.

The demand for sport-utility vehicles, or SUVs, provides a contemporary example. When gas prices were low and environmental concerns were not widespread, SUVs became popular. But with rising gas prices and global warming becoming accepted as fact, demand is falling. Some members of society lag behind the shift, continuing to spontaneously desire an SUV, while others speed ahead, demanding electric cars that have yet to be perfected.

Ideally the majority of a society would neither lag behind nor speed ahead. It would be right in step with commonsense advances. But those who are at the two extremes serve the social good by embodying the tension between development that is too fast and development that is too slow. Their tension, which produces such goods as healthy debates, is part of the dialectical relationship between common sense and sensitivity and spontaneous intersubjectivity that helps to generate a sustainable pace of progress. But if the creative tension swings too much to one side, it can also result in various problems that promote negative developments, or "decline," the subject of part 2 of this book.

Generally the problem is not so much decline as change that comes very slowly. As we have seen, with a change in the social situation, new desires and fears arise from people's sensitivity and spontaneous intersubjectivity. These desires and fears call for other changes in the social situation. These changes to the situation as a whole include changes to the people themselves, to their sense of taste, their thoughts, their emotions, their values, their actions, their habits, their relationships. And such complicated personal and interpersonal changes take time. For example, our need for food and our desire for tasty food have led to a myriad of technological changes in food production. For parts of the world this

---

reason, while the horses are the passions or desires. Both are important and have their roles. Desires move a person, but intellect should be in control. Without desire a person would go nowhere, but without the intellect, a person would crash.

has resulted in increased food production and decreased physical labor. A negative aspect of such progress is the rising rate of obesity in societies where personal and commonsense standards of self-moderation and spontaneous cravings have not yet adapted to the new bounty and inactivity.

The adaptation of sensitivity and spontaneous intersubjectivity requires not only time, but a laborious process of discovery, teaching, learning, writing, reading, and persuasion. "So it is that the present is ever a pattern of lags. No one can postpone his [or her] living until he has learnt, until he has become willing, until his sensitivity has become adapted."[47] In other words, we human beings must live before we have learned how best to live. Providentially, we have other resources built into emergent probability beyond commonsense insight and beyond the desires and fears of sensitivity and spontaneous intersubjectivity. In other words, there is more to human progress than insight and its creative tension with sensitivity and spontaneous intersubjectivity.

Reflection Questions for Chapter 2

- Have you experienced a desire to know? Lonergan says that children are often the best examples of this desire. They are a model of spontaneous and unrestricted wonder. They want to know what something means, where something came from, how something tastes. But most of all, perhaps, they want to know the answer to the question, "Why?" Why is the sky blue and plants green? Why do birds sing and cats meow? Why do some things taste bitter and others sweet?

- As we get older this type of wonder seems to diminish, perhaps even to die. This is partly due to the fact that as we get older, we tend to know more. Through the years we have asked many questions and received satisfactory answers. But the universe is vast, and some say that the more one knows the more one knows there is to know. Another cause of diminished wonder is that people get caught up in everyday life. When we do pause

47. *Insight*, 711.

to ask a question, we usually intend to use this information for some practical task. The ten-year-old in math class asking, "When am I going to use this?" is a good example of how we begin early on to measure things by their perceived usefulness. For a student such usefulness may be confined to whether or not the material will be on the test. For older people it may be how much money a thing will bring us.

• Practical matters like passing a test and making money are important, but with our limited knowledge, do we really know how something we encounter now may be useful later? Perhaps our society is too concerned with practicality; is it? If so, can we reawaken our childlike wonder? Should we? Why?

3 | Transcendental Method

As we learned from the cosmological context of Lonergan's anthropology, the world is ordered into a dynamic, interdependent hierarchy. Lower levels of recurrent schemes set the conditions for the more or less probable emergence and survival of higher recurrent schemes. Higher levels depend on the lower levels, but they also transcend or go beyond them. And they do so in a way that sublates the lower ones, or lifts them up into a greater, richer context that preserves and fulfills them. Lower levels are more essential to the whole, and higher levels are more excellent.

Humanity is a later and higher emergence in the cosmos. It transcends and sublates material, chemical, and biological recurrent schemes into a larger psychological context. We have considered insight and its role in the community's and the world's development, but insight is not the entire human contribution to emergent probability. The human person is complex. It is comprised of material, chemical, biological, and psychological levels. Moreover, on the psychological level there is a further multiplicity to the human person.

Thus far we have considered some of the lower, more essential psychological levels, starting with the human person's sensitive, intersubjective needs, desires, and fears, and moving up to a high-

45

er, intellectual level that seeks to direct and to fulfill the spontaneous drives of the lower level. We have seen that these two levels exist in a creative, dialectical tension that can produce both progress and decline. This is a rich picture, but it is not the full picture.

Published fifteen years after *Insight*, Lonergan's *Method in Theology* extends Lonergan's coverage of cognitive theory, epistemology, and metaphysics into the realms of ethics and religion.[1] Ethics deals with human decision-making in a social context, and religion pertains to human relationships with the absolutely transcendent—that is, God.[2] To *Insight*'s account of the human person as sensitive, spontaneously interpersonal, and intellectual, *Method* adds an expanded consideration of the person as concerned with value, exercising freedom, and falling in love. This fuller picture—on the human person as ethically and religiously self-transcendent—is the topic of this chapter.

✝ Four Levels of Conscious Intentionality

The core of Lonergan's anthropology as presented in *Method* is an analysis of human self-transcendence on four levels of consciousness. In each of these four levels, a person is *conscious* in the sense of being self-aware or self-present and *intentional* in the sense of seeking a goal.[3] Together Lonergan calls these levels "conscious intentionality." The four levels are: empirical, intelligent, rational, and responsible.[4] Each level is designated by one main operation: experience, understanding, judgment, and decision, respectively. So experience is the operation for the empirical level; this first

1. Lonergan writes that cognitive theory, epistemology, and metaphysics answer these questions, respectively: "What am I doing when I am knowing? Why is that knowing? What do I know when I do it?" Lonergan, *Method*, 25.

2. *Insight* ends with very brief, yet fruitful discussions on the possibility of ethics and a general notion of and heuristic for transcendental, religious knowledge; see Lonergan, *Insight*, chaps. 18–20.

3. See *Method*, 7–8. We will consider consciousness and its intended goals in brief sections devoted to each level.

4. Lonergan distinguishes between reason/rationality and logic. Reason is a broader term. It can be both logical and nonlogical. "The logical tend to consolidate what has been achieved. The non-logical keep all achievement open to further advance. The conjunction of the two results in an open, ongoing, progressive and cumulative process"; *Method*, 6. Logic operates on propositions, providing control and coherence. Reason facilitates discovery by an advertence to experience. It judges ideas based on both empirical evidence and logical coherence with known truths. More will be said in the following sections.

level is sometimes simply called "experience." Understanding is the operation for the intelligent level, and this second level is often called "understanding." Judgment is the operation for the rational level, and this third level is sometimes referred to as "judgment." Decision is the operation for the level of responsibility, also called "decision." Furthermore, for each of these levels, the overarching operation is comprised of multiple suboperations. Lonergan summarizes:

There is the *empirical* level on which we sense, perceive, imagine, feel, speak, move. There is an *intelligent* level on which we inquire, come to understand, express what we have understood, work out the presuppositions and implications of our expression. There is a *rational* level on which we reflect, marshal the evidence, pass judgment about the truth or falsity, certainty or probability, of a statement. There is a *responsible* level on which we are concerned with ourselves, our own operations, our goals, and so deliberate about possible courses of action, evaluate them, decide, and carry out our decisions.[5]

The operations relate to each other as levels generally do in a world of emergent probability—by transcendence or sublation: Later levels are higher and more excellent. They presuppose and build upon the lower, more essential ones. The higher levels include but go beyond the lower, and they lift the lower into greater contexts that fulfill the potential of the lower in ways the lower could not achieve on its own.[6] So understanding builds on experience, rational judgments presuppose and go beyond intelligent understanding, and responsible decisions presuppose and go beyond rational judgments about reality.

Lonergan uses the term "levels" because a person's movement from one operation to another raises or expands that person's consciousness. Movement from one level to another provides for personal growth and ultimately for social progress. As in the self-correcting process of learning, our experience, understanding, judgment, and decision both emerge from and transform the concrete social situation.

<hr />

5. *Method*, 9.
6. The "normal" movement of the transcendental method is from the lowest level to the highest, but there are two exceptions to this general rule by which the movement is from the higher levels down to the lower. More will be said on this in the next chapter.

The four levels do not constitute a rigid set of rules.[7] Lonergan's term for his presentation of the four levels as a whole is "method," which he defines as "a normative pattern of recurrent and related operations yielding cumulative and progressive results."[8] Lonergan affirms that experience, understanding, judgment, and decision are operations performed by people of all walks of life throughout their daily lives.[9] The operations are used in every human enterprise, from playing soccer to debating metaphysics.[10] The method is a kind of "third way" between art and science, and it is fundamental to both.[11]

Lonergan calls the four levels a "transcendental method" because the method is: (1) comprised of operations that include and go beyond each other; (2) the means of personal growth and social progress; and (3) used in all fields. Let us examine each operation of this transcendental method in greater detail.

Experience

The first level pertains to what Lonergan calls "experience." His use of this term is very particular, and it differs from common, contemporary usage in two ways: First, in everyday language, a person of experience is someone who has encountered a wide variety of situations and events, successes and failures, and thus has a great deal of first-hand knowledge as opposed to mere book smarts. Lonergan's use of "experience" is narrower and more basic than this. Experience for him does not necessarily lead to knowledge, but it can be a first step. Two people can have the same experience and not come to the same ideas and conclusions. For example, as mentioned in chapter 2, a two-year-old and a twenty-year-old watching a movie share an experience. But they will learn very different things from the movie. Or, to take another example,

---

7. *Method*, 6. 8. *Method*, 4.

9. *Method*, 3–4. Lonergan does not attempt to prove this method. Rather, he invites us in *Method* (14–21), as he did in *Insight*, to attend to our own consciousnesses and verify, augment, modify, or seek to deny his account.

10. Religion and theology, however, are more than human achievements. This method thus provides the "basic anthropological component" but not the "specifically religious component"; *Method*, 25.

11. *Method*, 4.

if two people are looking at the pages of a book written in English, but only one person understands English, only that person will have a chance of knowing what the book means.

The point is that for Lonergan, experience simply yields raw data. [A person requires further steps to transform such raw data into knowledge.] In this sense, as the first step toward knowledge, Lonergan's use of the word "experience" is narrower and more basic than the contemporary, commonsense definition of the word. However, in another way, it is broader. We tend to think of experience as the product of the physical senses—one experiences what one sees, hears, tastes, smells, or touches. This is experience for Lonergan, but Lonergan would broaden the term from simply the realm of sense data to include what he calls the "data of consciousness."[12] Consciousness for Lonergan is the self-awareness or self-presence that occurs to some degree in dreams, but more completely when one awakens. It is even more basic and pervasive to a person's psychology than sensory experience. The data of consciousness are what one gains when paying attention to one's ⭙ own conscious operations of desiring, fearing, questioning, understanding, judging, deliberating, deciding, and loving.

For Lonergan, thus, experience is twofold. There is the presence of physical objects through the data of our physical senses. Then there is the larger, more basic self-presence gained in the data of consciousness. Neither in itself is knowledge, but both may constitute a beginning of knowledge.

Understanding

A person's experience gives rise to questions. By our nature we wonder. We desire to understand. We want to know. Human experience is the source of a potentially endless number of questions. However, Lonergan asserts that all questions can be divided into two main types: *Quid sit?* (What is it?) and *An sit?* (Is it so?)[13] The

---

12. *Method*, 9, 201, 259, 263, 316.

13. *Method*, 335. Lonergan follows Aristotle and Thomas Aquinas in distinguishing the two; cf. *Insight*, chap. 9, and Lonergan, *Collected Works of Bernard Lonergan*, vol. 2, *Verbum: Word and Idea in Aquinas* edited by Robert C. Croken, Frederick E. Crowe, and Robert M. Doran. (Toronto: University of Toronto Press, 2004).

first is a question for intelligence. It aims at organizing data into intelligible relationships. Such is an understanding or an insight. In traditional terms it is an apprehension of the intelligible form, the nature, or the essence of a thing. The second question is for reflection, for rational judgment. It rests not merely on intelligible relationships, insight, or essences; rather, it depends on reality, the facts, or existence.

This is not to say that understanding and judgment are opposed. However, the distinction between understanding and judgment or between "What is it?" and "Is it so?" is crucial for Lonergan. The difference is similar to that between hypothesis and conclusion in modern scientific method.[14] The former is a more or less interesting *idea* and the latter is (ideally) the knowledge of *truth.*

Thus, as with experience, Lonergan uses the term "understanding" in a specific, technical sense that differs from its typical meaning in everyday language. This is true in two ways: First, in common usage, when one says, "I understand," one means, "I get it. I know what you mean. I know what's going on." On the other hand, the term "understanding" could also indicate a kind of sympathy, feeling what another feels. But by the term "understanding" Lonergan means neither knowing nor sympathizing.

Simply put, understanding is insight as well as the operation that produces an insight. Insight, as we have discussed in chapter 2, is the patterning or relating of multiple things (such as shapes, colors, letters, words, or events) into an intelligible whole. Understanding builds on experience and provides the foundation for judgment. It seeks to answer the question of *what* a thing is by grasping the internal relationships of the thing's parts as well as the thing's external relationships to other things. Complete understanding is obtained only by understanding all things in all of their relationships. Such understanding is enjoyed, of course, by God alone.[15] However, the absence of complete understanding does not preclude the possibility of any understanding.

14. *Method*, 5. The distinction between insight and judgment is so crucial to Lonergan's thought that I sometimes think his book *Insight* could have been called *"Judgment."*
15. See Lonergan, *Insight*, chap. 19.

For Lonergan, knowledge is not the product of experience alone, of understanding alone, or even of experience and understanding combined. Rather, knowledge is a composite of experience, understanding, and the further step called judgment. This term too he uses in a particular, technical sense.

Lonergan's distinction between understanding and judgment may seem abstract and unhelpful. But philosophers and other thinkers influenced by philosophy, including theologians, spend much time and energy debating the nature of reality and how it can be known. There are perhaps two dominant schools: (1) materialists or empiricists, who believe reality is physical and is known through the senses, and (2) idealists, who believe that the physical world is a deceptive appearance and that the real world of unchanging ideas is known by reason or intuition.[16]

Against these two schools, with their one-sided emphases on either experience or intellect, Lonergan acknowledges the important roles of both experience and understanding in the human effort to know reality. Experience provides the data (of sense and consciousness). Understanding takes the data and uses questions to come up with ideas or insights. Insights, however are "a dime a dozen," for understanding attains only *possible* intelligible relationships.[17] The next step of judgment is required for one to apprehend *actual* intelligible relationships, more commonly called "the facts" or "the truth." Insights are important, but they are simply ideas, and our ideas are often wrong. There are many possible ways of understanding one's experience, but reality is one. To know the facts about reality, a person must correctly judge the truth or falsehood of his or her understanding of experience.[18]

This method is reflected in the process that plays out in a court

16. *Method*, 213–14.

17. *Method*, 13.

18. *Method*, 230–33. Lonergan acknowledges that while reality is one, people's understanding and judgment of reality are multiple. Many will be correct, but incomplete. Then there is the possibility of error and bias. Lonergan asserts that error and bias are not necessary consequences of human subjectivity, but failures and aberrations; thus Lonergan takes a position against extreme forms of deconstruction, hermeneutics of suspicion, relativism, etc. Chapters 10 and 11 of *Method* ("Dialectic" and "Foundations") provide tools for identifying the causes of differences in opinion and for promoting authentic agreement. We will discuss bias in chapter 6 of this book.

of law. Here witnesses provide the empirical data through their testimony and other evidence. Lawyers present different understandings or interpretations of the data. The jury or a judge attempts to judge impartially which lawyer's interpretation is closest to the truth. All along the line, questions are asked. Lawyers raise various "What is it?" questions to the witnesses in their search for possible intelligible relationships of the events. Although multiple questions are asked of the witnesses, only one question is asked of the jury: Is the defendant guilty beyond a reasonable doubt?[19] This is a form of the second type of question, the question for judgment: "Is it so?"

Clearly, if judgment is the way people come to know reality in all areas of human living, it is very important to determine the standards for making correct, reasonable, or impartial judgments. If, as Lonergan believes, experience and intelligence alone are not reliable standards for objectivity, then what is? How do we make judgments? With instinct? Imagination? Gut feelings? Some external authority, such as scientific experts, the wisdom of the ages, tradition, scripture, or revelation? Lonergan affirms that all of these things are invaluable for human living.[20] However, the problem with these and other sources is that they too must be experienced, understood, and judged by a human person—if they are to be known by that person. Thus Lonergan's standard for making a correct judgment is not some element of human subjectivity or some external authority; rather it is the whole person operating properly on multiple levels of conscious intentionality. Such a person Lonergan calls an "authentic subject." And he maintains that such a person can make correct judgments: "Genuine objectivity is the fruit of authentic subjectivity."[21]

We will examine authenticity in general later in this chapter; however, let us consider precisely how one makes a judgment. Judgment presupposes and builds on experience and understand-

19. There is, of course, a fourth step after the witnesses have provided the data, the lawyers have presented possible interpretations, and the jury or judge has made a verdict—namely, the judge has the responsibility to decide what to do. This will be discussed in the next section.
20. The importance of belief for Lonergan follows in chapter 4 of this volume, under the section entitled "The Human Good."
21. *Insight*, 292; for more on judgment and objectivity, see chap. 10.

ing. Just as wonder or questioning promotes a transition from experience to understanding, so a question raises one's consciousness from understanding to the level of judgment. As already mentioned, the question that provides this second transition is, "Is it so?" This question may be formulated in many other ways, such as, "Is it true?" "Is it real?" "What is the case?" or "Is the defendant guilty?" (as was discussed in the courtroom example). No matter how the question is framed, what is at stake is whether some idea about reality is actually true.

This question about truth arises spontaneously. Once a person comes to some idea about his or her experience, he or she would fittingly begin to wonder whether or not his or her idea or insight is correct. One wonders, in other words, if one should assent to what one has apprehended.[22] Lonergan calls this second question, the one that pushes a person from understanding to judgment, the question for "reflection" or "critical reflection." ← *Understanding → Judgment*

In order to answer this question, one must gather the empirical data involved in the situation, or "marshal the evidence."[23] Then one must compare the data to one's insight/idea/apprehension/hypothesis and wonder, do the data support the hypothesis? If the evidence or data are deemed sufficient for supporting the insight or hypothesis, then a person judges whether the insight is correct, true, or factual. Such a judgment Lonergan calls a "judgment of fact."[24]

The key point above is that it is the sufficiency of evidence that grounds a judgment of fact. But what determines sufficiency? How does one know if one has enough evidence to make a judgment about objective reality? There are two factors immediately involved: the verification of empirical conditions required for the existence of a thing and the absence of "further pertinent questions" that might challenge the truth of an insight.[25] To understand the

22. *Insight*, 295–301; *Method*, 9–11. Lonergan's distinguishing between insight and judgment is based not only on Aristotle and Thomas, but also on John Henry Cardinal Newman's distinction between apprehension and assent in Newman's *An Essay in Aid of a Grammar of Ascent* (Notre Dame, Indiana: University of Notre Dame Press, 1992).

23. *Method*, 9.

24. *Insight*, 304–5.

25. *Insight*, 309, 661–62, 105–6, 296–99; cf. *Method*, 35.

first, we must understand Lonergan's distinction between the "virtually" unconditioned and the "formally," "strictly," or "absolutely," unconditioned. The formally, strictly, or absolutely unconditioned exists with no conditions, period. Only God exists as formally, strictly, or absolutely unconditioned. Creation as a whole and any part of creation exist as virtually unconditioned. These things do not have to be. There are conditions that must be fulfilled for them to exist. But when the conditions required for their existence are fulfilled, they exist and are called "virtually unconditioned."[26]

When a person knows the conditions for the existence of something and can verify that these conditions exist, then the person can know or judge for a fact that the thing exists. To take a simple example, if I know that the conditions to judge a TV as working are that the TV turns on and that it receives and communicates images and sounds from a broadcast station, and if I have indeed verified that the TV turns on and is receiving and broadcasting these images and sounds, then I know that the TV works.

The second factor, the absence of further pertinent questions, illustrates the more subjective aspect of authentic judgment. It also illustrates Lonergan's trust in the natural, human, unrestricted desire to know. This desire is also called "wonder," and for Lonergan it is a significant standard for knowing the truth that each person carries within her- or himself. Lonergan believes that if a person does not have sufficient evidence for judging her or his idea as true, then she or he ideally will reserve judgment. If the person continues to wonder, if further pertinent questions arise, then the person will know that the evidence is not sufficient.[27] That said, Lonergan is aware that there are many subjective conditions for a sufficient amount of pertinent questions to arise. A person, by temperament, may be "rash" or "indecisive."[28] He or she may not have the prior experience, understanding, and judgments necessary for further questions to arise, and/or he or she may simply not have enough time to allow them to emerge.

Despite the fragility of the process of coming to correct judg-

26. *Insight*, 305; *Method*, 75–76.   27. *Insight*, 308–9.
28. *Insight*, 312.

ments, people make concrete judgments and live by them all the time. One can increase one's chances of making correct judgment "by intellectual alertness, by taking one's time, by talking things over, by putting viewpoints to the test of action."[29] So while Lonergan admits that it can be difficult to make objectively true judgments, he defends the possibility of correct judgments from the fact that we make several of them, large and small, throughout our daily lives.

When one has correctly made a judgment and reached the knowledge of an aspect of created reality or of the virtually unconditioned, one has completed what Lonergan calls "intellectual self-transcendence." Intellectual self-transcendence is about knowing. One begins it in experience and makes qualitative leaps in it through questions for intelligence, insights, and questions for reflection. It is a type of self-transcendence, because by opening one's eyes and by wondering, one gets beyond oneself to other aspects of reality and improves oneself. However, a person attains a complete stage of intellectual or "cognitive" self-transcendence only in the judgment of fact or truth. "For a judgment that this or that is so reports, not what appears to me, not what I imagine, not what I think, not what I wish, not what I would be inclined to say, not what seems to me, but what is so."[30]

A correct judgment of fact is a complete act of intellectual self-transcendence. However, it is not the fullness of human self-transcendence as a whole, for human living does not consist merely in understanding and knowing, but also in valuing, doing, and loving.[31] Building on and going beyond intellectual self-transcendence is "moral self-transcendence."[32] The "initial thrust towards moral self-transcendence" occurs after one has completed an act of intel-

29. *Insight*, 310.

30. *Method*, 104–5. This quote from *Method* is taken almost verbatim from Lonergan, "Horizons," in *Philosophical and Theological Papers, 1965–1980*, 9.

31. "Horizons," 9. In addition, see "What Are Judgments of Value?" one lecture in a series Lonergan gave at Massachusetts Institute of Technology in 1972, published in *Philosophical and Theological Papers, 1965–1980*, 140–56.

32. And beyond moral self-transcendence, there is religious self-transcendence, to be discussed briefly in chapter 4 and thoroughly in chapters 8–10. For a wonderful, concise exposition of this threefold self-transcendence and an excellent introduction to Lonergan's thought in general, see his essay "Self-Transcendence: Intellectual, Moral, Religious," in *Philosophical and Theological Papers, 1965–1980*.

lectual self-transcendence, and this initial thrust is constituted by a yearning for an objective "judgment of value."[33]

In *Method in Theology* Lonergan builds on the cognitive analysis of *Insight* by adding an analysis of feelings as "intentional responses to value" and the judgment of value.[34] In much the same way that judgments of truth judge insights, judgments of value judge feelings. Feelings in *Method* play an expanded and perhaps substantially different role from that in *Insight*. Whereas *Insight* discusses feelings as arising from sensitivity and spontaneous intersubjectivity on a level *before* and *below* the intellectual search for intelligibility and truth, *Method* distinguishes between two types of feelings, "non-intentional states and trends" and "intentional responses."[35] The first of these functions before and below understanding and knowledge, while the second operates on a later, higher level than do insight and judgment of fact.

Examples may help to clarify the difference. Irritability is an example of a nonintentional state. Typically one will feel irritable before one understands why. Hunger is an example of a nonintentional trend. Hunger in general does not intend a particular object. It is not the result of intentionally apprehending and desiring some object. On the other hand, one may have a very specific, intentional longing for a particular type of food after seeing, smelling, imagining, conceiving, or discussing it. This particular, intentional longing is the type of feeling that arises after and above experience, understanding, and judgment of fact.[36]

Such an intentional feeling is subject to a judgment of value in a way parallel to how insight is subject to a judgment of fact. As insight grasps possible truth, so intentional feelings apprehend *possible value*.[37] Lonergan attributes an indispensable role to such

33. *Method*, 38.
34. Only once does Lonergan mention judgment of value in *Insight*, and that is in the limited context of a judgment of the value of belief (730). Again, much of *Method*'s discussion of feelings and judgment of value is taken almost verbatim from "Horizons," cited above. A helpful secondary source on moral self-transcendence, feelings, and judgments of value is Brian Cronin, *Value Ethics: A Lonergan Perspective* (Nairobi: Consolatia Institute of Philosophy, 2006).
35. *Method*, 30–31. Lonergan cites his dependence for these distinctions on Dietrich von Hildebrand's *Christian Ethics* (New York: David McKay, 1953).
36. *Method*, 30–31.
37. *Method*, 37.

feelings, calling them "the mass and momentum and power of . . . conscious living."[38] But while indispensable, they can be tricky. Lonergan asserts that a person's desire for an object may exceed its actual value, or one's fears may be misplaced. In other words, we do not always desire or fear something to the degree that it should be desired or feared. "What is agreeable may very well be what also is a true good. But it also happens that what is a true good may be disagreeable."[39] Hence the expression "bitter medicine."

Because feelings apprehend only apparent or possible value, the further step of a judgment of value is required if one wishes to reach true values or goods that exist in this world as independent of oneself or as "virtually unconditioned." Good judgments of value are not arbitrary impositions of the will. Bad ones may be, but good ones are not. In order to reach virtually unconditioned values, good judgments of value require self-transcendence—as much self-transcendence as good judgments of fact require, if not more. First of all, they build on all of a person's prior experiences, insights, and judgments of both fact and value. Furthermore, "the judgment of value presupposes knowledge of human life, of human possibilities proximate and remote, of the probable consequences of projected courses of action."[40] Ideally it considers not simply personal preferences, but the entirety of creation and history. One really needs to get beyond oneself to know what is truly good.

While the grasp of true, virtually unconditioned value is a difficult achievement, according to Lonergan a person identifies such value in a "simple" judgment of value. There is an additional "comparative judgment of value" that determines which value or values is/are better or more urgent in general or in a particular circumstance.[41] Comparative judgments are essential to human living, since people must choose not simply between apparent and actual goods, but also, and with more difficulty, from among multiple actual goods. Sadly we cannot have or do all good things. Saying

38. *Method*, 65.
39. *Method*, 31.
40. *Method*, 38; cf. Aristotle's treatment of pleasure in *Nicomachean Ethics* bks. VII and X.
41. *Method*, 31, 39; "Horizons," 16–17.

"yes" to one good typically involves "no's" to many others. Comparative judgments perform the needed task of sorting out and prioritizing different values.

As a general scheme for helping one to make such judgments, Lonergan orders values in a dynamic, interdependent hierarchy that is parallel to emergent probability's hierarchy of being.[42] He calls this hierarchy a "scale of values." On the first level are "vital values," such as physical health. Then come "social values," particularly the good of order that patterns or relates vital values and provides the context for their fulfillment. The economy is an example of a social value. Third, "cultural values" are grounded on vital and social values, yet they stand in judgment over vital and social goods, assigning meaning and value in a community. Freedom of speech would be an example. Fourth are "personal values," the values of persons themselves, persons as self-transcendent, as loving and beloved, as creative, as originators of value. Finally, there are "religious values," which regard ultimate value, the divine.[43]

The role of a compound judgment of value is to order and relate values within this scale according to their relationships to all things in the created world and to God. Judgments of value, both simple and compound, are, as stated above, the "initial thrust to moral self-transcendence." The fullness of moral self-transcendence lies not in judgments, however, but in the exercise of one's freedom in responsible decision and action.

Decision, Liberty, and Moral Self-Transcendence

"Decision" constitutes the fourth and final level of Lonergan's transcendental method—a method that, when used properly, promotes personal and social progress. Decision builds upon the knowledge gained through experience, understanding, and judgment. By decision one broadens one's consciousness from a "disinterested" focus on the true and the good independent of me and my desires to a more personal, "existential" concern for one's own role in relation to the whole of reality. One becomes interested not simply in knowing reality, but in acting to help shape reality. This con-

42. Discussed toward the end of chap. 1 of this volume.
43. *Method*, 31, 39.

scious shift of interest or intention from knowing to choosing and doing constitutes a movement from intellectual self-transcendence to moral self-transcendence.[44]

The turning point from judgment to decision, or from knowing to doing, is constituted by a question, just as it was for the transitions from experience to understanding and from understanding to judgment. However, the question for decision does not arise so much from the pure, disinterested desire to know as from a personal, practical, and existential concern. Now one cares not merely about what is true or good in theory, but what is true and good in this particular situation that one is facing. After the unrestricted desire to know has brought one to relatively objective judgments about reality and the possibilities for reality, one spontaneously begins to wonder in a more subjective manner: What should *I* do?[45]

Typically a person becomes aware of many possible courses of action, of several options to choose from. The decision-making process, or "deliberation," requires that a person evaluate each course carefully. An authentic, morally self-transcendent decision is made in accord not simply with a calculus of pleasure and pain, but with one's prior judgments of fact and value, with what one considers to be objectively true and good.[46] However, while a decision is based on one's prior judgments, it has a very different character from judgments. A judgment is made in light of the unconditional desire to know. This desire drives one with a certain necessity to assent to the virtually unconditioned truth or value of an existing thing. A deci-

44. The difference between knowing and intellectual self-transcendence and decision and moral self-transcendence is very similar to the difference between the intellect and the intellectual virtues that perfect it and the will and the moral virtues that perfect it—as contained in the faculty psychology of Aristotle, Thomas, and many who follow them. Lonergan finds much good in faculty psychology, but he believes that there is a danger, particularly in modern authors, that can lead to a separation and even a competition between intellect and will, the mind and the heart, reason and emotion, or facts and values; see *Method*, 95–96, 259–60, 268, 340–43; and Lonergan, *Topics in Education*, 82–83.

45. Lonergan discusses the four levels together throughout the first chapter of *Method*. The spontaneity of deliberative wonder is found on page 18. Lonergan acknowledges the possibility that one may not care to ask what one should do. The extreme of this he calls "psychopaths," and a milder type the "drifter." (On psychopaths see *Method*, 18, 122. On drifters see *Method*, 40; Lonergan, "Existenz and Aggiornamento," in *Collection*; *Topics in Education*, 46. More will be said on the drifter in chapter 9.

46. *Method*, 50. Authenticity is the topic of the next section, "Authenticity: Transcendental Precepts, Notions, and Desire."

sion, however, does not have the same exigent character of necessity. Rather, there is a great degree of personal freedom in decision.

This is not to say that decisions are completely unguided or open-ended. As mentioned above, they are based on and should be made in accordance with one's prior judgments of truth and value. Moreover, the existential character of decision gives it a tremendous weight of personal responsibility. When making a choice, a person is choosing not simply one good among other goods, but also what to make of him-/herself and of his/her world.[47] As the expression goes, "You are what you eat." And, according to another, "We vote with our pocketbooks." Thus decision is an exercise of freedom, but it can also transform the future context of one's freedom and decision, as well as that of others.

Lonergan sheds more light on the reciprocal relationship between freedom and decision by distinguishing two types of freedom. There is the theoretical "essential freedom" that human beings have in the abstract simply by virtue of being human. Then there is the actual "effective freedom" that a person has, based on the current social situation set up by the person's previous choices and the previous choices of others.[48]

To demonstrate the existential significance of decision and how decisions can increase one's effective freedom, Lonergan makes use of a spatial metaphor. First he distinguishes between the freedom to choose a particular good from a set of goods and thus to transform the set and a related but greater ability to choose oneself and thus to transform one's entire world. The difference between the two is the distinction between choosing from *particular goods* within one's horizon and choosing one's *horizon itself.* "Horizon" is Lonergan's term for the scope of a person's or a group's knowledge and interest.[49] "Horizontal liberty" is one's ability to select particular things within a given horizon. "Vertical liberty"

---

47. *Method*, 121.
48. See *Insight*, 643–47.
49. "There is a sense in which it may be said that each of us lives in a world of his own. That world is usually a bounded world, and its boundary is fixed by the range of our interests and our knowledge. There are things that exist, that are known to other men, but about them I know nothing at all. There are objects of interest that concern other men, but about them, I could not care less"; Lonergan, "The Subject," in *A Second Collection*, 69; cf. *Topics in Education*, 89.

is the ability to select a horizon. For just as one's physical horizon grows when one climbs vertically up a mountain, in a skyscraper, or in a hot-air balloon, so a person's range of options grows when that person makes a morally self-transcendent decision, one based on self-transcendent judgments of truth and goodness and a morally self-transcendent answer to the existential question of what one should do.

The positive exercise of vertical liberty is a substantial advance in effective freedom. It broadens one's entire horizon and thus radically increases the range of goods available for one to know and to desire, to love and to serve. But one's decisions could also have a negative effect on one's vertical liberty and one's effective freedom, causing the contraction of one's horizon and a decrease in the range of goods from which one has the capacity to choose.[50]

Not only do good decisions increase the range of choices one has, they also increase one's ability to make good choices. And, of course, bad decisions not only decrease one's range of choices, they also decrease one's ability to make good choices.[51] Thus decisions have consequences not only for one's freedom, but also for one's morality.

No one is born with unrestricted effective freedom and perfect morality. Over time a person grows in the discernment of values. Her or his feelings change. Ideally, true goods that once felt dissatisfying become satisfying, and lesser goods that were overvalued become viewed in proper perspective.[52] This development of knowledge and feeling often accompanies a growth in vertical liberty, and it increases one's effective freedom. One becomes less and less a slave to one's satisfactions and less and less attracted to merely apparent goods. One transforms from a pleasure/pain machine into a mature human person, a woman or a man, fully alive, at least as fully alive as is naturally possible.

---

50. *Method,* 40–41. Lonergan credits Joseph de Finance for the insights into vertical and horizontal liberty and refers us to de Finance's book, *Essai sur l'agir humain* (Rome: Presses de l'Université Grégorienne, 1962), 287 ff; cf. *Method,* 235–37; *Topics in Education,* 88–91; and the entire essay "Horizons."

51. This has much in common with Aristotle's presentation of moral virtues as good habits and vices as bad habits in his *Nicomachean Ethics* bks. II–V.

52. *Method,* 32.

Such a transformation, for Lonergan, is oriented toward love. He writes that when we decide to do the good that we have judged, and when we act on this decision, we achieve a full measure of moral self-transcendence, and we become "principles of benevolence and beneficence, capable of genuine collaboration and of true love."[53]

Authenticity: Transcendental Precepts, Notions, and Desire

As we have seen, human subjectivity plays a crucial role in Lonergan's ideas about transcendental method and human progress. Again, by "subject" Lonergan means simply a human person who is conscious. It is important to remember that when Lonergan uses the terms "subject" and "subjectivity," he is honoring the significance of human consciousness in human living. He is acknowledging the fact that human beings become conscious through various intentional operations. And he is attending to a way in which these intentional operations contribute to the progress or the decline of a person, a community, indeed our entire universe. But by attending to human subjectivity, Lonergan does not mean there is no objective truth or that anything goes, as types of subjectivism or relativism might imply. What makes the crucial difference is Lonergan's notion of what he calls "authenticity."

Thus far we have used the term "authentic" to identify correct judgments and good decisions, and we have said that Lonergan's standard for achieving objectivity is the authentic subject. Authenticity thus identifies a type of operation as well as a type of person. Furthermore, it is the result of, the cause of, and in some ways the same as personal self-transcendence and social progress.[54]

The possibility of authenticity underlies Lonergan's rather sunny views on human nature and human history. As stated at the beginning of this book, nature and progress are theoretical abstractions. The current, concrete reality of human existence is

---

53. *Method*, 35; cf. 104, 289. More on love will be said early in chapter 4.
54. See *Method*, 104: "Man achieves authenticity in self-transcendence"; and *Method*, 228: "Authenticity can be shown to generate progress."; complete quote to follow.

always a mixture of nature, sin, and grace—or progress, decline, and redemption. Reality is complex. Perhaps surprisingly, however, Lonergan believes that precisely because reality is complex, it is helpful to abstract these three aspects of reality in order to facilitate clear consideration of concrete problems and thereby to increase the likelihood of solving these problems.

To guard against an unrealistically positive image of the human situation or an equally unrealistic and negative view of Lonergan's thought, it is important to remember that, just as nature and progress are abstractions, so too is authenticity an abstraction, merely an aspect of the whole picture. As Lonergan writes, "Authenticity can be shown to generate progress, unauthenticity to bring about decline, while the problem of overcoming decline provides an introduction to religion."[55]

Authenticity is an ideal. But it is an ideal that can be very helpful for human living. Much of natural science depends on such abstractions and ideals. For example, physicists set the Earth's gravity at 9.8 meters per second squared. Nothing falls at this rate, however, because 9.8 meters per second squared is an abstraction or a selection of one variable from situations in which there are many variables, such as wind resistance. Nevertheless, the abstraction of gravity is tremendously helpful for understanding our planet and for contributing to all kinds of practical, technological advances, including space travel. Similarly, nothing on Earth is perfectly authentic, but authenticity affects everything, and understanding it is an outstanding aid for achieving one's potential and for promoting progress. Like progress in general, however, human authenticity is not simply the product of natural human capabilities, but also of divine grace. We shall leave the graced aspects of authenticity to part 3 of this book and focus now on three natural aids to promoting authenticity.

First, and very practically, Lonergan presents four guidelines for authentic observance of the transcendental method. They are called the "transcendental precepts": be attentive; be intelligent; be reasonable; and be responsible.[56]

55. *Method*, 288.   56. *Method*, 53, 55, 231.

On an empirical level one should *be attentive* in order to get the most out of one's experience. One pays attention by directing one's intentional consciousness to a particular object or objects, thus shifting one's awareness of this object(s) from the "background" of one's mind to the "foreground." When the subject pays attention to objects, she or he more authentically gathers data on objects in the world, including one's self.

On the next level, when understanding, it is best to *be intelligent.* [Intelligence is the ability to grasp patterns or relationships.] It is manifested in spontaneous questions. By intelligent wonder and by letting one's ideas be formed by intelligence rather than prejudice, one comes to better, more authentic ideas that relate the data in ways that more closely approximate their actual relationships.

To make good, authentic judgments, one should *be reasonable.* Being reasonable does not mean abiding always by logic, but [making critical conclusions based on the best ideas and verified by solid evidence.] Through reasonable judgments human subjects come to know objective truth and value. Thus such judgments fulfill one's potential for intellectual self-transcendence.

Finally, good decisions require that one *be responsible.* [Responsibility is the ability to conform one's actions to one's knowledge and one's values, as well as to the awareness that one's choices affect not merely the objects that one chooses, but also oneself and the entire world.] By being responsible a subject builds on the authentic experience, understanding, and judgment of what is objectively true and valuable, and she or he goes further to embody and to enact real values. Ultimately, personal responsibility entails moral self-transcendence in decisions and actions, thus making its practitioners "principles of benevolence and beneficence, of honest collaboration and of true love," as mentioned previously.[57]

These precepts are of fundamental import, not only to authentic personal self-transcendence, but to the entire range of practical and social progress:

Being intelligent includes a grasp of hitherto unnoticed or unrealized possibilities. Being reasonable includes the rejection of what probably would not

---

57. *Method,* 104. On moral self-transcendence, see the previous sections, "Judgment" and "Decision." Collaboration and love are topics for chapter 4 of this volume.

work but also the acknowledgement of what probably would. Bei.
sible includes basing one's decisions and choices on an unbiased ev
of short-term and long-term costs and benefits to oneself, to one's gr
other groups.

Progress, of course, is not some single improvement but a continu
flow of them.... So change begets change, and the sustained observance
the transcendental precepts makes these cumulative changes an instance o.
progress.[58]

[The transcendental precepts are internal commands built into
human consciousness. When followed they move us beyond ourselves to authenticity in our experience, understanding, judgment,
and decision. They are rooted in a vague awareness of a reality beyond our knowing. No matter how much a person knows or even
how much society as a whole knows, there are limits to this knowledge. When we become aware of our limits we encounter a "known
unknown," which we can probe in our questions.[59] Although our encounter with the known unknown may only be a vague awareness,
we will not be content to rest in ignorance, for the known unknown
causes a "radical intending that moves us from ignorance to knowledge" and to conscientious action in line with this knowledge.[60]

This radical intending of the unknown, which drives us through
questions to increase our knowledge, Lonergan calls the "transcendental notions." They are our second natural aid in authenticity:

The transcendental notions are the dynamism of conscious intentionality.
They promote the subject from lower to higher levels of consciousness, from
the experiential to the intellectual, from the intellectual to the rational, from
the rational to the existential.... Not only do the transcendental notions promote the subject to full consciousness and direct him to his goals. They also
provide the criteria that reveal whether the goals are being reached.[61]

There is a dual meaning to the transcendental notions. On the
one hand "*they intend* everything about everything," and on the
other "it is *by them that we intend* the concrete, i.e., all that is to be
known about a thing."[62] They are both "the *very dynamism* of our
conscious intending"[63] and "*what is intended*"[64] by our conscious

58. *Method*, 53.
59. *Method*, 23–24, 74, 77, 287.
60. *Method*, 11; see also 34–36.
61. *Method*, 34–35.
62. *Method*, 23, emphasis added.
63. *Method*, 12, emphasis added.
64. *Method*, 34, emphasis added. I believe this dual meaning has something to do with Aristotle's notion of the final cause—a good that is both the final goal and the original mover/motive.

operations. In other words, they are the object that we desire as well as something within us that moves us to desire them. Lonergan names the transcendental notions "beauty," "the intelligible," "the true," "the real" or "being," and "the good" or "value."[65]

The first four notions—beauty, the intelligible, the true, and the real or being—are intended on the first three levels of consciousness: experience, understanding, and judgment. This means that we are not content to appreciate the beauty of, to grasp the intelligible relations of, and to know the truth about one thing or one aspect of a thing. Deep down, when the noise of the world is stilled, we naturally want to know, to understand, and to appreciate "everything about everything."[66]

On the fourth level, decision-making, the transcendental notion of value or the good prevents one from finding *peace* until one has acted in a way that is truly good for all people, in both the short term and the long run. The notion of transcendent value drives consciousness into *conscience*. "The nagging conscience is the recurrence of the original question [What should I do?] that has not been met. The good conscience is the peace of mind that confirms the choice of something truly worthwhile."[67] This peace obtained by a healthy conscience no longer bugged by the transcendental notions is perhaps the best internal indicator that one is being authentic and helping the world to become a better place.

Lonergan summarizes his position—the transcendental notions function as standards for authenticity that are immanent in human consciousness:

The drive to understand is satisfied when understanding is reached but it is dissatisfied with every incomplete attainment and so it is the source of ever further questions. The drive to truth compels rationality to assent when evidence is sufficient but refuses assent and demands doubt whenever evidence is insufficient. The drive to value rewards success in self-transcen-

65. *Method*, 13, 34, 36. Lonergan cautions against confusing these transcendental notions with often mistaken, rigid concepts of them; *Method*, 12.

66. *Method*, 23; Lonergan, "Openness and Religious Experience," in *Collection*, 200; cf. *Insight*, 373. Beauty, art, and aesthetics play interesting but relatively undeveloped roles in Lonergan's thought; see *Insight*, 208–12, 291–92, 315; *Method*, 13, 61–64, 73–74, 272–74; and *Topics in Education*, chap. 9, "Art."

67. Lonergan, "Natural Right and Historical Mindedness," in *A Third Collection*, 174; cf. *Method*, 35, 40.

dence with a happy conscience and saddens failures with an unhappy co[n]science.[68]

This quote makes it seem as though a human person has mu[l]tiple drives and desires: one desire for intelligibility, another for truth, and a final one for value. In some ways this may be true; however, Lonergan writes that "the many levels of conscious intentionality are just successive stages in the unfolding of a single thrust, the eros of the human spirit."[69] This "eros of the human spirit" is the third natural aid for authenticity and is perhaps the most important and most fundamental of the three. It grounds and pervades all of Lonergan's thought.

In *Insight* Lonergan speaks of this eros as a "pure," "unrestricted," "detached," and "disinterested" desire to know. This fundamental human desire impels a person from experience to understanding and from understanding to judgment, prodding the person to perform each operation correctly. Lonergan expounds:

By the desire to know is meant the dynamic orientation manifested in questions for intelligence and for reflection.... The desire to know, then, is simply the inquiring and critical spirit of man. By moving him to seek understanding, it prevents him from being content with the mere flow of outer and inner experience. By demanding adequate understanding, it involves man in the self-correcting process of learning in which further questions yield complementary insights. By moving man to reflect, to seek the unconditioned, to grant unqualified assent only to the unconditioned, it prevents him from being content with hearsay and legend, with unverified hypotheses and untested theories.[70]

The domain of the pure desire to know is not limited to cold facts about existing realities. It seeks also to discern the value of things[71] and to identify various "practical possibilities"[72] for transforming the world. Lonergan asserts that human beings are doers as well as knowers, and that the pure desire to know unites these aspects of the human person, promoting a desire for harmony between them. In other words, "from that identity of consciousness there springs an exigence for *self-consistency* in knowing and doing."[73]

By our very nature we human beings desire not only to know

68. *Method*, 35.
70. *Insight*, 372.
72. *Insight*, 622.

69. *Method*, 13.
71. *Insight*, 624–25; cf. *Method*, 12–13.
73. *Insight*, emphasis added.

and to value reality wisely, we want to choose in line with this wisdom the best possible course of action, and we wish to actually follow this wisely chosen course of action. Without such self-consistency or integrity a person is tempted to do one or more of three things: (1) to "avoid self-consciousness" and the "precept of the sage ... 'Know thyself,'" in busy-ness, drugs, etc.;[74] (2) to rationalize one's inconsistencies—in other words, to lie to oneself, to dishonestly tell oneself that one's actions are not vicious or even that vices themselves are virtuous; and/or (3) perhaps most commonly to face one's wrongdoings and acknowledge that they are vices, but in an act of "moral renunciation ... [give] up any hope of amending" and claim, "If you please, it is very human."[75] In other words, to avoid the guilty conscience that comes from doing what we know is wrong, we can run from ourselves, lie to ourselves, or degrade our nature.

Affirming a good, natural desire to know the truth and to make our doing conform to our knowing is about as far as Lonergan goes in *Insight*. In *Method*, he develops this natural human desire within a broader context that emphasizes love and religion. *Insight*'s "pure," "unrestricted," "detached," and "disinterested" desire to know becomes in *Method* "a single thrust, the eros of the human spirit." This single eros drives human self-transcendence in and through all four levels of conscious intentionality. Since it is an "unrestricted thrust to self-transcendence," it will not rest when we have experienced, understood, judged, and decided in an authentic manner, one guided by truth and goodness. *Method*'s expanded, unrestricted thrust to self-transcendence finds its ultimate goal in the development of a loving relationship with an "other-worldly" love.[76] For Lonergan such unrestricted, other-worldly love and the possibility of self-transcendence into loving relationship with it are the proper topics of religion.

Religion, for Lonergan, is the study of ultimate, unrestricted reality and of how human beings find their origin and end in this reality. It is also a way of living in relation to this reality that, if taken

---

74. *Insight*.
75. *Insight*, 622–23; see also Lonergan, "Finality, Love, Marriage," in *Collection*, 25–26.
76. *Method*, 242, 289.

seriously, pervades all areas of one's life. The human being's natural, unrestricted desire for an ultimate fulfillment plays a central role in this study and way of living. There is a contrast between the more left-brain desire of *Insight* for infinite truth and *Method*'s more right-brain yearning for unrestricted love. But for Lonergan these desires are one. He links them in *Method* in a way that shows that *Method*'s eros for self-transcendence includes and goes beyond *Insight*'s desire for knowledge, which manifests itself in questions. "Just as *unrestricted questioning* is our capacity for self-transcendence, so *being in love in an unrestricted fashion* is the proper fulfillment of that capacity."[77] This quote points to the roots of *Method*'s language of self-transcendence in *Insight*'s language of questioning and knowing, since the human thrust toward self-transcendence begins with the natural spontaneity of our unrestricted questioning. So *Insight*'s pure desire to know that is fulfilled in infinite understanding, truth, and being is the same as *Method*'s single eros of the human spirit, which is fulfilled in unrestricted love.[78]

In the same way that human yearning for knowledge and love is one, there is a unity in this yearning's final fulfillment. Ultimately there is no competition between the true and the good. Those with training in traditional Catholic philosophy or theology will have recognized that the transcendental notions are traditional names for God, at least when they are capitalized to indicate their infinite, ultimate, or transcendent character. And they will have recognized that the seeming multiplicity of human fulfillment—in transcendent being, beauty, intelligibility, intelligence, truth, reality, goodness, value, and love—is in fact *one* single fulfillment, namely *God*.[79] Thus the natural eros of the human spirit is a natural desire for God.

In *Method* Lonergan writes directly and explicitly that the transcendental notions are notions about God, that the pure desire to know and the erotic thrust to self-transcendence are the desire

77. *Method*, 106, emphasis added; cf. 242: "Questions for intelligence, for reflection, for deliberation reveal the eros of the human spirit, its capacity and its desire for self-transcendence. But that capacity meets fulfillment, that desire turns to joy, when religious conversion transforms the existential subject into a subject in love, a subject held, grasped, possessed, owned through a total and so an other-worldly love."

78. *Insight*, 372–76, 680–708.

79. The traditional term for this is the "unity of the divine essence"; see, for example, Thomas's *Summa Theologiae* I, qs. 2–26.

for God, and that the natural human desire for unity with God has precedent in traditional Catholic theology, particularly in the thought of Thomas Aquinas. Lonergan connects his pure desire to know with Thomas's identification of lasting human fulfillment through the "beatific vision"—that is, an intimate unity with God conceived by an analogy of seeing or knowing God, neither through a likeness nor by faith, but by some measure of participation in and direct understanding of God's own essence.[80]

Never, to my knowledge, does Lonergan explicitly trace back this belief in a natural desire for God to Augustine's famous words at the opening of the *Confessions*: "You are great, Lord, and highly to be praised, ... you have made us for yourself, and *our heart is restless* until it *rests in you*."[81] However, Lonergan does allude to it. When discussing eloquently a "disenchantment" that arises when a person compares her or his limited achievements with the transcendental notion of the good, Lonergan mentions the possibility of *resting* in perfect goodness:

> That disenchantment brings to light the limitation in every finite achievement, the stain in every flawed perfection, the irony of soaring ambition and faltering performance. It plunges us into the height and depth of love, but it also keeps us aware of how much our living falls short of its aim. In brief, the transcendental notion of the good so invites, presses, harries us, that we could rest only in an encounter with a goodness completely beyond its powers of criticism.[82]

Eternal rest in loving relationship with God is the ultimate aim of human self-transcendence. In this life, however, God has given human beings not rest, but a restlessness caused by an unrestricted desire. This desire is a natural longing for a supernatural fulfillment, a human yearning for perfect, unrestricted love, good, truth, being, intelligibility, and beauty. This unified, transcendent desire underlies all human activities. It underlies the going beyond that begins when one opens one's eyes, when one attends to one's own feelings, and when one is moved to a spontaneous sense of

---

80. *Topics in Education*, 91, 173, 224. On page 91 the editors of Lonergan's *Collected Works*, vol. 10, note that Lonergan's notes cited Thomas's *Summa contra Gentiles* III, chaps. 25–63; and the *Summa Theologiae* I, q. 12, a. 1; a 8, ad 4m; q. 62, a. 1; and I-II, q. 3, a. 8.

81. Augustine, *Confessions*, translated by Henry Chadwick (Oxford: Oxford University Press, 1991), bk. 1, chap. 1, emphasis added.

82. *Method*, 36.

wonder. It is the source of a rushing stream of questions, of an earnest search for satisfying answers, and of the moral exigence toward conscientious action in society. The natural desire to know grounds transcendental precepts: Be attentive! Be intelligent! Be reasonable! Be responsible! It works with transcendental notions, providing a sense of peace when one has authentically carried out the operations of conscious intentionality.

"Man achieves authenticity in self-transcendence," Lonergan writes.[83] And self-transcendence is a single process comprised of four transcendental operations guided by four transcendental precepts, seeking four levels of transcendental notions, and driven by the natural, unrestricted thrust of the restless human spirit.

Even with these natural aids and impulses, authenticity is not automatic or even secure. A human person never fully possesses authenticity. We are always "on the way." Lonergan admonishes his readers:

> Human authenticity is not some pure quality, some serene freedom from all oversights, all misunderstanding, all mistakes, all sins. Rather, it consists in a withdrawal from unauthenticity, and the withdrawal is never a permanent achievement. It is ever precarious, ever to be achieved afresh, ever in great part a matter of uncovering still more oversights, acknowledging still further failures to understand, correcting still more mistakes, repenting more and more deeply hidden sins.[84]

In human history authentic self-transcendence promotes progress, while unauthenticity leads to decline. A full account of human authenticity would consider not merely the natural process of transcendental method and transcendent desire, but also the failure to perform the method well, the infidelity to the desire, and the resulting sins. Even more appropriately it would examine the effects on humanity of divine redemption, of God's gifts of grace and self-communication, and of the resultant conversion of human persons on intellectual, moral, and religious levels. But since sin, grace, and conversion belong to distinct vectors of Lonergan's analysis of human history, we save them for parts 2 and 3, on decline and redemption. As mentioned in the introduction, earthly reality is complex. It is always a product of nature, sin, and grace, or progress, decline,

83. *Method*, 104.   84. *Method*, 252; cf., 110.

and redemption. But as in the case of gravity, it is helpful for us to abstract elements of that complex, concrete reality and consider them individually. For now, let us now turn to another natural aid in human development, the original and greater context of personal transcendental operations: the cooperating human community.

Reflection Questions for Chapter 3

- Have you ever been wrong? Can you recall a particular occasion when you thought something was true, but it later proved incorrect? How did you find out you were wrong? Were there any negative consequences to your error? How did it make you feel to be wrong and to make other mistakes due to this error?

- We all make mistakes. Finding out that we have made one can be very humbling, even humiliating. It can make us lose trust in our judgment. The same goes when we find out that others have made mistakes. We can lose trust in them. We might even wonder if they were not simply mistaken, but deliberately deceptive. Such disappointment can make us suspicious. It can change our whole orientation toward ourselves, others, and the entire world. It can make us question anyone's ability to know the truth and to do good. It has even led some to believe that we cannot know anything, and that no one wants to do good. What do you think? Can we know that we can't know? Is it good to think that no one wants good?

- Lonergan believes that although we make mistakes, we can know through our experience, our intelligence, and our judgment, and we can choose to live authentically in accord with our knowledge. We have an infinite desire for this, a desire that sets us on a quest and will not be satisfied until we reach infinite truth and unite with unrestricted love. Have you felt this unrestricted desire, the longing to know everything about everything, to love and be loved by everyone? Have you craved experiences, delighted in ideas, been desperate for the truth, or agonized about what to do? Have you paid attention, been intelligent, reasonable, and responsible? Have you learned and grown? Have you ever been able to transcend yourself?

4 | The Cooperating Human Community

In the preceding chapter we considered the larger picture of Lonergan's account of anthropology—his transcendental method.
We discussed how an unrestricted desire for ultimate truth and
goodness drives the human person through multiple operations on
four levels of conscious intentionality. This larger picture remains
incomplete, however, for progress is driven not by the operations
of isolated individuals, but by the cooperation of persons in community. Ideally these cooperating persons are bound together by
mutual love and shared meaning into a dynamic communal matrix
that Lonergan calls "the human good."

Love

[Authenticity in experience, understanding, judgment, and decision leads to intellectual and moral self-transcendence. But there
is a higher authenticity caused by a third transcendence that Lonergan sometimes calls "affective." It transcends intellectual and
moral self-transcendence, advancing beyond their limits:

[W]e noted that the human subject was self-transcendent *intellectually* by the
achievement of knowledge, that he was self-transcendent *morally* inasmuch
as he sought what was worth while, what was truly good, and thereby became
a principle of benevolence and beneficence, that he was self-transcendent *af-*

fectively when he *fell in love*, when the isolation of the individual was broken and he spontaneously functioned not just for himself but for others as well. Further we distinguished different kinds of love: the love of intimacy, of husband and wife, of parents and children; the love of mankind devoted to the pursuit of human welfare locally or nationally or globally; and the love that was other-worldly because it admitted no conditions or qualifications or restrictions or reservations.[1]

Affective self-transcendence and moral self-transcendence are intimately linked. The peak of moral self-transcendence reaches to the base of affective self-transcendence. Thus, as quoted earlier, Lonergan wrote that it is through morally self-transcendent, responsible decision that people "can be principles of benevolence and beneficence, capable of genuine collaboration and of true love."[2] Moral self-transcendence does not seem in itself to attain the affective self-transcendence that is an effective love: willing the good (benevolence), doing the good (beneficence), and collaborating with others in this. Rather, moral self-transcendence is the condition for the possibility of these things. As Lonergan states in a very similar passage later in *Method*, "moral self-transcendence is the *possibility* of benevolence and beneficence, of honest collaboration and true love, of swinging completely out of the habitat of an animal and becoming a person in human society."[3]

Love is the key component of affective self-transcendence—falling in love, staying in love, and growing in love.[4] There is, however,

1. Lonergan, *Method*, 289, emphasis added.
2. *Method*, 35; cf. 289. This passage was quoted at the end of chapter 3 of this volume.
3. *Method*, 104, emphasis added. It is important to note, however, that in concrete reality love actually *precedes* moral deeds, as we shall see in "The Way From Above Downwards" in this chapter and in chapter 9 of this volume, "Religious, Moral, and Intellectual Conversion."
4. Some scholars believe Lonergan's affective self-transcendence and affective conversion to be the same as eminent Lonergan scholar Fr. Robert Doran's psychic conversion. I would disagree, however. Fr. Doran's psychic conversion, which Lonergan endorsed, seems to involve a specific type of feeling—namely, *Insight*'s precognitive spontaneous sensitivity and intersubjectivity or *Method*'s nonintentional states and trends. And while it is clear that affective self-transcendence, affective conversion, and affective development pertain to feelings, it seems that only affective development (*Method*, 65–66) pertains to the precognitive feelings involved in psychic conversion, while affective self-transcendence and affective conversion both deal with higher feelings—the postcognitive, intentional responses to value and love that pertain to moral and religious conversions. As quoted above from page 289 of *Method*, Lonergan seems to identify affective self-transcendence with religious self-transcendence when he says that affective self-transcendence involves falling in love, and he lists affective self-transcendence in a trio with intellectual and moral self-transcendence. Furthermore, in "Natural Right and Historical Mindedness," in *A Third Collection*, 179, Lonergan mentions affective conversion in a trio with intellectual and moral conversions, thereby seeming at least to identify af-

a great complexity to love. First of all, love is of many types, as Lonergan mentions in a quote similar to the one above: "There is the love of intimacy, of husband and wife, of parents and children; the love for one's fellow men with its fruit in the achievement of human welfare. There is the love of God with one's whole heart and whole soul, with all one's mind and all one's strength (Mk 12, 30)."[5]

When speaking of moral and affective self-transcendence, Lonergan is building on Aristotle's, Augustine's, and Aquinas's discussions of virtue, love, and friendship. At the end of his presentation of moral self-transcendence, Lonergan mentions that the fundamental principle of morality is not some set of rules, but the authentic person or "a fully developed self-transcendent subject." He states that this morally developed, authentic person is what Aristotle named a "virtuous person."[6] This is similar to Augustine's claim that "if one loves God, one may do as one pleases, *Ama Deum et fac quod vis*."[7]

In other words, there is a way in which a person who is genuinely in love is not bound by rules, and yet through this love this person acts more morally than a person who is following the rules. Love does this because it helps one to order values correctly; in particular, it helps a person to value others above or at least equally to oneself. In addition, rules are devised in order to protect various values. A person in love cares more about these values than a person motivated simply by concern for following rules. This is incomparably so if one is in love with God. Thomas Aquinas brings together the insights of Aristotle and Augustine when he writes that the love of God, called "charity," is a virtue and "the mother and root of all virtues."[8]

---

fective conversion with religious conversion. That said, in both cases Lonergan seems to mean something broader than religious conversion and religious self-transcendence, since in these two cases (the only ones I can find) affective self-transcendence and affective conversion include falling in love with other human beings as well as with God. Of course, religious self-transcendence and conversion include falling in love with other humans, but they stress the priority of one's relationship with God. And these passages seem to place the two loves on equal footing.

5. *Method*, 105; cf. 289. The last type of love mentioned here is charity. We will discuss it briefly in this chapter and in more detail in chapter 6 of this volume.

6. *Method*, 41. In a footnote Lonergan adduces a few references from Aristotle's *Nicomachean Ethics* II that indicate that the standard for virtue is the virtuous person.

7. *Method*, 39. Lonergan is paraphrasing Augustine's "*Dilige et quod vis fac*," found in his seventh homily on the letter of John, "*Epistula Ioannis ad Parthenos*" VII.8.

8. Thomas Aquinas, *Summa Theologiae* I-II, q. 62, a. 4, resp.; cf. q. 62. More will be said on the love of God in part 3 of this volume.

Additionally, when Lonergan speaks of the possibility of "benevolence and beneficence" and "of genuine collaboration and of true love," he is speaking of the mutual love that Aristotle called "friendship." In particular he means the friendship Aristotle considered "genuine" or "perfect," the kind that can be formed *only* by those with shared "virtue" or "excellence."[9] Virtues are good habits that orient a person to good acts. Classic examples from Plato and Aristotle include wisdom, justice, courage, moderation, generosity, and many others. Love, if real and not the possessive, blinding kind depicted in romance novels, is a virtue. So Lonergan affirms that like friends who share other virtues, those in love treat one another as valuable. And they do this not simply for the pleasure each brings the other, nor for any external goods they may stand to gain from the other, but because that person is valuable in him- or herself. Those who love thus truly enjoy the other person for his or her own sake. They wish each other well through benevolence, and they work for the good of each other through beneficence. Often such work is done in collaboration.

There are additional ways love is special for Lonergan. True love is the peak in a person's development of feelings as intentional response to value. It is "the supreme illustration" of "feelings so deep and strong ... that they channel attention, shape one's horizon, direct one's life."[10] For Lonergan love is a feeling, an intentional response to value, but it is also much more than a feeling. It is the fullness of human authenticity, the fulfillment of self-transcendence and unrestricted desire. It is a dynamic state that is at once a principle of rest and of movement.[11] Lonergan writes most eloquently of love in a kind of breathless and bursting way:[12]

One can live in a world, have a horizon, just in the measure that one is not locked up in oneself. A first step towards this liberation is the sensitivity we

9. Lonergan does not cite Aristotle on friendship in *Method*, but he does in other writings, such as "Finality, Love, Marriage," in *Collection*, 24–25. Aristotle treats friendship in his *Nicomachean Ethics*, particularly in bks. 8 and 9.

10. Lonergan, *Method*, 32, as well as in his soteriological writings.

11. Love as a principle of rest and of movement is mentioned many times in *Method*, but in "Natural Right and Historical Mindedness," 172–75, Lonergan discusses the roots of this in Aristotle's definition of nature.

12. In fact, I know of atheist couples who have used excerpts from Lonergan's discussion on love in *Method* in their wedding ceremonies.

share with the higher animals. But they are confined to a habitat, while man lives in a universe. Beyond sensitivity man asks questions, and his questioning is unrestricted....

The transcendental notions, that is, our questions for intelligence, for reflection, and for deliberation, constitute our capacity for self-transcendence. That capacity becomes an actuality when one falls in love. Then one's being becomes a being-in-love. Such being-in-love has its antecedents, its causes, its conditions, its occasions. But once it has blossomed forth and as long as it lasts, it takes over. It is the first principle. From it flow one's desires and fears, one's joys and sorrows, one's discernment of values, one's decisions and deeds.[13]

For self-transcendence reaches its term not in righteousness but in love and, when we fall in love, then life begins anew. A new principle takes over and, as long as it lasts, we are lifted above ourselves and carried along as parts within an ever more intimate yet ever more liberating dynamic whole.[14]

A man or woman that falls in love is engaged in loving not only when attending to the beloved but at all times. Besides particular acts of loving, there is the prior state of being in love, and that prior state is, as it were, the fount of all one's actions. So mutual love is the intertwining of two lives. It transforms an "I" and "thou" into a "we" so intimate, so secure, so permanent, that each attends, imagines, thinks, plans, feels, speaks, acts in concern for both.[15]

Love for Lonergan is at the centerpoint or crossroads of an individual person's conscious intentionality and the society's common good. It overlaps the natural process of progress and the supernatural grace of redemption. In this chapter on progress we must limit ourselves to the love that is theoretically possible to a nature that itself is a theoretic construct, yet immensely helpful.[16] In part 3 of this book we will examine the supernatural aspects of love—i.e., the summit of being in love with God.[17]

13. *Method*, 104–5; cf. Lonergan, "Horizons," in *Philosophical and Theological Papers, 1965–1980*, 11; and Lonergan, "Self-Transcendence: Intellectual, Moral, Religious," in *Philosophical and Theological Papers, 1965–1980*, 325–27.

14. Lonergan, "Natural Right and Historical Mindedness," 175.

15. *Method*, 32–33.

16. For Lonergan's excellent account of the historical development within Catholic theology of the theoretical category of nature, see the first chapter of his dissertation, published as Lonergan, *Collected Works*, vol. 1, *Grace and Freedom: Operative Grace in the Thought of St. Thomas Aquinas*, (Toronto: University of Toronto Press, 2000).

17. Without grace, it is possible, but not probable, for a person to love God. In "Finality, Love, Marriage," 25, Lonergan cites Thomas in *Summa Theologiae* I-II, q. 109, a. 3 c., as saying, "Even without grace man naturally loves God, but, from the corruption of nature, rational will seeks self." The editor notes that the quote is "*ad sensum.*" In *Insight* Lonergan affirms a natural love for God, as primary intelligence, primary truth, primary good (679–81). But this is not the full love of God with one's whole heart, soul, mind and strength of scripture that Lonergan speaks of in *Method*.

The Way from Above Downwards

Love for Lonergan is the fullness of human authenticity. It is the fulfillment of humanity's unrestricted desire and its capacity for self-transcendence. It is the result of an affective self-transcendence that surpasses both moral and intellectual self-transcendence.

But in addition to being a final end, love for Lonergan is a new beginning. As simultaneously the principle of movement and rest, it brings peace and friendship, new personal feelings and new communal cooperation. In addition to being a foundation for personal authenticity and for social collaboration, love has the intriguing ability to reverse the order of the operations in human conscious intentionality. In other words, love can reorder the flow of the four levels of Lonergan's transcendental method from experience, understanding, judgment, and decision to decision, judgment, understanding, and experience.

Typically, knowledge precedes love, as formulated in the scholastic expression *Nihil amatum nisi praecognitum*: "Nothing is loved if it is not first known." For Lonergan this is true "ordinarily."[18] Decision ordinarily presupposes judgment; judgment ordinarily presupposes understanding; and understanding ordinarily presupposes experience. Despite this norm, "there is a knowledge born of love. Of it Pascal spoke when he remarked that the heart has reasons which reason does not know.... The meaning, then, of Pascal's remark would be that, besides the factual knowledge reached by experiencing, understanding, and verifying, there is another kind of knowledge reached through the discernment of value and the judgments of value, of a person in love."[19]

To the ordinary way of knowing Lonergan distinguishes two exceptions, a "minor" and a "major." Both reverse the ordinary priority of knowing to loving. Both are forms of "a knowledge born of love." The major exception flows from God's love flooding our hearts, and will be discussed later in part 3. The minor exception begins when

---

18. *Method*, 122; cf., 278, 283, 340.

19. *Method*, 115; cf "Horizons," 19. This passage in *Method* is taken from "Horizons," where the Pascal quote is quoted in French: "*Le Coeur a ses raisons que la raison ne connaît point; on le sait en milles choses*" and located in *Pensées: D'après l'édition de L. Brunschvicg* (London: M. Dent and Sons, n.d.; Paris: Georges Crés en Cie, n.d.), no. 277, 120.

people fall in love with each other. This love, like all loves, is "a new beginning, an exercise in vertical liberty in which one's world undergoes a new organization."[20] Love is an exercise in vertical liberty because, while the world remains largely unchanged, the lover's personal world or horizon expands. Love reveals new values, and because values are related, one is confronted with the need to reevaluate all of one's older values in light of the new ones. Thus love reorganizes one's world. It occasions a new beginning.

Love's revelation of new values and its transformation of old ones flip upside down the typical order that moves from experiencing through understanding and feeling, to making judgments of truth and value, and eventually to commitment and decision. Using a spatial metaphor, Lonergan calls this ordinary process the way "from below upwards" and love's reversal of this process the way "from above downwards."[21]

In this second way love operates primarily on the fourth and highest level of conscious intentionality. There it creates new existential commitments. These commitments shape the decisions we make about how to live in society. Moving down to Lonergan's third level of consciousness, the commitments and decisions of love inform new judgments of value and truth. Such judgments informed by love are not necessarily subjective and biased. They may be, if the love that informs them is biased. But for Lonergan genuine love flows into objective, authentic judgments.[22]

Continuing our move "downwards," love provides a new horizon for understanding. A person dedicated to love and to judging with love will be more likely to come to certain ideas or insights and less likely to have others. Finally, love transforms the way we experience the world. When we fall in love, we not only have new commitments, new judgments, and new ideas, but also new ways of being sensitive and spontaneously intersubjective.[23] At the very least, our prior decisions, judgments, and ideas influence the way

20. *Method*, 122. Vertical liberty was first discussed in chapter 3 of this volume under "Decision, Liberty, and Moral Self-Transcendence."

21. "Natural Right and Historical Mindedness," 180–81.

22. More on this will be said below, in this chapter, on belief; in chapter 6, on bias, and in chapter 9, on conversion.

23. One might say, particularly if the love in question is the love of God, that "the world is charged with the grandeur of God," as Gerard Manley Hopkins wrote in his poem "God's Grandeur."

we attend to our experience, the things to which we pay attention. A beautiful quote by Jesuit Superior General Pedro Arrupe expresses this in poetic form:

> Nothing is more practical
> than finding God, that is, than falling in love
> in a quite absolute, final way.
> What you are in love with, what seizes your imagination,
> will affect everything. It will decide
> what will get you out of bed in the morning, what you do with your evenings,
> how you spend your weekends, what you read, whom you know,
> what breaks your heart, and what amazes you with joy and gratitude.
> Fall in Love, stay in love, and
> it will decide everything.

The World Mediated by Meaning and Belief

Love is not always the fiery experience of romance novels, the kind that consumes all of one's energy and focuses all of one's attention on a single object to the exclusion of others. Love can slip into the background, unnoticed, particularly as it ages. But even then it is no less operative and orienting. Such, perhaps, is the general love one may have for one's community.

The shared commitments of a community—the truths and the values it holds, its commonsense fund of understanding, and even the ways it structures one's experiences through common architecture, design, music, and food—provide the background that conditions the possibilities for one's personal growth in discovery and commitment. As we have seen, experience, understanding, judgment, and decision take place within a horizon. The human community forms much of this horizon. But what is community? How is it formed and of what is it constituted?

As usual, Lonergan's answer is complex. Simple physical proximity in a fixed geographic region is not enough to form human communities, nor are communities founded on some deliberate social contract. The individual does not join society out of a rational calculation of its usefulness. Reason and deliberation do shape various communities; however, human society is not initially the product of experience, understanding, judgment, and decision, or even of love. Lonergan asserts that society is founded on something more basic: "Prior to the 'we' that results from the mutual love of an 'I' and a 'thou,' there is the earlier 'we' that precedes the distinction of subjects and survives its oblivion."[24]

This "prior we" is caused by the "spontaneous intersubjectivity" reflected upon earlier. Lonergan believes that by nature human persons have some measure of "fellow-feeling." This is manifested, for example, by the fact that one spontaneously reaches out one's arms to save another person from falling, just as one spontaneously raises one's arms to protect oneself.[25]

Spontaneous intersubjectivity and fellow-feeling are the basic foundation for human communities, but much more than this, human communities are constituted by "common meaning, common values, common purposes, common and complementary activities."[26] For Lonergan common meaning is most basic, and it unites these commonalities. Where does common meaning come from? Lonergan believes it arises much like personal meaning. Thus common meaning develops from experience and questions, but from common experience and common questions. It becomes formal in common understanding, actual in common judgment of truth and value, and realized in common decision and activities.[27]

While the common meaning of a community as a whole develops "from below upwards" by the addition of new insights of creative people who meet new problems and old problems in new ways,[28] an individual's entry into the community's common fund of meaning occurs by means of the way "from above downwards." From birth, or perhaps even in the womb, a person is educated into a tradition. In each tradition there are certain common commitments to values, certain truths held in common, and certain common ways of doing things. Only after one has learned and followed these traditional meanings, values, and practices does one grow in critical understanding of them.[29]

24. *Method*, 57.
25. *Method*, 57; see the passage cited in chap. 2, note 41 of this volume.
26. *Method*, 211.
27. *Method*, 79; see also Lonergan, "Existenz and Aggiornamento," in *Collection*, 243–47.
28. This was discussed early in chapter 2 of this volume.
29. For an excellent discussion and extension of Lonergan's thought on education in a tradition and personal discovery, see Frederick Crowe, *Old Things and New: A Strategy for Education* (Atlanta: Scholars Press, 1985).

A major step in one's education in a tradition begins when one learns the language. Language is not simply a child's achievement, but a community's accumulation. It is the primary means for making common its common meaning.[30] Through language a person's horizon is radically altered. One transcends from the infant's "world of immediacy," characterized by mere sensitivity and intersubjective spontaneity, to enter a far richer mode of existence—what Lonergan calls "the world mediated by meaning."

The infant's world of immediacy is "the world of what is felt, touched, grasped, sucked, seen, heard. It is a world of immediate experience, of the given as given, of image and affect without any perceptible intrusion from insight or concept, reflection or judgment, deliberation or choice. It is the world of pleasure and pain, hunger and thirst, food and drink, rage and satisfaction and sleep."[31]

However, as one's command of language develops, one's world expands exponentially. "For words denote not only what is present but also what is absent or past or future, not only what is factual but also the possible, the ideal, the normative." But perhaps more important, at least from the standpoint of community, is the fact that words express the memories and aspirations, the problems and the solutions, the successes and failures of other people in all walks of life. Through language we can learn "from the common sense of the community, from the pages of literature, from the labors of scholars, from the investigations of scientists, from the experience of saints, from the meditations of philosophers and theologians."[32]

In itself "the world mediated by meaning" is enormous compared to the infant's world of immediacy. But entry into this larger world is no guarantee of participation in it. The initial entry is through language, but one participates in it to the extent that one *believes*. Belief tends to be associated almost exclusively with the realm of religion, but Lonergan reminds us of its integral role in any human activity. For example, people around the world orient

---

30. Meaning has other carriers, "in human intersubjectivity, in art, in symbols, in language, and in the lives and deeds of persons"; *Method*, 57; for sections covering each of these carriers, see *Method*, 57–73.
31. *Method*, 76.
32. *Method*, 77.

themselves geographically with maps. But how many have verified for themselves empirically the positions of cities on a map? When using a map we implicitly believe the mapmaker. Furthermore, not only users, but makers of maps rely on belief. Larger maps tend to be compilations of smaller ones. And the compiler does not verify all the work of the smaller mapmakers, who themselves rely on the work of surveyors. Every day, however, the accuracy of the maps and the value of belief are verified by the travel of cars, planes, and boats.[33]

Scientists, too, whose knowing is often contrasted with that of religious believers, depend to a great degree on belief. The advance of science depends on a division of labor that extends across both space and time. No scientist checks all the findings of all other scientists currently working, let alone all that went before him or her. This would require repeating all of their experimental observations, formulating all of their hypotheses, verifying all of their conclusions. Scientists verify each other's work to some degree, but without belief among scientists there would be no scientific progress.

This highlights the general social and historical character of human knowledge, without which human progress itself would operate on a much smaller and slower scale, if at all:

There is a progress in knowledge from primitives to moderns only because successive generations began where their predecessors left off. But successive generations could do so, only because they were ready to believe. Without belief, relying on their own individual experience, their own insights, their own judgment, they would have ever been beginning afresh, and either the attainments of primitives would never be surpassed or, if they were, then the benefits would not be transmitted.

Human knowledge, then, is not some individual possession, but rather a common fund, from which each may contribute in the measure that he performs his cognitional operations properly and reports their results accurately.[34]

In fact, Lonergan writes, compared to the community's "common fund" of knowledge the "immanently generated knowledge"

33. *Method*, 42. This is not to say that maps are perfect; cf. Lonergan, "Belief," in *A Second Collection*, particularly 88.
34. *Method*, 44.

that comes from a person's own experience, understanding, and judgment is only a "small fraction of what any civilized man considers himself to know."[35] Because of this communal, historical aspect to knowing, and in order to promote progress, we must be attentive, intelligent, reasonable, and responsible, not only in our personal acts of discovery, but also in the communication of our discoveries in writing or other media. On the other hand, because we are aware of the possibility and the actuality of our own error, we must be aware of the possibility of others' error, and we must make prudent judgments about whom to believe, about what things, at what times.[36] Still, this does not eliminate the indispensability of belief. It simply means that belief must be critical and that progress is "advancing not merely from ignorance to truth but error to truth."[37] In fact, progress requires that we must continually correct our own errors and the errors of those who preceded us. Due to belief's central role in human cooperation and progress, authenticity in reporting, judging, and correcting is of paramount importance.

The Human Good

We have said that for Lonergan, the human community is constituted primarily by meaning. This is not idealism, for the real is not merely what can be rationally conceived, nor is it simply what can be sensed, as a materialist might think. Rather, it is all that can be known, whatever can be judged to be true.[38] "Now the common meanings constitutive of community are not some stock of ideal forms subsistent in some Platonic heaven. They are the hard-won fruit of man's advancing knowledge of nature, of the gradual evolution of his social forms and of his cultural achievements."[39]

---

35. *Method*, 41.

36. Error is not the same as sin; see *Insight*, 690, where Lonergan distinguishes sin from "inadvertent failure."

37. *Method*, 44. For more on the critical process of coming to believe, see *Method*, 41–47; and *Insight*, 725–40.

38. *Method*, 20, 38, 93; *Insight*, chaps. 9, 10; cf. Lonergan, "The Subject," in *A Second Collection*, 69–86.

39. Lonergan, "Transition from a Classicist World-View to Historical-Mindedness," in *A Second Collection*, 4.

Lonergan's term for the advancing human community in all its meaningful and material aspects is "the human good." All that we have discussed has been part of the human good. The human good is a higher integration of general natural processes, of an authentic individual's intellectual, moral, and affective self-transcendence, as well as of a community formed by common meaning.

For Lonergan the human good, like anything good, is concrete.[40] The good is not just an abstract aspect of a thing. The good is comprehensive. It includes everything about everything. As the common scholastic formula states, being and the good are convertible.[41] We have seen that for Lonergan, the good is a transcendental notion. No matter how much we think we know, choose, act according to, or love the good, the good impels us on to further good. Along with Christian tradition, Lonergan believes that God alone is good by essence, while everything else is good by participation.[42]

Aristotle affirmed famously that the good is "what everything seeks."[43] Lonergan insists that not just the object of human desire is good. The desire itself is good, as are the capacity to desire, the concrete situation in which desire can be fulfilled, and the human operations and cooperation that bring fulfillment.[44] This set of object, desire, concrete situation, operations, and fulfillment provides the outline for what, in *Topics in Education* and *Method in Theology*, Lonergan calls "the invariant structure of the human good." Let us consider first Lonergan's earlier and simpler development of the human good in *Topics* and then his later, more complex framework in *Method*.

Like the good in general, the human good includes all of creation, starting with "the forest primeval."[45] The specifically human aspect of the human good is what is realized by human knowledge, choice, and activity. It is a developing reality, progressing

---

40. "What is good, always is concrete"; *Method*, 27. Note that for Lonergan, "concrete" does not mean physical. It means what is real, what can be judged to be true.

41. "*Ens et bonum convertuntur*"; Lonergan, *Topics in Education*, 27. We will discuss the existence or nonexistence of evil in chapter 5.

42. *Topics in Education*, 31.

43. *Topics in Education*, 28.; cf. Aristotle, *Nicomachean Ethics* I.1.1094a 2.

44. *Topics in Education*, 28.

45. *Topics in Education*, 33, citing Henry Wadsworth Longfellow's "Evangeline."

with each generation's new insights, judgments, choices, actions, and changed situations. Thus "the human good is a history, a cumulative process."[46] It is something to which we all belong, something to which we all contribute, and something from which we all draw. It shapes us, and we shape it. Concretely, it is a compound of human achievement, human sin, and divine redemption. On it depends our "eternal destiny."[47]

Lonergan analyzes the human good into levels. First and most basic are "particular goods," as we have seen. A particular good can be any particular thing, such as a pizza or pad thai. It can be an event, a satisfaction, or an activity. Lonergan tends to identify it with any satisfaction of a particular appetite, but, as noted, it would include appetites themselves.

A related set of particular goods organized in a particular way Lonergan calls a "good of order." The good of order is "the setup," a network and a flow of particular goods, similar if not identical to how a scheme of recurrence is comprised of an interdependent set of things or events. The good of order is not one more good among other particular goods, but the proper organization of a set of particular goods. The economy is an example. All the pieces required for a robust economy may be in place, such as raw materials, factories, labor, and consumers, but if these parts are not related harmoniously, there is no good of order.

Economic depression exemplifies the lack of a good of order. The good of order provides for a regular and recurrent production and distribution of particular goods. Without the order, particular goods may come, but not regularly or recurrently. This is important, because "Man is intelligent; he is not satisfied with breakfast today; he wants lunch and dinner too, and he wants them every day."[48]

The third and final level of the human good is "value." Particular goods and the good of order are evaluated and criticized as more or less worthwhile based on a society's values.[49]

Particular goods, the good of order, and values are related in a way similar to experience, understanding, and judgment. Particu-

46. *Topics in Education*, 33.
48. *Topics in Education*, 39.
47. *Topics in Education*, 34.
49. *Topics in Education*, 39–40.

lar goods are similar to the data gained by experience. The good of order is a pattern, similar to those produced by understanding. And values stand in judgment of both particular goods and the good of order.

Each culture will have different particular goods, different goods of order, and different values. But every culture will have *some* particular goods, *some* good of order, and *some* values. Thus for Lonergan these three levels constitute an "invariant structure" to the human good.[50] Particular goods are relatively self-explanatory, but let us consider further the good of order and value.

In *Topics in Education* Lonergan writes that there are many elements of a good of order, but he chooses to discuss four: "a regular recurrence of particular goods, coordinated human operations, a set of conditions of the operations, and personal status."[51]

First, "a regular recurrence of particular goods" is not to be achieved by "mechanist planning," since in a mechanist model the plans must be perfect. They must work out every detail, or the whole system will go awry. Instead of comparing the good of order to a machine, Lonergan likens it to the way water circulates on the surface of the earth. Its circulation operates on probabilities more than certainties. Consequently some parts of the earth are very dry and some are very wet. Rain may fall for many days in a row and disappear for months. Nevertheless, there is a statistical regularity to precipitation in certain geographic areas at given times.[52]

Second, in affirming that the good of order is about "coordinated human operations," Lonergan denies that human development is produced mainly by the unrelated achievements of isolated individuals. Instead he affirms that most human operation is cooperation. "Coordinated human operations" occur because of an interdependence formed by spontaneous interdependence, love, and the communal bonds of common meaning, value, and purpose. Persons separated by time and space may still influence one another mutually, albeit less directly. Such human cooperation is essential to the proper functioning of any human enterprise.[53]

50. *Topics in Education*, 33.
52. *Topics in Education*, 35.
51. *Topics in Education*, 34.
53. *Topics in Education*, 35.

Third, for this cooperation to occur there is required "a set of conditions," including (1) "habits" and "skills" of the heart, mind, and body; (2) "institutions," which are like habits on a social level —something in society that regularly handles certain sets of operations (for example: schools, courts, post offices, athletic organizations); and (3) "material equipment," such as books, desks, pens.[54]

"Personal status," the fourth aspect of the good of order, is produced by the pattern of cooperation in and among institutions. Each of us is a part of a larger whole. Different people perform different functions and fill different roles. We are who we are as persons in relation to others.

The standard for evaluating, criticizing, and improving both particular goods and the good of order is Lonergan's third level of the human good, "value." Just as a society can choose from a variety of potential products which goods it will produce, there are many possible ways of setting up a society, or goods of order. Commenting on the Cold War, Lonergan writes, "Children fight about particular goods, but men fight about the good of order."[55] Such fights arise and are settled by the values held by the participants.

Lonergan selects three types or approaches to value: The "aesthetic" approach realizes the true and the good in the sensible. When a good of order is good, its goodness is transparent in its products and in the happiness of its members. Second, the "ethical" approach asks if its members are becoming more "autonomous, responsible, free." And third, the "religious" approach to value judges all things as when we stand before God, with our neighbor, in the context of history.[56] It is religious in the sense of pertaining to ultimate things, but not necessarily in adhering to any particular organized religion. Any given society will have some measure of all three approaches.

Lonergan's basic point in *Topics in Education* thus is that the human good is not simply an accumulation of things that fulfill particular desires, but the whole system, which includes and provides for the fulfillment of these desires. The particular goods that

54. *Topics in Education*, 35–36.   55. *Topics in Education*, 37.
56. *Topics in Education*, 37–38. These three approaches parallel the three ways of living Søren Kierkegaard identifies in many of his works, including *Fear and Trembling.*

Figure 4-1.

Individual			
Potentiality	*Actuation*	Social	Ends
capacity, need	operation	cooperation	particular good
plasticity, perfectibility	development, skill	institution, role, task	good of order
liberty	orientation, conversion	personal relations	terminal value

Note: *Method*, 48. I am grateful to the University of Toronto Press for permission to reproduce this chart.

fulfill our desires and the whole system that produces and distributes these goods are not values-free. They are the embodiments of a community's judgments of value and their decisions based on these values.

To present the invariant structure of the human good in *Method*, Lonergan selects eighteen terms and divides them into three categories: individual potentialities and actuations, social, cooperating groups, and ends or goals. Figure 4-1 is the reproduction of a chart from *Method in Theology* that depicts these terms organized under their categories.

The following is my attempt to relate these eighteen terms among themselves clearly, accurately, and briefly. (At their first mention, the eighteen terms are italicized, and their above-mentioned categories are in bold.) *Method*'s main additions to *Topics in Education* are "liberty," "orientation," and "conversion." These I treat at greater length than other terms.

Each **individual** has **potentialities**. Basic among these potentialities are *needs* and *capacities* to fulfill the needs. The capacities are **actuated** on an individual level by *operations* that obtain the **ends** of *particular goods*. To a great extent, since we live in cooperating groups, or **society**, the operations are *cooperations*. The capacities for operating are *plastic* and *perfectible*, so *skills* can be *developed*. Development is largely in the context of social *institutions*, which also facilitate cooperation by assigning individuals different *roles* with respective *tasks*.

The *good of order* is the sum of these things in a related whole.

It is individuals in society developing their plastic and perfectible capacities to operate and cooperate into skills that give them roles and tasks in institutions that provide particular goods. The good of order is not a design for a utopia, nor is it a theoretical ideal or a set of laws.[57] The good of order as a whole and the individuals within it are characterized by a *liberty* that is not indetermination, but a self-determinism (oriented toward the good). The liberty of self-determination is experienced by individuals in their choosing and acting. Real liberty is the result of responsible decisions, exercised within *personal relations* that are determined by more or less shared needs, commitments, expectations, experiences, feelings, meanings, and values. *Terminal values* are the values chosen by an "originating value" or an authentic chooser, whose choices create valuable goods, and who personally grows in liberty with each choice and realization of true value. These originators of value, these self-transcendent people, are also themselves worthy of being sought after as terminal values.[58]

By their choice of terminal values, exercised in liberty, individuals and societies *orient* themselves and shape the direction of their development. As individuals or social groups people may also choose to change the direction or orientation of their development. *Conversion* is a tremendous change in orientation, particularly a positive change. It frees one from inauthenticity for greater authenticity. Conversion causes a radical shift in one's fears and desires, satisfactions and values, beliefs and scales of preference.[59] Lonergan expounds on conversion:

It is not merely a change or even a development; rather it is a radical transformation on which follows, on all levels of learning, an interlocking series of changes and developments. What hitherto was unnoticed becomes vivid and present. What had been of no concern becomes a matter of high import. So great a change in one's apprehensions and one's values accompanies no less a change in oneself, in one's relations to other person, and in one's relations to God.... Conversion may be compacted into the moment of a blinded Saul falling from his horse on the way to Damascus. It may be extended over the slow maturing process of a lifetime.[60]

57. *Method*, 48–49.   58. *Method*, 50–51.
59. *Method*, 51–52. Conversion is treated at length in chapter 9 of this volume.
60. "The Subject," 65–66.

In part 3 of this book we will examine in greater detail the role of conversion, but let us end this discussion of the human good by returning to *Topics in Education*, which contains Lonergan's strongest presentation of the human good as it develops. In chapter 2 of *Topics*, Lonergan discusses the development of the human good on two levels: civilization and culture. "Intellectual development corresponds to civilization, reflective development to culture."[61] Lonergan analyzes the development of civilization along the lines of technology, economy, and polity.[62] Civilization is driven by ideas, while culture is driven by values. Culture stands above civilization as values stand above the good of order. In other words, culture provides the standards for evaluating and critiquing a civilization. It provides the "aims and values" by which one may judge the ideas embodied in a civilization's various ways of relating things.[63]

The mutual development of civilization and culture follows a pattern of "challenge-and-response" that Lonergan learned from a leading contemporary historian, Arnold Toynbee.[64] Basically "challenge-and-response" means that challenges arise in a human community. The challenges invite responses by members of the community, and the responses create new challenges that again call for new responses, and so forth. This is also the process of *Insight*'s self-correcting process of learning and *Method*'s transcendental method.

Revealing the interdependence of the human good in a world ordered by emergent probability, Lonergan notes that the process of challenge-and-response may start small, with a single insight in response to a minor, localized problem, but swiftly it

will involve repercussions all through the good of order. New ideas will start popping up everywhere. There will result augmented well-being, and it affects each of the aspects of the human good: the flow of particular goods becomes more frequent, more intense, more varied; new equipment is produced; institutions are remodeled; new types of goods are provided; the so-

---

61. *Topics in Education*, 50.
62. *Topics in Education*, 55; cf. *Insight*, chap. 7.
63. *Topics in Education*, 50.
64. *Topics in Education*, 51, with note to Arnold J. Toynbee, *A Study of History*, 12 vols. (London: Oxford University Press), vol. 3, *The Growth of Civilizations* (1934); vol. 6, *The Disintegration of Civilizations* (1939); and vol. 10, *The Inspiration of Historians* (1954), index, "Challenge-and-Response"; see also *Insight*, 234.

ciety enjoys more democracy and more education; new habits are formed to deal with the new equipment in the new institutions; there is status for all, because everything is running smoothly; everybody is too busy to be bothered with knifing other people; there are happy personal relations, a development in taste, in aesthetic value and its appreciation, and in ethics, in the autonomy of the subject; finally, there is more time for people to attend to their own perfection in religion.[65]

The agents of this change are "creative personalities." And although small changes can spread quickly, sustained progress requires a long succession of these personalities, "who are not simply sunk into the existing situation, immersed in its routines, and functioning like cogs in a wheel, with little grasp of possibilities, with a lack of daring."[66] To become creative, such personalities must withdraw from society and become detached, at least mentally, in order to see how things could be different, to "become themselves." This withdrawal is not a permanent, final goal. It is for the sake of a return to the world to transform it. Lonergan notes that Karl Marx, who, for better and for worse, was perhaps the most influential person of the twentieth century, spent years of obscurity and solitude writing in the British Museum.[67]

On return these creative types must be prepared to struggle. Toynbee assesses four steps in a difficult process of social adaptation to creative ideas: (1) enthusiasm, led by poets; (2) sedation, when systematizers take over; (3) disillusion, with conflicts caused by change; and (4) general acceptance, when "the prophets are honored by the sons of those who had stoned them." Ideas slowly spread by imitation. Toynbee calls this *mimesis,* and it involves charmed followers who feel something is afoot but need a leader to provide direction, hierarchy, law, loyalty.[68]

A major aspect of the difficulty faced by the creative class involves a change in culture. Along with changes in the technological, economic, and political structures of a civilization, and in ad-

65. *Topics in Education.*

66. *Topics in Education,* 51–52. For more on the need for change, particularly within the context of the church and classicism, see "Existenz and Aggiornamento," especially, 247–49.

67. *Topics in Education,* 52. Lonergan relies here as well on Toynbee, particularly his concepts of "withdrawal for return" and a "creative minority." For the full reference to Toynbee's work, see note 65.

68. *Topics in Education,* 52. Lonergan does not provide citations for this or for the ideas referenced in notes 65 and 68.

dition to changes in the particular goods, the good of order, and the concrete ways of realizing value, there must be a concomitant change in the public's apprehension, reflection upon, and expression of those changes in the society's symbols, customs, laws, stories, and traditional wisdom.

As a culture develops, so too do its tools for reflection. In *Topics in Education* Lonergan discusses this as progress "from the compactness of the symbol to the differentiation of philosophic, scientific, theological, and historical consciousness."[69] Thus a very important part of progress occurs within human consciousness as a "differentiation" of consciousness. Lonergan's account of four differentiations of consciousness constitutes our final section in this chapter on progress.

Realms of Meaning

The "realms of meaning" are communal developments on a level of culture. They arise when any group of people develops its own technical language, its own distinct methods for gaining and sharing knowledge, and perhaps even its own formal cultural, social, or professional organizations.[70]

Lonergan typically counts four basic realms of meaning, leaving the possibility open for more.[71] These realms, or at least the first three realms, emerged at different historical stages. All four can be found in our world today, but a particular culture or a particular person may be fluent in as little as one or as many as four of the realms of meaning. When a person becomes fluent in more than one realm, her or his consciousness becomes "differentiated," so Lonergan calls the effect within consciousness of each fluency a "differentiation of consciousness." He enumerates at least thirty-one possible combinations of differentiated consciousness, plus one undifferentiated consciousness (a consciousness restricted to the most basic realm).[72]

The first and most basic realm of meaning is "common sense."

69. *Topics in Education*, 55.   70. *Method*, 81–85, 257–62.
71. *Method*, 272. Here Lonergan adds a realm of "art," focused on beauty, and a realm of "scholarship," which aims at the meaning of words and the intentions of deeds.
72. *Method*, 272.

One's entry into common sense is the same as one's entry into the world mediated by meaning: language.[73] We have discussed common sense as a set of insights, meanings, and values, which considers things in relation to ourselves or our group, and which aims at providing practical knowledge for everyday living.

We have also already considered the second realm, "theory," and this in terms of the scientist's quest for knowledge that moves from description to explanation, or from things as they are related to us and our senses to things as they are related to each other. This distinction comes from "the Aristotelian designation of the *priora quoad nos* and *priora quoad se*.[74] A simple example of the commonsense description of things in relation to us would be to call something hot or cold. But to relate temperatures to each other and explain the things in terms of a Celsius or Fahrenheit scale would be to shift into the scientific realm of theory.[75]

Common sense extends back to time immemorial, since the practical concerns of common sense are basic to human communities. But theory, at least in Western civilization, seems to have developed with what Lonergan, following Bruno Snell, calls "the Greek discovery of the mind."[76] Theory develops when questions arise from real or apparent contradictions in a culture's myths.[77] Parmenides is a key figure in the development of theory, because he challenged sense evidence and therefore established a distinction between sense and intellect. Furthermore, the thrust to theory is well exemplified in Socrates' search for universal definitions.[78]

Lonergan distinguishes between two stages within the realm of theory. In the first stage, philosophers represent the paradigm for theory, so all academic thinkers, including scientists, seek logical control over meaning.[79] In this stage classical law reigns. But in the second stage of theory, the natural sciences are given an inde-

73. *Method*, 86–90.   74. *Method*, 120.
75. *Method*, 82, 342.

76. *Method*, 90, citing Bruno Snell, *The Discovery of the Mind* (New York: Harper Torchbook, 1960), chap. 1, 3, 5, 9. Lonergan writes that as *stages* of meaning they are "ideal constructs" and that "in the main" he has "in mind the Western tradition"; *Method*, 85.

77. *Method*, 89–91. For Lonergan this is true of the development of Christian theology. In one's reading of scripture, questions arise that scripture itself does not answer. Lonergan traces the development of one such question: If there is one God and the Father is God, then what is the Son? This is the subject of Lonergan's work *The Way to Nicea* (Philadelphia: Westminster Press, 1976).

78. *The Way to Nicea*, 82, 92.   79. *The Way to Nicea*, 85.

pendence from philosophy, and developments such as statistical law emerge.[80] Both stages within theory give rise to the pursuit of wisdom and culture *for its own sake* in what Lonergan, following Marx, calls a society's "superstructure," namely its schools, libraries, research institutions. Commonly, some members of society may think such developments are useless, but they are for enrichment of the mind, the ennobling of the will, and many other unforeseen purposes.[81]

The third realm or stage of meaning, "interiority," is developed from questions raised by conflicts between common sense and theory, between those who value stories and parables and those who prefer logical and scientific precision. Such questions might include: Is common sense with its emphasis on narrative and myth simply "primitive ignorance"? Is science with its rigor and practical applications the "dawn"? Or are the stories by which we come to take part in a community what make us human, and is science with its cold precision really dehumanizing? Are commonsense thinkers short-sighted? Do theorists have their heads in the clouds? What is the truth? How can we know?[82]

In Western culture the rise of interiority as a distinct realm of meaning on a social level began in the Enlightenment with the slow replacement of faculty psychology (which analyzes the person into various parts, such as intellect and will) by intentionality analysis (which focuses on our interior intentions). It occurred through the challenges and advancements of such thinkers as Galileo, Descartes, Spinoza, Kant, Hegel, Kierkegaard, Schopenhauer, Nietzsche, Blondel, Brentano, Husserl, and the pragmatists.[83] Though he does not agree completely with their answers, Lonergan credits them with raising the right questions and conceiving important ideas. Lonergan believes that interiority is becoming dominant in culture today as the influence of the classicism of an early stage within theory diminishes.[84] This is the realm of meaning Lonergan calls us to in his books *Insight* and *Method*. While interiority arises from questions about how one comes to know, its

---

80. As discussed in chapter 1 of this volume, in the section "Classical and Statistical Law."
81. *Topics in Education*, 75–76.   82. *Method*, 83.
83. *Method*, 96.
84. *Method*, 96.

domain extends to questions about decision-making, loving, and the relationships among knowing, deciding, and loving. What is love? How does one know one is in love? Does love cloud or aid one's objectivity? Here Lonergan advises us that, "As always, enlightenment is a matter of the ancient precept, Know thyself."[85]

The fourth basic realm of meaning, "transcendence," regards necessary being, unrestricted intelligibility, absolute truth, the value beyond criticism, and unconditional love. It is "the realm in which God is known and loved" that a person may reach in "religiously differentiated consciousness."[86] Not limited to some future stage, and not restricted to Christian mystics, like Teresa of Avila, Lonergan finds that genuine mystics from other religions inhabit this realm as well (although they may not name what they encounter in it "God," and some may even be hostile to the term).

Speaking generally about Western civilization, however, Lonergan's view is that the four realms of meaning are historical developments that arose in stages or plateaus. Common sense is the earliest development, with its practical concerns and its emphasis on narrative. Theory developed over two thousand years ago with Greek philosophers and scientists challenging popular myths, asking for universal definitions, and studying the stars. Interiority arose during the Enlightenment with thinkers like Descartes, Hume, and Kant focusing on the question of how we come to know. And transcendence, while as old as the various mystical traditions, is becoming pervasive in contemporary society, as seen in the deep popular interest in spirituality, an interest that is often connected with a suspicion for traditional forms of religious thought and practice.

Society has exhibited a progression from the simple, undifferentiated consciousness of common sense to a differentiated consciousness that includes all four realms of meaning. Still, individuals within that society may remain content in an undifferentiated common sense, sometimes marveling at and sometimes mocking the scientists, academics, poets, artists, and saints who have stretched their minds to further realms of meaning.

85. "Natural Right and Historical Mindedness," 279; this essay discusses the three historical stages as plateaus: 277–79.
86. "Natural Right and Historical Mindedness," 272.

Conclusion

This ends part 1's presentation of Lonergan's tremendously complicated, but equally enriching thought on what drives human progress. For Lonergan, progress is a more or less abstract notion. He affirms that in concrete reality human beings do make real progress.
But Lonergan studies progress in a particular, theoretical way: as it
flows from human persons and human society to the extent that we
are strictly "natural," in other words abstracted from the negative
effects of sin, which cause decline, as well as the positive effects of
grace, from which flows redemption.

For Lonergan this nature that drives human progress is: (1) on
the move within time, or, historical; (2) part of a creative world order
governed less by necessity than by emergent probability; (3) driven
by an intelligence that is infinite in its desire; (4) self-transcendent
through a larger experiential, intellectual, reasonable, and responsible authenticity; (5) comprised of common life in community, bound
by shared meaning, value, and love; and (6) productive, through
social cooperation, of a developing human good. While Lonergan's
views on nature and progress are complicated, still, they comprise
just one of three factors or differentials operative in Lonergan's
analysis of the concrete human situation. In part 2 we will consider
Lonergan's thought on the second differential—namely, the decline
caused by sin.

Reflection Questions for Chapter 4

• When I was a kid, I sometimes daydreamed about being completely independent. I even went so far as to fantasize about escaping society to a deserted island. First I figured I would need
some tools: at least a knife, maybe a lighter and a waterproof
tent, probably some survival books. But then I thought that if
I read the right books before I went, I wouldn't need to bring
anything; I could make my own knife, fire, and shelter out of
what I found on the island. Eventually, however, it dawned
on me that anything I accomplished on the island would have
been due in part to the human community that educated me.
Even if I were dropped naked in the wilderness, so many of my

thoughts would have been shaped by my culture. So I imagined myself being born in the wilderness without any upbringing in society. Would I survive past infancy, though? And if by some tiny chance I did, what kind of a person would I be without anyone to have taught me anything, even a language? How would I think? Would I be human? Tracing this line of thought back further still, I realized that even if I could teach myself a language and form thoughts, I could never be completely independent, because I could never give birth to myself.

- And I am not alone. No one gives birth to himself or herself, literally or figuratively. Yet to some degree, we all seem to share this myth of being a self-made individual. This may not be surprising, since our culture champions free-thinking, self-made individuals to the point that, ironically, everyone believes he or she is totally unique, creative, and self-sufficient.

- Our dependence on our communities is true not simply for our physical selves, but also for the meanings and values by which we conduct our lives. The majority of what we know we have learned from others whom we believe. We were told, for example, that our parents are our own. But how can we know for sure? Are even DNA tests infallible? We have been informed the world is round. But have we experienced this for ourselves? People claim that there are countries like Egypt, Japan, and Finland. Have we been there personally? If we think we have, how much of this relies on believing an airline, friends, and others? Can we ultimately know that we are not merely brains in jars, being stimulated by some advanced computer or an alien intelligence? It is amazing how much we rely on others for what we think we know.

- Do we acknowledge the extent to which we depend on the love and the learning of our community, to say nothing of the constant flow of goods that comes from its economic, scientific, political, scholarly, artistic, and religious systems? Do we appreciate how it nourishes us in body and mind, in heart and spirit? Do we respect it enough to give back to it, to contribute to others with our bodies and minds, with our hearts and spirits?

Part 2 Decline

NATURE AS FALLEN

The utopian idea that progress in human affairs is automatic and unbroken was perhaps the biggest mistake made by early modern proponents of progress, according to Bernard Lonergan.[1] In his view these theorists failed to account for slowdowns and breakdowns, particularly those caused by sin and evil. Accompanying the many positive contributions of modernity to the natural and human sciences came an arrogance that believed that human intelligence at the service of personal egoism was the sufficient engine for progress, and human sin was what transforms an ordinary, unimportant person into a unique, free-thinking individual.[2] Modern liberals thus were aware of sin, but they held the illusion that unfettered, competitive self-interest would fuel progress more than derail it.[3]

Progress, as one vector in the analysis of human history, is Lonergan's transposition of the classical category of "nature" into a more dynamic, historical context. In reality no person and no soci-

1. Lonergan, *Insight*, 264, 710–11; Lonergan, *Topics in Education*, 47.

2. Lonergan, Existenz and Aggiornamento," in *Collection*, 247.

3. "Modern" liberals are not the same as contemporary liberals, and in fact are in some ways their opposites, particularly on economic issues. The modern liberal prefers as little government control of the economy as possible, while contemporary liberals believe that government must intervene to keep businesses from harming the public. For more on modern liberalism, see note 5 in this book's introduction.

ety is ever in a pure state of nature, and so progress is never pure. Human beings are all affected by what Christian tradition calls "the Fall,"[4] "original sin,"[5] and the resultant "darkening of intellect and weakening of will."[6] The human person as concretely alive in this world is a composite, more or less affected by both the intrinsic goodness of nature and the inherent evil of sin. The result is that we are, as Pascal observes, both "wretched and great."[7]

"Decline" is Lonergan's term for sin's cumulative effect on human history. It is why our world does not function in a rosy, continuous succession of improvement following improvement. Just as human persons and societies are always mixtures of nature and sin, so human history is always a combination of progress and decline. Because of decline we remain intelligent and free, rational and loving, but we are so in potential more than in truth.[8] Decline flows from our repeated failures to observe the transcendental precepts and act authentically in our individual operations and social cooperation. As progress depends on our being attentive, intelligent, reasonable, and responsible, decline is the result of "inattention, obtuseness, unreasonableness, irresponsibility." And as progress was a series of insights improving the human situation, so decline causes successive, "objectively absurd situations."[9]

Decline is the result of a twisting or perversion of the natural, unrestricted desire for beauty, meaning, truth, value, goodness, and love—in other words, of the human longing for God. Sinful acts suppress and distort this desire. Over time they form multiple

4. Lonergan, "Openness and Religious Experience," in *Collection*, 200.
5. Lonergan, "Healing and Creating in History," in *A Third Collection*, 101–2.
6. "Healing and Creating in History," 102; cf. Lonergan, Collected Works, vol. 1, *Grace and Freedom*, 16. On the universality of sin and its effects, Lonergan cites Rom. 1:18–3:20; 7:14–24; and Eph. 2:3 in his "Transition from a Classicist World-View to Historical-Mindedness," in *A Second Collection*, 8.
7. Blaise Pascal, *Pensées*, translated by A. J. Krailsheimer (London: Penguin, 1995). This is a recurrent theme in the *Pensées*, and it is the focus of I.7 Similarly, though with an understanding of goodness that was confined strictly to grace, Luther wrote the phrase "simultaneously justified and sinner" (*simul justus et pecatur*) in the margin of his Bible. The theme is expressed in his *On Christian Liberty* as "free lord" and "dutiful servant"; Martin Luther, *On Christian Liberty*, translated by W. A. Lambert (Minneapolis, Minn.: Fortress Press, 2003), 2.
8. Lonergan comments that because of sin, we are rational animals only in potency. In reality, he believes, we are more symbolic animals than rational animals, since symbols affect both saints and sinners; *Topics in Education*, 79–80.
9. Lonergan, *Method*, 54–55.

biases that shrink a person's natural orientation to truth and goodness, to beauty and love. In turn these biases increase the probability of future sins, and thus produce a downward spiral of more and worse sin and bias—in a word, "decline."

In this part we will examine decline in three chapters: the traditional cause of decline in chapter 5, "Sin and Evil"; the mutual effect and cause of sin in human consciousness in chapter 6, "Bias"; and the result of sin and bias in history in chapter 7, "Decline."

5 | Sin and Evil

Creation, the Fall, and Original Sin

In the very first chapter of the very first book in the Bible, nature is proclaimed to be worthy of celebrating. All of its parts, the light and the dark, the sky and the sea, the plants and the animals are all created "good." As a whole, it is "very good." Human beings are further privileged to be made "in the image and likeness of God."[1]

In the Bible sin is not something created by God. It is not natural. It does not enter into the picture until the third chapter, where we see human beings choose to listen to the serpent's temptation and disobey God. God does not create us to sin, nor does the devil make us do it. Rather, sin and its evil consequences enter into the world through the bad decisions of human persons.[2]

Mainstream Christian tradition, like the Jewish tradition that preceded and accompanies it, does not take these stories to be literally true. But literal truth is not the only reason to value a literary work. The comics are prized for their humor, novels for their ability to entertain, and speeches for their potential to inspire. While some parts of the Bible are meant to be taken literally, the stories of creation and the fall are not. The first chapter contains one creation story, the most famous one, summarized above. In it God creates the world over a period of six days, starting with the light

1. Gen. 1:4, 10, 12, 18, 25, 26, 31.
2. Gen. 3:1–19.

and the dark and ending with human beings. The second chapter presents another creation account. This one begins like the first one with the creation of a basic environment, the heavens and the earth. But then it talks about a stream rather than the sea. It has God creating *a man* first, not plants, then animals, then human beings (which is, interestingly enough, the same order laid out by evolutionary science. The biblical order even gets the details right of fish and birds coming before land animals.) This second creation account has God then create various plants for the man's food and animals for the man's partners. When none of the animals is thought to be a suitable partner, God creates a woman from one of the man's ribs. So instead of being created together, as they are in the first account, they are created with a pause between the man's creation and the woman's.[3]

The Bible thus contradicts itself on a literal level within the first two chapters of the first book, Genesis. This is not some new discovery. The original compilers of the Bible had to know of their contradiction. It is apparent at first glance. So why would they still include both accounts? We cannot know their exact thoughts, but we may surmise that since literal truth is not the only thing worthwhile in a text, they left both accounts in there for some other reason. The traditional view is that while the first three books of Genesis may not be literally or superficially true, they reveal a deep wisdom about the fundamental relationships of things in the world, including us and our role. They tell us that the things in this world come not from competing interests, but from one intelligent, just, caring, and powerful source, called "God." They tell us that God made the world good, that all its parts are interdependent, that human beings are a late, great emersion in the world. And, combined with the third chapter of Genesis, they teach us that even though we humans derive our living from the larger environment, we are given God-like powers that, if we choose to use them badly, can cause great damage to ourselves and the rest of creation.

Such wisdom can be very helpful for ordering our lives. If everything comes ultimately from one source, from one God who

3. Gen. 2:4–24.

loves us all, then our wars cannot have an ultimate character to them. "Our" God does not fight exclusively on "our side." Since the world God created is made of interdependent parts that we can damage, we must behave responsibly. To do otherwise would be devastating. The stories of the first three chapters of Genesis, though not literally true, teach such deep wisdom in a way that is much more memorable and more moving than if they were to express their insights in a direct, literal way. In other words, putting this wisdom into the form of a story was a wise move.

Nevertheless, there are disadvantages to stories. They have all of the advantages and all of the disadvantages of common sense. They are great for relating things to us, particularly to our affect and thus to our spontaneous behavior. But in the inquisitive minds of those raised in the twentieth and twenty-first centuries, to those familiar with recent advances in theory by the natural sciences and history, these narratives give rise to questions. We want to know not only *that* we can use our freedom badly and *that* this has poor consequences, we want to know *why* we choose poorly and *why* this causes devastation. To answer the questions that arise from commonsense narratives, we turn to theory.[4] And the theoretical discipline we use in particular is theology.

As mentioned in chapter 1 of this book, Catholics define theology as the use of our natural gifts, including reason and the secular forms of knowing (philosophy, chemistry, history, psychology, and so forth), to gain some measure of fruitful insight into revealed truths.[5] "Original sin" is a very common term in Catholic and Protestant theology; however, the term itself is not found in scripture. It was developed by Augustine in debates against a contemporary of his named Pelagius. Pelagius argued in general that human beings do not need grace to do good works and in particular that infants do not require baptism. (In fact, to this day, those who believe that hard work is all one needs to do good are called "Pelagian.") Augustine countered that "the Fall" of Adam and Eve

4. For more on the relationship between common sense and theory, see chapters 2 and 4 of this volume and Lonergan's *The Way to Nicea*.

5. See also the Vatican I document *Dogmatic Constitution on the Catholic Faith*, chap. 4 in Henry Denzinger, *The Sources of Catholic Dogma*, translated by Roy Deferrari (St. Louis: Herde, 1957), 1795–1800.

caused by their "original sin" of disobeying God and eating of the tree of knowledge of good and evil resulted in all human beings needing grace, particularly the waters of baptism, which wash away the effects of this original sin as well as one's own personal sins.[6] Augustine's teaching was made official Catholic doctrine by the Council of Carthage in 418 A.D.

Lonergan does not discuss original sin by name in any great detail. And he would probably reject some of the more common metaphors for the effects of original sin, such as a "stain" on one's soul, since they are often more misleading than helpful. Still, he would agree that through the sins of others (those who went before us as well as those around us currently), we are reoriented to some degree from our natural orientation to do good to a sinful orientation to do evil. The sins of others, in other words, do not *necessarily* cause us to sin, but they increase the *probability* of it. So, for example, if one is born into a racist or sexist family or society, one will be more likely to be racist or sexist.

Thus, instead of describing original sin in terms of a stain or a handicap, Lonergan seems to agree with those who call original sin a "social sin." Lonergan explains the doctrine of original sin as the negative influence of a society in decline or a "sinful social process." For example, he writes, "Decline disrupts a culture with conflicting ideologies. It inflicts on individuals the social, economic, and psychological pressures that for human frailty amount to determinism. It multiplies and heaps up the abuses and absurdities that breed resentment, hatred, anger, violence."[7]

Personal Sin and Its Consequences

To go back to the debate between Augustine and Pelagius, Lonergan would agree that in a state of pure nature, completely unaffected by sin, we can do good without grace. He would agree that it may even

6. People often wonder why God would want to keep us from the knowledge of good and evil. One answer is that knowledge can be painful. "Ignorance is bliss," the expression goes. Ignorance is not always bliss, nor is knowledge always painful. But sometimes they are, such as when a child discovers Santa Claus does not exist or when anyone discovers the betrayal of a friend. Knowledge may be helpful, even in such cases, but it is not always pleasant. Like the biblical Fall, it may prompt a radical change in one's world.

7. *Method*, 117.

be theoretically possible in this world, which is affected by sin. But realistically—given various social pressures with roots that span generations, prejudices like racism and sexism, or the pressures to conform to others' standards of beauty and success—the chances are slim to none. Consequently Lonergan affirms with traditional Christian theology that, to the degree that human beings do good, we are God's instruments, and when we do evil, we are the sole initiators of the act. Following Thomas Aquinas in particular, Lonergan affirms that God is the sole creator and the ultimate sustainer of all that exists and of all that is good. Directly, God wills only what is good. Among the goods that God wills are the free wills of human persons. In willing the good of free will, God allows or permits the evil of sin, but in no way does God will it.[8]

In *Insight* Lonergan distinguishes "basic sin" from "moral evil" and "physical evil." In the traditional terms of faculty psychology, basic sin is a failure of the intellect and the will, respectively, to identify the good rationally and to choose it morally. In terms of Lonergan's transcendental method they are breakdowns in the natural thrust toward intellectual and moral self-transcendence. Lonergan emphasizes the negativity of basic sin by calling it not simply a failure *of* the will, but a failure *to will*. Similarly, sin is not only a failure of the intellect and reason; it is *unintelligible* and *irrational* in itself.[9] "If there were a reason it would not be sin. There may be excuses; there may be extenuating circumstances, but there cannot be a reason, for basic sin consists, not in yielding to reasons and reasonableness, but in failing to yield to them; it consists not in inadvertent failure but in advertence to and in acknowledgment of obligation that nonetheless is not followed by reasonable response."[10]

Simply put, sin is choosing something we know is wrong—choosing a lower good over a higher one. This makes no sense. In the traditional terms of faculty psychology, it is a failure of our intellect and our will. As a failure of the intellect and will, Lonergan

8. Lonergan, "Moral Theology and the Human Sciences," in *Philosophical and Theological Papers, 1965–1980*, 304. Lonergan cites Thomas's *Summa Theologiae* I, q. 19, a. 9 c., and ad 3m; see also *Insight*, 688–90. The relationship between God and evil will be covered more thoroughly in chapter 6.
9. *Insight*, 689–90.
10. *Insight*, 690.

calls basic sin a "contraction of consciousness."[11] In the language of Lonergan's intentionality analysis, this contraction can be understood as a failure on all four levels of conscious intentionality. It would be a failure to heed the self-transcendent desire to know and to be good, and thus a failure to experience attentively, to understand intelligently, to judge reasonably, and to decide responsibly. Such failures by a person amount to basic sin or, as it is more commonly called, "personal sin."

"Moral evil" is Lonergan's term for the inauthentic actions and any other results or "consequences" of basic sin. Such consequences include damage done to the sinner, to people close to the sinner, to the entire society, including generations not yet born, and even to other aspects of creation. Basic sin and its resultant moral evil not only cause direct damage; they also increase the probability that future sins and evils will occur, as mentioned above. They do this by heightening the "tension and temptation in oneself or in one's social milieu."[12] As scripture asserts, it is through sin that suffering and death enter the world.[13]

Moral evil is to be distinguished from "natural evil," which includes such occurrences as natural disasters and birth defects. Natural or "physical" evils are in no way caused by sin, but rather constitute "all the shortcomings of a world order that consists, insofar as we understand it, in a generalized emergent probability."[14] The universe is developing from lower to higher material and biological and spiritual forms. This development is not a matter of fixed determinism, but of risk. From a limited perspective, hurricanes, illnesses, and the like are evil. But from the point of view of the entire world order, they can be seen as tending to the good. As an evolutionary biologist might put it, great leaps in evolution are often caused by some defect in the environment or the organisms themselves.

In fact, even moral evil (the harmful consequence of sin), which is indirectly willed by God in the creation of a just world or-

---

11. *Insight*, 689.   12. *Insight*, 689.

13. Lonergan, "Transition from a Classicist," in *A Second Collection*, 8; Lonergan cites Gen 2:15; 3:19; Rom. 5:12; 6:22–23.

14. *Insight*, 689.

der, can be viewed in this way. "For the imperfection of the lower is the potentiality for the higher; the underdeveloped is for the developed; and even moral evils through the dialectical tension they generate head either to their own elimination or to a reinforcement of the moral good."[15] We can learn and grow from suffering the consequences of our sins or even others' sins. Sin causes problems, and it raises questions. This drives us to seek answers and solutions. Thus it *can* help us to learn and grow. But such positive developments do not happen necessarily. We must use our freedom to learn instead of responding to sin with sin, to violence with more violence, and thus creating an ever-worsening social and global situation.

In *Topics in Education* Lonergan identifies deliberate human sin, rather than natural evils, as the cause of such potential decline. He examines sin and its effects as "crime," as "social process," and as "aberration." They parallel his analysis of the human good as particular goods, the good of order, and value.[16] But they parallel these components of the human good in an oppositional way. So crime destroys particular goods, sin as a social process harms the good of order, and aberrations are the negations of value. But let us consider each in turn:

Considered as *crime*, sin can be studied statistically and may be dealt with mainly by laws, police, courts, and prisons. The law is a fundamental instrument for apprehending good and evil. "As St. Paul says in Romans 3:20, 'Through the law there is knowledge of sin.' And again in Romans 5:13 he writes, 'Before the law there was sin in the world, but the sin was not counted as sin since there was no law.'" Under the laws of the government, ignorance of the law is no excuse. But if a law is not properly propagated or proclaimed, it is not considered a law. And sin in any case is not the same as a crime, since one truly has to know what one is doing is wrong for it to be a sin. Still, there are helpful similarities between sin and crime. Both are done by people who do not fully under-

---

15. *Insight*, 691.
16. They also to correspond to the first three levels of Lonergan's transcendental method, to his analysis of communities on material, social, and cultural levels, and to Aristotle's potency, form, and act; see chapter 4 of this volume.

stand the social network and/or who do not wish to be a part of it, people whom society has failed to bring up in its ways or those who refuse to live by society's ways. Viewing sin as a crime makes sin easy to recognize; it would simply be a matter of looking it up in the law. However, the great disadvantage of this approach is that it is a minimal standard for the good. The good, so defined, has no real positive value. It becomes merely not breaking the law or perhaps just not getting caught.[17]

Lonergan believes that, due to these shortcomings, it is best to supplement this view with an understanding of sin as a component in a *social process*. Reminding us that the good of order does not in fact develop in the "glorious fashion" he outlined in his discussion of progress, Lonergan writes that the good of order:

> develops under a bias in favor of the powerful, the rich, or the most numerous class. It changes the creative minority into a merely dominant minority. It leads to a division of classes not merely by their function, but also by their well-being. This division of classes gives rise in the underdogs to suspicion, envy, resentment, hatred, and in those that have the better end of the stick, to haughtiness, arrogance, disdain, criticism of "sloth," of "lack of initiative," of "short-sightedness," or in earlier times, of "lowly birth."[18]

So in the world process sin introduces biases in favor of some types of people and against other types. To the extent that these biases are operative in society, it is not enough to have good ideas and to work hard. One must have some measure of wealth, power, and popular support if one's ideas are to be realized. Management seeks ever more power because it desires control. Bureaucratic hierarchies arise. Eventually the only ideas that have a chance of success are those that come from the people at the top. This is how personal sins lead to original sin, which leads to further personal sins, and so forth.

In a better world good ideas could come from anywhere and still be effective. They could come from "the man on the spot who

---

17. *Topics in Education*, 59. It would seem that another disadvantage to viewing sin as a crime is the individualization of sin. A court of law must hold some individual or group of individuals responsible. Original sin, however, adds a social component that falls under social process and decline. Lonergan does not state this weakness of considering sin as a crime, but it may have been at least part of the reason for his addition of sin as part of the social process.

18. *Topics in Education*, 60. Sin as social process seems to me to be the closest Lonergan gets to the traditional doctrine of original sin; see note 5 of this chapter.

is intelligent, sees the possibilities, and goes ahead at his own risk. But in the bureaucracy the intelligent man ceases to be the initiator.... Activity is slowed down to the pace of routine paperwork. Style and form, which are inevitable when the man who has the idea is running things, yield to standardization and uniformity."[19] Small, independent businesses are taken over or forced to close. "You have to be in big business to be in business at all, and in big business you have nothing to say."[20] Work becomes drudgery. People seek distraction in frivolity. The universities become ivory towers, with no concern for the way people actually live.

Lonergan finds that many attempts to improve the social situation end up perpetuating or increasing the damage. One such attempt is archaism, or a return to ancient virtues, even when the ancient virtues are no longer relevant. Another is futurism, the expectation that utopia will come in some leap, probably through technology. Alternatively, the state may create "'times of troubles,' wars to arouse social concern, to give people a stake in the nation, to give them the feeling that they belong together in one nation."[21] Any of these, for Lonergan, perpetuate sin as a "social process."

Finally, sin may be considered as *aberration*, as an evil opposed to the reflective development of the individual and the broader culture. For Lonergan an aberration causes a negative outcome, whether in the individual's consciousness or the society's cultural history. "As aberrant [individual] consciousness heads to neurosis and psychosis, similarly aberrant [social] history heads to cataclysm."[22] Ideally, both persons and communities are oriented to the totality of the true and the good. But the aberration of sin shrinks human concern, blocking off important ideas, questions, and aspects of experience. It corrupts or negates "the higher aspirations of the human spirit and the human heart."[23] Such damage to individual consciousness results in damage to society's culture, and vice versa.

In advanced civilizations the higher aspects of culture (art, literature, philosophy, religion) function as arenas to work out the

19. *Topics in Education*, 60–61.
20. *Topics in Education*, 61.
21. *Topics in Education*, 61–62.
22. *Topics in Education*, 63.
23. *Topics in Education*, 63.

natural human unrestricted desire for beauty, truth, and goodness. However, the "chain reactions" of sin transform high culture into "a high-level rationalization" for society's sins.[24] In response to the evils of a culture in decline, virtuous observers may be tempted to wholesale condemnation, but Lonergan warns that this is not the best response: "the Catholic may wish to retire to an ivory tower, to condemn the new good because of its association with new evils; but that is another form of the aberration."[25]

Not just culture, but the whole human good is affected. As there are particular goods, a good of order, and the values by which particular goods and a good of order may be judged, so too there are particular evils, an organization of evil, and a negation of value. Particular evils include personal privations, suffering, harm, and destruction. Organized evils include chronic schemes of recurrence, such as crime waves, depressions, and war. These organized evils are evil schemes of recurrence. People involved in a cycle of evil can gain skills and habits, just as they do in a good of order. But these skills and habits are oriented toward evil operation and, to some degree, cooperation. When cooperating in evil, people set up institutions for it. The results twist or pervert other elements in the social order. "There can be the destruction of personal relations and status through hatred, envy, jealousy, lust, resentment, grievance. People with grievances, nations with grievances, very easily can become warped in their entire outlook."[26]

On top of particular evils and their recurrent scheme there is a "negation of value." Aesthetically, particular goods become dysfunctional and ugly. The good of order becomes either too complex to be transparent or so loose it exists in name only. Ethically, the liberty that flourishes in a good of order becomes perverted into "a reign of sin, a despotism of darkness" that makes all people its slaves.[27] The freedom of humanity that is "essential" to its nature becomes less and less an "effective" reality.[28] If there is an order, it is mechanical. Most individuals become "drifters" who

24. *Topics in Education*, 67.
25. *Topics in Education*, 64–65.
26. *Topics in Education*, 43–44.
27. *Insight*, 714.
28. *Insight*, 715. On effective and essential freedom, see chapter 3 of this volume, toward the end of the section "Four Levels of Conscious Intentionality."

do not think for themselves, but just go with the flow, conforming unthinkingly to those around them. Some become "the complementary type with the will to power, social engineers, the hidden persuaders, who dominate the drifting masses ... [who] are controlled without their knowing it—the propaganda ministry of the totalitarian state. And there can be its equivalent in the advertising setup, big institutions for control of people's choices without their knowing it."[29]

Against religious value are the evils of "estrangement from God, secularism, the negation of the idea of sin, complete and full self-assertion." Social thinking becomes dominated by "vast illusions," such as automatic progress, utopias, supermen, the illusion of the individual, and scientism. People neither "fear God" nor "respect man."[30]

Finally, there is a "theological dimension" to sin and its consequent particular evils, evil schemes of recurrence and negation of value. Sin is not merely an intentional failure to observe the natural desires of the human person and the natural patterns of the social order. Sin is also a "revolt against God, an abuse of his goodness and love, a pragmatic calumny that hides from oneself and from others the absolute goodness and perfect love that through the universe and through men expresses itself to men."[31] Sin is a rejection of the wise, divinely willed order of the universe as well as of humanity's role of "cooperation with God in the realization of the order of the universe."[32] Tradition distinguishes between venial and mortal sin, with mortal sin being a deadly blow, a total rupture of the sinner's relationship with God or, as contemporary moral theologians might say, a "fundamental option" against God.[33]

In *Method in Theology* Lonergan does not detail the evils of sin. Rather, he focuses on spelling out the good, proper performance of a human conscious intentionality that is in right relationship with God and all things. In this context, however, I believe it safe to say

29. *Topics in Education*, 46.   30. *Topics in Education*, 46–47.
31. *Insight*, 722.   32. *Insight*, 714.
33. Lonergan, "Philosophy of God, and Theology," lecture 2, "The Functional Specialty 'Systematics,'" a lecture given at St. Michael's Institute, Gonzaga University, Spokane, Washington, 1972, published in *Philosophical and Theological Papers, 1965–1980*, 197.

that sin is a failure of conscious intentionality to be authentically self-transcendent in one's experiencing, understanding, judging, and deciding, as discussed in chapter 3. It comes from and causes various types of inauthentic relationships. Ultimately basic sin and moral evil lead to a "sinfulness," which "is distinct from moral evil; it is the privation of total loving; it is a radical dimension of lovelessness."[34] One might even decline to the point of loving evil, to nursing hatred rather than fostering love.[35] But because by nature we humans desire unrestricted love and the lasting peace that only such love can bring, the hatred associated with sin leads us to engage in

sustained superficiality, by evading ultimate questions, by absorption in all that the world offers to challenge our resourcefulness, to relax our bodies, to distract our minds. But escape may not be permanent and then the absence of fulfillment reveals itself in unrest, the absence of joy in the pursuit of fun, the absence of peace in disgust—a depressive disgust with oneself or a manic, hostile, even violent disgust with mankind.[36]

Along with this disgust comes *alienation,* on which Lonergan writes briefly: "Sin is alienation from man's authentic being, which is self-transcendence, and sin justifies itself by ideology."[37] While rationalization is a lie an individual tells him- or herself to feel good about doing something he or she knows is wrong, ideology is such self-deception on a social level. Alienation in the context of transcendental method is a disregard of the transcendental precepts: be attentive, be intelligent, be reasonable, be responsible. Since these are natural, interior commands that bring one to authenticity, alienation is a distancing from one's nature and interiority. It is the opposite of authenticity. Concretely and socially, it results in decline.[38]

In a public lecture a year after *Method*'s publication, Lonergan summarizes the above aspects of sin, defining it simply as "a turning against yourself, and against God, and against your neighbor."[39]

34. *Method,* 242–43.
35. *Method,* 40: "So one may come to hate the truly good, and love the really evil."
36. *Method,* 243.
37. *Method,* 364. More on alienation and ideology will follow in our discussion of decline in chapter 7.
38. *Method,* 55.
39. "The Functional Specialty 'Systematics,'" 8.

Reflection Questions for Chapter 5

- Sometimes we think sin does not exist. There are so many voices in our heads championing such different ways of life. There have been a multitude of nations, cultures, and religions that have generated so wide a variety of laws, customs and ultimate ends. All too often, their standards for ethical action conflict. Can any of them be right? Is anything objectively good or bad, true or false?

- Some things seem very clearly to be wrong: rape, genocide, torture, murder. The tremendous and lasting damage that they do is hard to deny. On the other hand, we may wonder: Who are we really to judge the actions of another?

- Maybe we can only judge ourselves and our own actions. Have you ever chosen to do what you thought was wrong? Why did you think it was wrong? Was it merely because your society, your family, a friend, or a religion said so? Or did you believe it personally? How deep was your conviction? Where did it come from?

- Do you think you are naturally oriented toward choosing good things or bad ones? Do you think that your culture, your family, your friends, and your religion have oriented you toward good things or bad ones? Maybe a little bit of both? Can you think of any examples?

- To answer this, it may help to consider the consequences of your choices. How have they benefited you, other people, or the environment? How have they harmed you, others, the environment? Have they served and promoted the truth, justice, beauty, harmony, love? What can we learn from the consequences of our actions? Can they teach us anything about sin?

6 | Bias

Sin and evil are categories traditional to Catholic theology, even if Lonergan's analysis of them is his own. Bias, an inauthentic orientation caused by and causal of inauthentic actions, decisions, judgments, ideas, and experiences, is a concept more original to Lonergan. It is both the result of sin and a cause of further sin. As such, bias functions in a way I find similar to Aristotle's bad habits, or vices.[2] However, while Aristotle discusses vice as an extreme on either side of a golden mean, Lonergan analyzes bias in terms of conscious intentionality, social dynamics, and history. Sinful personal judgments of value, decisions, and actions damage the social and historical situation. Such actions and situations cause the hardening of bias, which is the shrinking of one's horizon of concern as well as a harmful, habitual orientation of the heart and the mind. This shrinking of horizon, this harmful habit of the heart and mind, corrupts a person's or a community's decisions, judgments, understandings, and experiences.[3]

Let us examine in greater detail the four biases that Lonergan identifies: dramatic, individual, group, and general.

1. Lonergan, *Topics in Education*, 60.

2. See Aristotle, *Nicomachean Ethics* bks. 2, 4, 7. I am not sure if, when translated into Aristotle's terms, Lonergan's bias would be an intellectual vice or a moral one. It certainly involves knowing, but as a shrinking of one's horizon of concern, it opposes charity, which Thomas says perfects the will primarily.

3. Lonergan, *Method*, 231. Notice the movement "from above downwards," similar to how

Dramatic Bias: Lack of Integrity

Dramatic bias operates largely on a subconscious basis. It negatively affects the psychic activity of the person, which controls the underlying physical, chemical, and biological schemes of recurrence, and which sets the conditions for the emergence of higher-level functions of consciousness: experiencing, questioning, understanding, judging, and deciding.

Even in the ideal authentic person, experience is not completely raw or unfiltered. It is patterned by "interest, anticipation, and activity."[4] For example, all of one's conscious operations can be geared toward fulfilling biological needs, such as getting food to live or escaping possible death, or toward attending to the beauty of the world and experiencing for the sake of experiencing, as hikers or children at play do. Like Archimedes, all of one's consciousness could be focused on getting an insight or figuring out a problem. In general, however, people are engaged in the general task of daily living. This task takes up the biological, aesthetic, and intellectual concerns and brings them into a richer context of crafting the drama of one's own life. When one is focused on crafting one's own drama, Lonergan says one is living the "dramatic pattern of experience." In this pattern, food, art, insight, and other things get taken up into larger contexts of meaning. "[C]lothes are not a simple-minded matter of keeping warm. They are the colored plumes of birds as well as the furs of animals. They disguise as well as cover and adorn."[5]

In the dramatic pattern of experience by which we live our lives, higher mental functions reach down into the neural processes that set the preconscious conditions for conscious operations. All conscious operations have counterparts in preconscious neural functions. There is a preconscious operator that Freud calls a "censor," which does the "selection and arrangement," and thus the "rejection and exclusion" of both sensitive and affective expe-

---

genuine love and its horizons and habits shape a person or community's decisions, judgments, understandings, and experiences; see chapter 4.

4. *Method*, 210.

5. *Method*, 210. For more on such patterns of experience, see Lonergan, *Insight*, 204–12; *Method*, 286. To the biological, aesthetic, intellectual, and dramatic patters of *Insight*, *Method* adds the mystical or worshipful.

rience.[6] Normally the censor functions in a positive, constructive manner by raising helpful schemes of images and feelings. In the person who seeks genuine insight into the drama of living, the censor is neutral to whatever insight may arise from the question's interaction with the scheme.

However, "[j]ust as insight can be desired, so too it can be unwanted. Besides the love of light, there can be a love of darkness."[7] This Lonergan calls a "flight from understanding."[8] When a person has intentionally done something wrong, she or he tends to prefer to remain in darkness and flee from understanding. Truly, the flight from understanding is a flight from one's natural human desire for transcendent truth, goodness, love, beauty, justice. This flight is caused by the natural human desire to have all of these things together in unity, harmony, or integrity. We want our choices to be in accord with our knowledge of reality. As mentioned in part 1, we want by nature to live with integrity, with a kind of wholeness and harmony among the four levels of our consciousness, with their transcendent orientations to the transcendental notions. Deciding to do something that one has judged to be wrong makes one feel uncomfortable. It presents one with the pangs of conscience.

To avoid an uneasy conscience, one may tell oneself more or less conscious lies—that is, one may rationalize.[9] For example, if I steal candy as a kid or clothes as a teenager, I may try to assuage my uneasy conscience by telling myself, "My parents and I spend a lot of money in this store. The store marks up its prices to unjust levels. I'm just taking back what's owed to us." I would know that stealing is wrong. I would know that I should not have decided and acted to steal. But I did it anyway. It was selfish and irrational. But the core of myself, my natural orientation to integrity, wants me to act in a loving, rational way. So I made up "reasons" for my action. I know I acted unjustly, but I tell myself otherwise.

Through such conscious lies, sinful acts harm not only their victims, but also their perpetrators. Performed often enough, they

6. *Insight*, 214.   7. *Insight*, 214.
8. *Insight*, 5, 220–23.
9. *Insight*, 215; cf. 264–65, 621–23. For more on rationalization see chapter 3, "Authenticity: Transcendental Precepts, Notions, and Desire," in this volume.

come to affect a sinner not only on his or her conscious levels, shaping his or her decisions, judgments, insights, and experiences; they penetrate deep into the hidden depths of one's subconscious self, forming a largely unconscious bias. This bias damages the way one lives with oneself. It twists the inner dialogue one has with oneself on conscious and subconscious levels. It thus has devastating consequences for the spontaneous way one crafts the drama of life. It is what Lonergan calls "dramatic bias."

If a person has a dramatic bias, the censor's positive function of selecting and arranging images and feelings to produce insights becomes primarily repressive. "Just as wanting an insight penetrates below the surface to bring forth schematic images that give rise to the insight, so not wanting an insight has the opposite effect of repressing from consciousness a scheme that would suggest the insight."[10]

Perverted by dramatic bias, the censor represses insight by inhibiting neural demand functions that allow needed images and feelings to arise. Feelings may arise, but only when they have been detached from their proper image or insight. They then bubble up, attached to some incongruous object that may be more or less associated with the original object. Without the proper connections between feelings and images, insights get blocked, causing "blind spots" or "scotomas" in one's understanding.[11] The repression of just one insight can have far-reaching effects, as Lonergan explains: "To exclude an insight is also to exclude the further questions that would arise from it, and the complementary insights that would carry it towards a rounded and balanced viewpoint. To lack that fuller view results in behavior that generates misunderstanding both in ourselves and in others. To suffer such incomprehension favors a withdrawal from the outer drama of human living into the inner drama of fantasy."[12]

Dramatic bias fosters a bad kind of introversion, one contrary to the natural human extroversion on biological, aesthetic, intel-

10. Lonergan, *Insight*, 216; cf. Lonergan, "Moral Theology and the Human Sciences," in *Philosophical and Theological Papers, 1965–1980*, 305–6.
11. *Insight*, 215.
12. *Insight*, 214.

lectual, and social levels. A person who suffers from it is no longer at home in the real world, and so he or she must generate "a differentiation of the persona that appears before others and the more intimate ego."[13] Individuals may seek release from division of the persona and the ego in certain dreams, in therapy, or in the "mass therapy" and "catharsis" of theater, of totems and taboos. In any case, a cure will require insight. Lonergan reminds us that, though associated with very serious neuroses and psychoses, dramatic bias is common to all people and elementary to all our sins.[14]

Individual Bias: Egoism

Egoism is generally acknowledged as a negative bias. However, it is difficult to identify exactly what constitutes egoism. It is not an animal hunting down its prey, just as altruism is not the animal parent fostering its young. Both of these acts are instinctual rather than deliberate. This distinction extends to some human behavior. Egoism is not simply the spontaneous desire to satisfy one's own appetites, and altruism is not just the tendency of spontaneous intersubjectivity to help others to gain their satisfactions.[15]

Furthermore, egoism is not the same as self-love, at least not genuine self-love. Aristotle brings this to light in his *Nicomachean Ethics*. True friendship excludes self-love in its popular sense— namely, egoism. However, he asserts, to be a good friend to another person one must have genuine love for oneself. This is so first because, to the extent that we do not love ourselves properly, we tend to use others to bolster our self-esteem. We will value another only to the degree that the person makes us feel better about ourselves. Second, genuine self-love can improve one's friendships, because if one loves oneself rightly, one seeks the best things for oneself. This may seem like it is opposed to friendship and love. Is not the egoist precisely the person who takes the best things for him- or herself?

13. *Insight*, 214.
14. *Insight*, 214–27. The significance of proper understanding in mental health is emphasized by Holocaust survivor and psychiatrist Victor Frankl in his works, particularly the classic *Man's Search for Meaning* (New York: Washington Square Press, 1985).
15. *Insight*, 244.

Aristotle's insight hinges on one's definition of the best things. He believes that wisdom, generosity, and other virtues are truly the best things. So a person with genuine self-love would strive to possess these virtues. In fact, for Aristotle, being virtuous, as we discussed in part 1, is the necessary prerequisite for a person to be a true friend to others. It is also required if one is to be a true friend to oneself. Only a wise and otherwise virtuous person would act in a way that truly benefited her- or himself.

[Thus self-love, if it is intelligent and genuine, is quite compatible with love of others and true friendship] Since love of self and love for others are intertwined, egoism and altruism are not ultimate categories. Lonergan agrees with all of this from Aristotle. Nevertheless, as Lonergan writes, egoism is in some sense always wrong, and altruism is "its proper corrective."[16]

To explain egoism on his own terms, Lonergan returns to his distinction between common sense on the one hand and sensitivity and spontaneous intersubjectivity on the other. Human living is the result of a dialectical development of these two things. Egoism is caused by an overemphasis on spontaneity to the point where it interferes with the development of common sense and other forms of intelligence. Egoism is a failure to ask if one's actions are capable of being generalized and if they are compatible with the social human good. This overemphasis on spontaneity does not come with the destruction of common sense or intelligence in general, for an egoist may also be "the cool schemer, the shrewd calculator, the hardheaded self-seeker." Such an egoist is adept at instrumentalizing intelligence for his or her purposes. Thus egoism can be intelligent to some degree, but it always is caused by and causes an incomplete development of intelligence.[17]

This incompleteness accompanies a perversion of the detached and disinterested desire to know. Egoism brushes aside the "further pertinent questions" that would cast doubt on its selfish acts. "[I]t fails to pivot from the initial and preliminary motiva-

16. *Insight*, 244, citing Aristotle, *Nicomachean Ethics* IX, 8. The editors note that this text of Aristotle is discussed at greater length in Lonergan, "Finality, Love, Marriage," in *Collection*, 16–17. Christ's command that one love one's neighbor as oneself implies this as well, as we shall see in part 3 of this volume, on redemption.

17. *Insight*, 245.

tion provided by desires and fears to the self-abnegation involved in allowing complete free play to intelligent inquiry."[18] Questions about fairness or the effects of one's action on the group are dismissed or are answered improperly in a way that creates further difficult questions that again are brushed aside.

Like dramatic bias, individual bias causes an aberration in one's understanding. It contradicts the wisdom of commonsense proverbs like, "What's sauce for the goose is sauce for the gander." It rejects the golden rule that advises us to treat others as we would like to be treated, as well as the multitude of other rules that people are held to in common. This rejection is often rationalized by the protestation that exceptions should be made, since each person and each situation is different.

Lonergan acknowledges that there are differences among people and situations, and he concedes that common sense is incomplete without further insights into a situation's unique circumstances. But he insists that although persons and situations have their particularities, they are not completely different, so "it does not follow that the golden rule is that there is no golden rule. For the old rule did not advocate identical behavior in significantly different situations; on the contrary, it contended that the mere interchange of individual roles would not by itself constitute a significant difference in concrete situations."[19]

So while exceptions can and should be made, the egoist thinks that *he or she* is the exception to any rule in whichever situation he or she chooses. The egoist is more or less proactive in this, devoting much time and energy "to sizing up the social order, ferreting out its weak points and its loopholes, and discovering devices that give access to its rewards while evading its demands for proportionate contributions."[20]

Contrary to some early modern thinkers, such as Thomas Hobbes, Lonergan maintains that egoism is not something people are born with that arises spontaneously from human nature. Rather, any egotistical choices we make (at least until they become

18. *Insight*, 245–46. The role of further pertinent questions was explained in chapter 3 of this volume, under "Judgment."
19. *Insight*, 246.
20. *Insight*.

habitual) have to overcome systematically the fellow-feeling of our natural intersubjectivity as well as the spontaneous questions that arise from our natural desire to know.

Individual bias operates on a more conscious level than dramatic bias, so while egoists may try to flee from their actions through self-deception, they will be made aware of their lack of integrity on "the fourth level of human consciousness, the level on which consciousness becomes conscience."[21] Lonergan explains: "The egoist's uneasy conscience is his awareness of his sin against the light. Operative within him there is the eros of the mind, the desire and drive to understand. He knows its value, for he gives it free reign where his own interests are concerned; yet he also repudiates its mastery, for he will not grant serious consideration to its further questions."[22]

The egoist may "get away" with breaking the written or unwritten rules of social reciprocity, but even if he or she avoids a jail sentence or some other extrinsic punishment, the person's own conscience will bug him or her. The "further pertinent questions" that were brushed aside in rationalization will at times creep up or flare up, particularly when a person is alone and in silence.

Group Bias: Egoism of the Group

Like individual bias, group bias involves an incomplete development of common sense. It shares a disregard for any reciprocity implied by the golden rule. And it too rationalizes its selfishness and suppresses further pertinent questions about the world and one's actions. "But while individual bias has to overcome normative intersubjective feeling, group bias finds itself supported by such feeling. Again, while individual bias leads to attitudes that conflict with ordinary common sense, group bias operates in the very genesis of commonsense views."[23]

The community as a whole has a common sense, but each subgroup within a community has its own additional, particular common sense that comes from the particular situations in which its

21. *Method*, 268.
22. *Insight*, 247. On essential and effective freedom, see chapter 3 of this volume, under "Decision, Liberty, and Moral Self-Transcendence."
23. *Insight*, 247.

members tend to live and operate. From living together, working together, or sharing a trait that makes them encounter the world in a similar way, people can form many healthy types of communal bonds. But group bias is an aberration of common sense that creates ["a loyalty to one's own group matched by a hostility to other groups."]24 It is this matching hostility to others, particularly an irrational hostility, that constitutes group bias.

When analyzing group bias Lonergan devotes special attention to social classes. He does not find their mere existence to be necessarily bad. Ideally these groups would arise from and be distinguished by their roles in the many interrelated schemes of recurrence that underlie the production of a community's technology, the economic distribution of its goods and services, and the political arenas of deliberation and decision. So, for example, research scientists are distinguished from technicians, foremen from managers, and judges from lawyers. If group bias arises, however, one group may manipulate the social order for its own good to the detriment of others. "Classes become distinguished, not merely by social function, but also by social success," and that social success is obtained at the expense of others.25 It leads to privilege in areas of life where privilege is unmerited or unjust. The "body social" becomes unhealthily divided into "those who have and those who have not."26

In Lonergan's opinion, times of great change (caused by new material conditions and/or transformative ideas) set fertile conditions for the genesis and hardening of group bias. Social classes are often but not always caused by a group's seizure of power or wealth. They may also result from the failure of a group or groups to adapt their lives to a change somewhere in the technological, economic, or political order. Changing technology and diminished demand for some product, for example, can lead to the workers, managers, and owners of one factory losing their source of income while another group of people take advantage of the new situation. The disenfranchised group may blame the resulting inequalities on the group that benefited, or it may find some other scapegoat.

24. *Method*, 53.
26. *Method*, 54.

25. *Insight*, 249.

Either way, continued experiences of inequality and even inferiority can lead to a type of ill-feeling, called *"ressentiment."* This is the longstanding re-feeling of a clash in value in which a person or a group felt both unequal to another and unable to attain equality.[27] Such resentment may be accompanied by real injustices and oppression. And it often is. But at times it may simply be caused by difficult circumstances or a group's poor choices. As the subject has blind spots and the egoist seeks conclusions compatible with his or her egoism, so also groups of people are prone to developing blind spots and resisting questions and insights that threaten their social advantages or the usefulness of their social roles.[28] As those who suffer from individual bias seek to soothe their uneasy consciences by the lies of rationalization, so do group egoists reinforce their irrational and uncaring acts by the shared systematic rationalization of ideology.[29]

Despite their similarities, group egoism is likely to be more damaging than individual bias. The individual egoist is resisted by the mass of society, but those who succumb to group bias have the reinforcement from others and from shared theories and doctrines. The broad effects of group bias and the difficulty of its reversal make group bias the cause of a "shorter cycle of decline," to be discussed after general bias.

General Bias: Shortsightedness

Common sense, as discussed in chapters 2 and 4, is a differentiation of human consciousness by which individuals in society learn a community's shared sets of meanings and values. It is a common fund of accumulated wisdom. On it people of all walks of life base their daily decisions, actions, and interactions. Common sense is a wonderful human development, but it is not its only development. General bias "takes the narrow and complacent practical-

27. *Method*, 33. Lonergan relies on Max Scheler's reworking of Nietzsche's term, citing Manfred Frings, *Max Scheler* (Pittsburgh: Duquesne University Press; Luvain: Nauwelaerts, 1965), chap. 5. Lonergan read this book after writing *Insight*, and did not directly apply *ressentiment* to the development of group bias as the result of one group's slow adaptation to change, but I believe it accounts concisely for the meaning of the process he describes at greater length in *Insight*.

28. *Insight*, 248.

29. *Method*, 55, 357–58.

ity of common sense and elevates it to the role of a complete and exclusive viewpoint."[30]

Americans are particularly prone to this bias, and we are known for it. A German friend once teased me about the way we measure all things by how useful they are, or how useful we think they are. He told me this joke: Three scientists went to the savanna to study elephants. They studied the exact same herd of elephants and then went back to their home countries to write very different books. The French researcher's was "The Love Life of the Elephant." The German's was "A Brief Introduction to Elephants, Vols. 1–10." And the American's was "How to Build a Bigger, Better Elephant." The French are enamored with romance; Germans are known for their detailed scholarship; and Americans are obsessed with what is immediately practical.

We often forget that practicality is not everything, and that common sense is a specialized form of knowing with an expertise in the immediate, the concrete, and the particular. It helps us to solve a multitude of everyday life problems, both major and minor. But there is much that lies outside its reach. Unfortunately, we are prone to forgetting its limitations as well as to rationalizing its limitations by saying that other forms of knowledge, like theory, are useless or even untrue. Lonergan attributes this to the thought that, "Every specialist runs the risk of turning his specialty into a bias by failing to recognize and appreciate the significance of other fields."[31] Lonergan does not quote Plato on this, but it is reminiscent of a passage from Plato's "Apology," in which Socrates describes his failed quest to find people of genuine wisdom:

Finally I went to the craftsmen, for I was conscious of knowing practically nothing. And I knew that I would find that they had knowledge of many fine things. In this, I was not mistaken; they knew things I did not know, and to that extent they were wiser than I. But, men of Athens, the good craftsmen seemed to me to have the same fault as the poets: each of them, because of his success at his craft, thought himself very wise in other most important pursuits, and this error of theirs overshadowed the wisdom they had.[32]

30. *Insight*, 256.
31. *Insight*, 251.
32. Plato, *Five Dialogues*, translated by G. M. A. Grube, edited by John Cooper (Indianapolis, Ind.: Hackett, 2002), 27.

Such overconfidence is a temptation for those who know any-thing about any area of life. But with common sense, the tenden-cy is very strong. Its great competence in the indispensable tasks of living makes it easy for us to mistake common sense for being omni-competent. It is indifferent to the worthwhile tasks of reach-ing abstract and universal laws, attending to larger issues of the greater whole and, most importantly, considering the long-term consequences of human action. Common sense's main role is to make swiftly a multitude of pressing decisions. It may consider an action's effects on more than one person and even on more than a particular group. But in its focus on the immediate situation, com-mon sense does not consider adequately the effects of a decision on the surrounding environmental conditions, on the next genera-tion, or on the ones following.

This is a significant problem because, as discussed in part 1, humans can direct world orders of emergent probability with tre-mendous consequences to ourselves and other parts of the uni-verse. We can grasp the conditions for and the probabilities of the emergence of various schemes of recurrence, and with this knowledge we can act to transform conditions and shift probabili-ties—increasing the likelihood that some schemes will arise and decreasing the likelihood that others will emerge. In other words, human beings become in some measure the executors of human and global development. To do this reasonably and responsibly, we need to recognize how our present insights, decisions, and ac-tions will influence our potential future insights, decisions, and actions.

Looking even further into the future, we can recognize how the efforts of one generation can affect the possibilities open to succes-sive generations. Common sense takes into account the next step or two, but what of the next five or ten? Common sense can get a student to care if the day's lesson will be on the test, but it would not see as much value in the pursuit of insight and wisdom for its own sake. It is common sense to educate our young, but can com-mon sense alone teach them how to make informed, considerate decisions, ones that account not only for their immediate desires, for their own objective good, or even simply for that of their group, but for the benefit of multiple groups across generations?[33] Lonergan believes that common sense is

unequal to the task of thinking on the level of history. It stands above the scotosis of the dramatic subject, above the egoism of the individual, above the bias of dominant and of depressed but militant groups that realize only the ideas they see to be to their immediate advantage. But the general bias of common sense prevents it from being effective in realizing ideas, however appropriate and reasonable, that suppose a long view or that set up higher integrations or that involve the solution of intricate and disputed issues.[34]

These are matters for science and theory, both natural and social, from physics to history. "The challenge of history is for man progressively to enlarge the realm of conscious grasp and deliberate choice."[35] This is true both for the history "that is written about" (our actions in time) and the history "that is written" (the academic discipline that studies these actions). We cannot know everything, but the more we know, the better our decisions, and the better their consequences. As time goes on, we would hopefully learn from various academic disciplines and integrate their insights into our culture's common sense.

If we allow general bias to cut off all academic debate and discovery, we stand to lose these insights and make irresponsible decisions. Compounding the limited competence of common sense is general bias's rationalization of common sense's limits. General bias adds "sins of refusal" to common sense's "sins of omission." In its one-sided emphasis on immediate practicality, it makes "insistent desires and contracting fears" of the immediate situation the only standard for ideas.[36] It ridicules the far-ranging views of history and science as irrelevant and impractical. This leads to a whole succession of problems, which we will discuss in the next chapter, on decline.

Reflection Questions for Chapter 6

- Have you ever dropped a stone into a still pond and watched the ripples spread throughout the entire body of water? If the

33. *Insight*, 252.   34. *Insight*, 253.
35. *Insight*, 253.   36. *Insight*, 253.

water is calm enough, you may observe the effects of even a small pebble as tiny waves lapping up against the shores. From early Native Americans to modern natural scientists, people teach that this ripple effect is true throughout the natural world. Or, to take another metaphor, they say that everything is connected into one big "web of life." Touch one part, even a far corner, and it affects the rest of the whole.

- Sadly, however, we tend not to care about the far-reaching consequences of our actions. We wall up our personal worlds, making our "horizon of concern" increasingly smaller. We think, "All that matters is this generation, and really just me and my friends, the ones who have the right look, live in the right neighborhoods, listen to the right music. Of course, when push comes to shove, what really matters is just me. And the only part of me that matters is my immediate, superficial desires." Not only do we all think this way at times, but we act like it too, although we may more readily admit that others do this. It is easy to point fingers, and we indulge ourselves all too often.

- Perhaps it is worthwhile to wonder, how broad is my own horizon of concern? When I make decisions, how far into the future do I think ahead? Do I think about others? When I don't, and I hurt myself and others, how do I respond to this fact? Do I lie to myself? Do I make up excuses? Do I flee from understanding myself and others? How can I stop this? Is it possible for me to make amends?

7 | Decline

Lonergan asserts that it is easy to fall into the aberrations of bias, but difficult to correct them:

Egoists do not turn into altruists overnight. Hostile groups do not easily forget their grievances, drop their resentments, overcome their fears and suspicions. Common sense commonly feels itself omnicompetent in practical affairs, is commonly blinded to long-term consequences of policies and courses of action, is commonly unaware of the admixture of common nonsense in its more cherished convictions and slogans.[1]

The extent of aberration is variable. "The greater it is, the more rapidly it will distort the process of cumulative change and bring to birth a host of social and cultural problems."[2] Such is decline.

Decline is a negative, cumulative process caused by sinful biases. These biases have harmful consequences throughout a vicious cycle. They result first in oversights, rather than insights. Oversights cause "unintelligent policies and inept courses of action." Unintelligent policies and inept actions lead to absurd situations.[3] This scheme of bias, oversight, unintelligent policy, inept action, and absurd situations recurs again and again, getting worse each time. And so biases deepen, oversights abound, policies become increasingly unintelligent, actions become more and more inept, and situations extend ever more brutally the bounds of the absurd.

1. Lonergan, *Method*, 53.   2. *Method*, 53–54.
3. Lonergan, *Insight*, 8.

It is important to remember that Lonergan uses the word "decline" in a technical sense intended to transpose traditional notions of sin into an enriched context that incorporates recent insights from psychology and history. Thus we devoted chapter 5, the first chapter of this part, to discovering the biblical roots of traditional thought on sin, as well as Lonergan's own contribution to the topic. While psychology and history played some role in chapter 5, chapter 6, on bias, emphasized the psychological aspects of decline, and this chapter concentrates on its historical dimensions. This chapter, the final chapter of part 2, is the shortest of its chapters. This brevity does not mean it is of least significance. Though smallest in size, it is of greatest comprehensiveness, because it draws from the terms and relations discussed in the previous chapters and raises them into a fuller historical context; for sinful actions and biased psyches cause decline over time.

The Shorter Cycle

Lonergan distinguishes between shorter and longer cycles of decline. The shorter cycle is caused by group bias. We have discussed its origins and how it accompanies aberrant social inequalities. However, we have not discussed its contribution to the accelerated, cumulative formation of harmful and absurd elements in a society, which, in a word, is decline.

Lonergan's exposition of the shorter cycle of decline picks up where his analysis of group bias and aberrant social classes leaves off. When one group's success comes at the expense of other groups, the successful group must seek increasing amounts of power in order to stay in power. Ideas that benefit society as a whole are increasingly left behind as the powerful group only backs ideas that increase its hold on society. Lonergan does not analyze the various types of power, but since he sees development as coming from the bottom up or the top down (ideally through people's intellectual ability to discover good options and the effective freedom to choose from these options). It would seem that power, for Lonergan, might be wielded by anyone with the technological, economic, political, or cultural resources to force or to persuade others to do what they wish. Of course, those on the top would tend to have a disproportionate share in these resources.

Lonergan discusses the cumulative effects of group bias: "[T]hose in favor find success the key to still further success; those unable to make operative the ideas that are to their advantage fall behind in the process of social development." The "haves" become more and more separated from the "have-nots." The "haves" divert an increasing amount of social resources from institutions that benefit all to "devising and implementing offensive and defensive mechanisms."[4]

But there is hope. This shorter cycle of decline caused by group bias creates the principles for its own reversal. In its growing power and abuse of power, the successful group calls into being "an opposed group egoism."[5] Imperfect ideas and sinful choices that are forced on society by one group at first may go unrecognized as such, except perhaps by a few experts. But eventually the ideas and choices that come from group bias cause negative consequences. As these consequences bring palpable damage to peoples' lives, the imperfection and sin of the system are increasingly brought to light for all. Groups made unsuccessful become motivated to work for reform or to fight for revolution. Dominant groups respond to this pressure by reactionary means, progressive ones, or a mixture of both. To the degree that they are reactionary, their suppression of other ideas calls forth revolutionaries, and the situation heads toward violence. The moderates on both sides, the progressives who aim at correcting their own oversights, and the liberals who wish to increase freedom for all may meet in the middle to agree on a goal while still debating "the pace of change and the mode and measure of its execution."[6]

The hope one can afford during a short cycle of decline is not the same as a hope for full redemption. One group may end another's reign, but it will tend eventually to impose its new rule with its own group bias. There is a tendency to "correct old evils with a passion that mars the new good."[7] What is needed is not simply the rise of one group and the fall of another, but the return to attentive, intel-

---

4. *Insight*, 249.   5. *Insight*, 249.
6. *Insight*, 250.   7. *Insight*, 8.

ligent, reasonable, and responsible rule, one that allows for insights to come from wherever and whomever they arise and for their implementation to be just as attentive, intelligent, reasonable, and responsible.

The Longer Cycle

When general bias is added to group bias, the result is a more deeply rooted decline. Group bias alone can initiate a cycle of decline, but this cycle tends to be short, because the practical plans discarded by the dominant group are "championed later by depressed groups."[8] But if the society's problems are compounded by general bias's neglect of long-term solutions good for the whole of society, then all groups neglect the kind of ideas that would reverse decline. There begins the longer cycle of decline.

In a normal process of positive development, questions lead to insights, problems lead to solutions, higher viewpoints are attained, and better situations are achieved. But caught in the longer cycle of decline, society consistently disregards "timely and fruitful ideas."[9] This precludes their implementation for society's benefit, and it prevents the emergence of conditions for the possibility of other ideas and other developments to arise in the future. Consequently the social situation deteriorates at an accelerating rate. Bad ideas lead to bad situations, which result in worse ideas and to worsened situations. Social schemes and functions become corrupted, some die, and some grow out of control. The effects can be seen on technological, economic, and political levels. Sluggishness leads to stagnation. The best that one can hope for is a balance of powers. "What is worse, the deteriorating situation seems to provide the uncritical, biased mind with factual evidence in which the bias is claimed to be verified. So in ever increasing measure intelligence comes to be regarded as irrelevant to practical living. Human activity settles down to a decadent routine and initiative becomes the privilege of violence."[10]

In addition to deteriorating social relations, general bias has

8. *Insight*, 252.   9. *Insight*, 254.
10. *Insight*, 8.

negative effects on cultural systems that evaluate and criticize the society's values. Its disregard for intellectual pursuits and all that is not deemed "immediately practical" banishes art and literature into an ivory tower, makes philosophy a mere curiosity, and constricts religion to the private sphere if it allows it at all:

Cognitional self-transcendence is neither an easy notion to grasp nor a readily accessible datum of consciousness to be verified. Values have a certain esoteric imperiousness, but can they keep outweighing carnal pleasure, wealth, power? Religion undoubtedly had its day, but is not that day over? Is it not illusory comfort for weaker souls, an opium distributed by the rich to quiet the poor, a mythical projection of a man's own excellence into the sky?[11]

It is normal for common sense to be in tension with such higher cultural pursuits. But ideally this tension is creative, and people of common sense can find "a profoundly satisfying escape from the grim realities of daily living by turning to men of culture, to representatives of religion, to spokesmen of philosophy."[12] But general bias wipes out any validity to these other ways of thinking. Without them people lose humanizing sources of play and exaltation, so life becomes more and more like that of subhuman animals. Life is just about survival. People care only about what they will eat, where they will sleep, whom they will have sex with, how they can get ahead of the competition. Culture, religion, and philosophy may remain in name, but their goals and methods become those of common sense. There can still be discovery and development, but the culture will be uncritical. There will be limited concern for possibilities, no standard of truth, and no normative measurement of value. Without the higher aspects of culture, human life gets truncated, loses its meaning, and eventually becomes absurd.

It is bad enough for general bias to banish culture to an ivory tower; worse yet is the co-opting of science, culture, religion, and philosophy into justifying the absurdities of decline. Through the perversion of these higher pursuits, spontaneous rationalizations are sustained, hardened, and handed on in ideology. "Imperceptibly the corruption spreads from the harsh sphere of material advantage and power to the mass media, the stylish journals, the

---

11. *Method,* 243.
12. *Insight,* 255; cf. *Method,* 242–44.

literary movements, the educational process, the reigning philosophies. A civilization in decline digs its own grave with a relentless consistency."[13]

On all levels of the human good, from material conditions to higher culture and personal value, there is created the "social surd" —that is, the elements of a social situation that exist and are influential, but are unintelligible.[14] In the longer cycle of decline, the surd expands exponentially, "and so there is an increasing demand for further contractions of the claims of intelligence, for further dropping of old principles and norms, for closer conformity to an ever growing manmade incoherence immanent in manmade facts."[15]

At the root of decline and the resultant social surd is a frustration of our core selves, the center of human nature, the "eros of the human spirit," our self-transcendent desire for truth, goodness, and love. "As self-transcendence promotes progress, so the refusal of self-transcendence turns progress into cumulative decline."[16] The frustration of this eros to self-transcendence is a crucial, basic sin, because "the social surd resides least of all in outer things and most of all in the minds and wills of men."[17] Basic sin is not disobedience of social or religious rules but rather failure to obey the promptings of one's deepest self to be attentive, intelligent, reasonable, and responsible.

So sin and bias, as well as rationalizations and ideologies, alienate people from reality, from each other, and even from themselves. The basic form of alienation is the disregard of the transcendental precepts. As these precepts are disregarded, there increasingly is formed a "familiar opposition between the idealism of human aspiration and the sorry facts of human performance."[18]

In the longer cycle of decline, this opposition is unfortunately reduced, not by an improvement in human performance, but by the lowering of human ideals. Ideology perpetuates the alienation of persons from their self-transcendent cores.[19] It transforms the entire culture, which should function as "social conscience," into

13. *Method*, 55.
14. *Insight*, 254–57, 651–52, 712–16.
15. *Method*, 256.
16. *Method*, 55.
17. *Insight*, 712.
18. Lonergan, "Finality, Love, Marriage," in *Collection*, 25, cf. 26; see also *Method*, 55, 357–58.
19. *Insight*, 712; cf. *Method*, 55, 364.

a social justification for the social surd.[20] For a community in the longer cycle of decline and confronted by increasingly absurd situations, culture becomes pervaded by an "ultimate nihilism."[21] Lonergan explains that this nihilism comes about when:

after repeated failure man begins to rationalize, to deform knowledge into disorderly loves. Such rationalization may involve any degree of culpability, from the maximum of sin against the light which rejects known truth, to the minimum of precluding such futurible advance in knowledge and virtue as without even unconscious rationalization would have been achieved. Moreover, this deformation takes place not only in the individual but also and much more convincingly in the social conscience. For to the common mind of the community the facts of life are the poor performance of men in open contradiction with the idealism of human aspiration; and this antithesis between brutal fact and spiritual orientation leaves the will a choice in which truth seems burdened with the unreal and unpractical air of falsity. Thus it is that a succession of so-called bold spirits have only to affirm publicly a dialectical series of rationalizations gradually to undermine and eventually to destroy the spiritual capital of the community; thus also a culture or a civilization changes its color to the objectively organized lie of ideology in a trans-Marxian sense, and sin ascends its regal throne (Romans 5:21) in the Augustinian *civitas terrena* [earthly city].[22]

When a culture is pervaded by ideology and sin "ascending its regal throne," it heads toward war with others and totalitarianism within its borders. This process begins with a seemingly minor error —the mistaking of common sense's narrow practical standards for the ultimate standard of truth and value. But in the longer cycle of decline, the results of this mistake spread damage to all aspects of the society. Lonergan details what would happen in a totalitarian regime ruled by the short-sightedness of general bias:

On the totalitarian view every type of intellectual independence, whether personal, cultural, scientific, philosophic or religious has no better basis than nonconscious myths. The time has come for the conscious myth that will secure man's total subordination to the requirements of reality. Reality is the economic development, the military equipment, and the political dominance of the all-inclusive state. Its ends justify all means. Its means include not merely every technique of indoctrination and propaganda, every tactic of economic and diplomatic pressure, every device for breaking down the moral conscience and exploiting the secret affects of civilized man, but also the ter-

---

20. "Finality, Love, Marriage," 26.   21. *Insight*, 259.
22. "Finality, Love, Marriage," 26.

---

rorism of a political police, of prisons and torture, of concentration camps, of transported or extirpated minorities, and of total war.[23]

As wars increase in violence, the longer cycle heads to complete destruction of the world. However, as emergent probability teaches, nothing is necessarily inevitable. The longer cycle need not end in total destruction. This cycle is long because it teaches a lesson of utmost difficulty—namely, that the needs of human living are not adequately met by common sense alone, not even by a combination of the practical pursuits of technology, economics, and politics. Many things are needed at this point if the decline is to be reversed. One thing any society needs, but particularly one in decline, is what Lonergan calls a "higher viewpoint."[24]

Literally, a higher viewpoint, like that of a mountain peak, an airplane, or a skyscraper, is a perspective that allows one to experience many things, and thus to come to understand and to operate in relation to these things. It expands one's horizon of possibilities. And as Lonergan uses the term, it allows one to expand one's horizon of concern. Such expansion enables a person, a group, or a society to make more responsible decisions. In a more general sense, a higher viewpoint is reached not simply by physical ascent, but by self-transcendence—that is, by heeding one's natural, unrestricted desire and authentically following the transcendental precepts on four levels of consciousness.

When a society is under the sway of general bias and in the throes of the longer cycle of decline, it needs the higher viewpoint made possible by disciplines that belong to the higher realms of meaning. It needs theory, including all the natural and social sciences. And it needs interiority, which helps its members to avoid sin and bias and teaches them self-appropriation and thus increased mastery of the transcendental method.

However, a full and lasting solution—one that would shift probabilities to favor progress over decline, one that could dissolve the longer cycle of blocked insight, worsening situations, banished culture, hardened ideologies, totalitarianism, and total war—would require an absolutely transcendent viewpoint. Such a viewpoint

23. *Insight*, 256–57.
24. *Insight*, 259.

would be part of a supernatural vector in human history. It would have to be introduced by an absolutely transcendent reality. We may take heart, because, for Lonergan at least, this solution is already present in our world through the divine gift of grace. This solution is redemption.

Conclusion

For Lonergan, human history is always a mixed product of nature and sin, progress and decline. We are good by our natures, which causes progress. But we can and we do choose to sin, which leads to decline. Though good by nature, we are born into a world that is already marked by sin. Every generation that has gone before us has left a legacy that is both positive and negative. We enjoy many benefits from their technological, economic, political, academic, and spiritual developments. But we suffer numerous effects of their sins. And the more we suffer them, the more likely we are to add our own sins to the world and thus to continue a negative cycle of sin.

This cycle begins with individual acts of evil, but it spreads throughout the community and the world, causing particular evils, destroying environmental and social processes, and negating a culture's ability to judge true value.

Sin is the free and willing choice to do what one knows to be wrong, to choose a value one has judged to be lower than others available. It might be overindulging one's desires for food and sex and thus preventing the emergence of higher goods like growth in wisdom and justice. It could be settling for short-term satisfaction rather than persevering in one's aspiration for a long-term good. Or sin might take the form of acting for one's own lower, short-term good when it leads to great, long-term harm to others.

The external consequences of such sins are plain to see: exploitation of the environment, oppression of whole groups of people, death by starvation, wars, torture, rape, and genocide. Then there are the inner consequences to the sinner himself or herself. Doing what one knows is wrong goes against a person's core desire for truth and goodness, integrity and wholeness, so it causes an alienation from oneself. It brings about a restless, painful conscience. We can attempt to soothe ourselves with a flight from understanding through lies, rationalizations, ideologies. But because we know deep down that we are lying, we may develop dramatic biases that ruin our psyches. Since a major rationalization is to think sin is natural and we are all in competition with others, we may develop the individual bias of egoism. Or we may seek to console ourselves in the company of like-minded others, forming various groups that have a biased love for their own based on a *ressentiment* of others. We might simply succumb to the practical concerns of everyday life, forming a general bias against what we do not find personally useful.

Such sins and biases result in decline. One thing leads to another. This is true for the good as well as for evil. Evil acts produce not just a vicious cycle, but a downward spiral. Evil choices cause evil consequences in the world and in us, increasing the likelihood that we will sin again and sin more severely. The vector of decline points ultimately to an unbridled struggle for totalitarian power and the mutually assured destruction of a total war.

Still, there is hope. Sin has not totally destroyed the goodness of nature. And the object of our desire, the unrestricted being who is perfect truth, goodness, beauty, justice, and love has entered into our world. Such is grace, the cause of redemption.

Reflection Questions for Chapter 7

- When I was a kid, my parents and teachers said that if I told one lie, it would require me to tell other lies to cover up the first lie. Throughout my childhood this proved to be true. And it was true not only about lies, but about doing anything I knew was wrong: stealing, cheating, bullying, letting others bully. One sin led to another, and I was getting to be worse and worse of a kid. I can think of many examples, but one sticks out. My mom was very strict about schoolwork. As a result, I studied hard, learned a lot, and had great grades to show for it. When I was fourteen, I rebelled. So my mom left me alone. I stopped studying, and my grades dropped. To bring them up, I asked friends for answers, or for hints, at least. That kept my grades up a bit. And I figured I was smart enough that I didn't need to do the work. How could I not think this? I had a reputation as one of the smartest kids in school.

- But then things changed. I lost my reputation. I lost friends. I lost my knowledge. I lost some ability to think. And I lost my self-respect. I had been lazy, using my friends, letting myself and my relationships fall into decline. And I did it for the short-term "practical" goal of getting good grades. I chose the lower goods of reputation and "success" over higher values like wisdom, self-discipline, honesty. In a way, it was "common sense" to cheat. Many did it. And why not if you could get away with it? Anyone else is a sucker, right?

- At some point, I got turned around. By what, I'm not exactly sure. Part of it was the realization that I wasn't gaining even the lower goods of reputation and success. Part was a sense of loss over my diminished academic knowledge and abilities. Part was the interior awareness of my "sins against the light." And part of it, I'm sure, was grace.

- Can you think of a way in which you have experienced decline? Have you seen a friend suffer through it? A school, a team, a family? What was it like? How did it affect you and others?

Part 3　Redemption

NATURE RAISED INTO SUPERNATURE

Everyday life can be problematic. Whether simple or difficult, the challenges we face raise questions. At some point our questioning of life leads to what Lonergan calls "ultimate questions." Such questions seek insight into the meaning of life, the reason things are the way they are, whether things can improve, and how improvements might be made. Those who pursue such questions with rigor eventually seek insight into the ultimate origin and end of existence. Put in traditional Christian terms, life leads us to questions about the universe, about God, and about God's relation to the universe as its creator and redeemer:

The facts of good and evil, of progress and decline, raise questions about the character of our universe. Such questions have been put in very many ways, and the answers given have been even more numerous. But behind this multiplicity there is a basic unity that comes to light in the exercise of transcendental method. We can inquire into the possibility of fruitful inquiry. We can deliberate whether our deliberating is worth while. In each case, there arises the question of God.[1]

We praise progress and denounce every manifestation of decline. But is the universe on our side or are we just gamblers and, if we are gamblers, are we not perhaps fools, individually struggling for authenticity and collectively

---

1. Lonergan, *Method,* 101.

endeavoring to snatch progress from the ever mounting welter of decline? ...
Such is the question about God.[2]

Indeed, since God is the first agent of every event and emergence and development, the question really is what God is or has been doing about the fact of evil.[3]

Redemption is Lonergan's answer to the question of what ultimate reality, or God, is doing and has been doing in a universe confronted by "the facts of good and evil, of progress and decline."[4] Chapter 8 will first clarify what is meant by the "absolutely supernatural" aspect of grace and then will consider the distinction between two general aspects of grace: its "healing" of nature from a fallen state and its "elevation" of nature into the absolutely supernatural order. From this distinction, chapter 9 proceeds to the concrete, personal effects of grace in religious, moral, and intellectual conversion. Chapter 10, the final chapter of this part and of the book as a whole, presents Lonergan's thought on two redemptive communities formed by and formative of human persons divinized by grace and conversion. They are a natural "cosmopolis" and a graced Body of Christ.

As in parts 1 and 2, on progress and decline, this consideration of redemption moves (1) from more traditional, classical theories to more contemporary, historical ones, and (2) from surrounding conditions to personal factors to social orders to historical implications.

2. *Method*, 102–3.
3. Lonergan, *Insight*, 709.
4. Interestingly, Lonergan called redemption "renaissance" in some of his earliest formulations of the dialectic of history. This is seen in the unpublished essays "Outline for an Analytic Conception of History" and "Analytic Conception of History"; see Shute, *Origins*, 148–54, 182. Shute does not say why or when Lonergan changed from "renaissance" to "redemption."

8 | Grace

The Supernatural, Relatively and Absolutely

The theology of grace is both simple and complex. Not just any gift from God is a gift of grace. All that humanity has and is has been given by God. Grace, however, is an extraordinary gift. It is God's gift to creation, which goes beyond the natural goodness of creation. Defined simply, grace is God's gift of Godself to the world.

But what does it mean for God to give God's self to the world? This is complex and ultimately mysterious, for God is absolutely supernatural, as is God's gift of Godself in grace. What does "absolutely supernatural" mean? We may remember that for Lonergan, oxygen's operation on chemical levels is natural.[1] Its operation on higher levels, such as human respiratory schemes, is supernatural. Nevertheless, it is only "relatively supernatural," since chemical and biological schemes are both part of the created, natural order. In contrast, the absolutely supernatural transcends all of created nature, including our ability to understand it comprehensively.[2] Our minds, like all of creation, are finite and imperfect, while divine reality is infinite and perfect.

Despite transcending all of created nature, divine grace re-

1. See chapter 1 of this volume, under the subsection entitled "A Dynamic, Interdependent Hierarchy."
2. We shall consider the mysterious nature of the supernatural and our limited ability to understand in chapter 9, under "Faith."

mains harmonious with nature. The absolutely supernatural is not destructive of, counter-operational to, or completely independent of nature. Rather, as natural biological rhythms presuppose, sublate, and go beyond natural chemical levels, so supernatural grace as it operates in us presupposes, sublates, and goes beyond created nature as a whole. As the biological schemes are higher orders of what is systematic and nonsystematic on a chemical level, the supernatural order of redemption is a higher order of what is systematic and nonsystematic in human progress and decline. In short, God's supernatural gift of grace cooperates with and augments the natural world order of emergent probability.

Lonergan speaks eloquently about the harmony of supernatural grace with the natural order:

[A] concrete plurality of essences has an upthrust from lower to higher levels.... [This is] conspicuous to one who looks at the universe with the eyes of modern science, who sees sub-atoms uniting into atoms, atoms into compounds, compounds into organisms, who finds the pattern of genes in reproductive cells shifting, *ut in minori parte*, to give organic evolution within limited ranges, who attributes the rise of cultures and civilizations to the interplay of human plurality, who observes that only when and where the higher rational culture emerged did God acknowledge the fullness of time permitting the Word to become flesh and the mystical body to begin its intussusception of human personalities and its leavening of human history.[3]

The general harmony of supernature with nature notwithstanding, there is one crucial difference. The supernatural grace that flows from the divine missions of the Son and the Spirit is utterly, absolutely beyond what nature could achieve on its own. Grace is not a scheme of recurrence that more or less probably emerges from natural processes. There is nothing a human person or human societies can do to earn or merit the supernatural gift that is grace.

This is just a general word on grace. A full picture of a traditional Christian theology of grace would include many other terms used to distinguish various aspects and effects of grace, such as "actual" and "habitual," "operative" and "cooperative," "healing"

3. Lonergan, "Finality, Love, Marriage," in *Collection*, 21. In a footnote Lonergan mentions an affinity between modern statistical law and Aristotelian *contingens ut in maiori parte* and between modern chance variation and *the contingens ut in minori parte*.

and "elevating."[4] Here we do not pretend to consider all aspects and effects of grace. We shall instead focus on its healing and elevating effects, since this distinction helps to clarify the relationship of redemption to progress and decline.

Healing and Elevating Grace

In the work that was originally his doctoral dissertation, Lonergan traces the development of the distinction between healing and elevating grace to Philip the Chancellor in the early 1200s. Lonergan writes that this was part of a "'Copernican revolution' in theory" that distinguished between the two orders of nature and supernature, between "the familiar series of grace, faith, charity, and merit" and "nature, reason, and the natural love of God."[5] By nature we have reason, through which we can discover the order of things in the natural world, and we have a natural love of God in our natural desire for a perfect, transcendent reality. By grace we are given faith, which enables us to grasp truths we could not know by nature, and we are given charity and merit, which enable us to unite with God and to love as God loves.

As mentioned earlier, nature and grace are harmonious and cooperative with each other. They are not equal partners, however. Grace transcends nature in that grace, or supernature, includes, goes beyond, perfects, and augments nature. Cognitively the supernatural knowledge of faith transcends the natural knowledge of reason by including, going beyond, perfecting, and augmenting it. So, for example, tradition affirms that we can know *that* God exists by our reason. Faith can tell us both *that* God is and *what* God is.[6] It can tell us God's essence as well as God's existence. Affectively, charity has the same relationship to justice. Charity transcends the natural orientation toward justice by including, going beyond, perfecting, and augmenting it. In particular, justice enables us to easily and joyfully give people what they deserve. But

---

4. For a very detailed account of grace, see Lonergan, *Collected Works*, vol. 1, *Grace and Freedom*.

5. *Grace and Freedom*, 17.

6. See Thomas Aquinas, *Summa Theologiae* I, qs. 1–13, on knowing God's existence and essence, and II-II, qs. 1–9, on faith.

by charity we go beyond justice into the realms of mercy and give people more than they deserve.[7]

The parable of "The Workers in the Vineyard" told by Jesus in the gospel of Matthew illustrates how the grace of charity transcends the natural expectations of justice. In the story Jesus explains "the kingdom of heaven" (a state of perfection when God will put all things in proper order or right relationship) through the analogy of a landowner who hires several sets of laborers for his vineyard. To each of them he says he will give them the "just" daily wage. At the end of the day, the various sets of laborers gather together to be paid. The group hired last is paid first, and its members receive the usual daily wage. Those in the earliest group are paid last, and they become upset when they receive the same amount as the last group. They complain to the landowner that it is unfair that they, who worked all day and through the hottest part of the day, were paid the same amount as those who worked for only one hour. The landowner replies to them, saying, "My friend, I am not cheating you. Did you not agree with me for the usual daily wage? Take what is yours and go. What if I wish to give this last one the same as you? Am I not free to do as I wish with my own money? Are you envious because I am *generous*?"[8]

The usual interpretation of this parable is that the workers stand for human beings and the owner represents God. All the workers are given in the end what they are due by justice, but some are given more. The point, however, is not that God loves some people more than others. The point is that God loves all of us with a generous, even wasteful love that gives us more, much more, than we deserve.[9] If any of us were to receive our just due, we would receive nothing. For none of us even created ourselves. Moreover, because of our sins, we deserve punishments, not rewards. But that is the point of grace; it is a gift that we do not deserve, earn, or merit. It is a gift freely given that goes beyond all

7. See Aquinas, *Summa Theologiae* I, q. 21, on God's justice and mercy, and II-II, qs. 21, on charity, 30 on mercy, and 58 on justice.

8. Mt. 20:1–15, *The New American Bible*, emphasis added.

9. See also the parable of the Prodigal Son. Some say the story should be called the "Prodigal Father," since the father's forgiving, overabundant love seems wasteful (the true meaning of "prodigal").

natural possibilities and expectations. And just as in the story, the generosity of divine charity fulfilled and went beyond the wages of justice, so grace in general fulfills and goes beyond nature.

To bring this distinction to bear on healing and elevating grace, we must consider the fact that in concrete reality, we are not in a state of pure nature, governed by the natural standards of reason and justice. We are mixed up in sin with its irrationality, injustice, suspicion, and hatred. Grace has a twofold effect of (1) lifting us up out of sin and back to the state of pure nature, as well as (2) raising us higher, from a state of pure nature to a divine, graced, supernatural state. By its first effect, grace is called "healing." And by its second, it is called "elevating."

In Latin "healing grace" is *gratia sanans,* and thus is translated as the grace that saves, cleanses, cures, or heals. It cures humanity of the negative effects of sin and restores nature to its original, good state. In traditional terms, *gratia sanans* frees us of the vicious habits that dispose us to sin. It "plucks out the heart of stone that made the sinner a slave to sin; it implants a heart of flesh to initiate a new continuity in justice."[10] In terms of Lonergan's dialectic of history, healing grace counteracts the forces of decline and enables their reversal. It is "the liberation of human liberty."[11] Overcoming bias, it allows human persons to become more attentive, intelligent, reasonable, and responsible and thus to perform better their natural operations of experiencing, understanding, judging, and deciding.

The second type of grace is an elevating or sanctifying grace called *gratia elevans.* Elevating grace causes things to emerge that are not possible to the natural world of emergent probability. It enables human beings to operate on levels beyond their "own steam." Traditionally conceived, *gratia elevans* "infuses" us with (or gives us) the supernatural virtues of faith, hope, and charity,[12] and it allows us to know God face to face, to know as we are known.[13] For Lonergan its primary effects are on cognitive, moral,

---

10. *Grace and Freedom,* 58.   11. *Grace and Freedom,* 50.
12. Cf. Lonergan, *Topics in Education,* 242–43. We will discuss faith, hope, and love further in chapter 9, "Religious Conversion."
13. Lonergan, "Openness and Religious Experience," in *Collection,* 200–201.

and affective levels of humanity. But its implications quickly move into the social realms of personal relations as well as the cultural realms of shared meaning and value. Eventually its effects extend to all of creation.

Reflection Questions for Chapter 8

- Our world can be so dark and depressing at times. The news is often full of crimes, natural disasters, and tragic accidents. Friends and family may disappoint us. We do the same to them and even to ourselves. Life seems like one big competition, a rat race in which each individual must do "whatever it takes to get ahead."
- But sometimes we are surprised. We encounter not senseless acts of violence, but gratuitous acts of kindness. C. S. Lewis, the British author most famous for his children's series *The Chronicles of Narnia,* once wrote an autobiography called *Surprised by Joy.* It described how he would sometimes be struck by a strong, inexplicable feeling of happiness that he called "joy." As time went on and he converted to Christianity, he began to associate this experience with divine grace. Coincidentally, after writing the book, he met and married a lively American woman named Joy Gresham. This happened late in his life, when he no longer expected to marry; so people would say that in more ways than one, he was surprised by Joy.
- Have you ever experienced such unexpected, inexplicable joy? Have you known generosity or been given something you did not earn? Have you been granted mercy or forgiveness? Has anyone ever loved you, not for how useful you may be, but simply for being who you are?
- Have you ever loved anyone this way? Have you ever been the source of a random, undeserved act of kindness, mercy, or forgiveness?

9 | Religious, Moral, and Intellectual Conversion

As mentioned in chapter 4 within the section, "The Human Good," Lonergan defines conversion in terms of horizontal and vertical liberty. Horizontal liberty allows a person to make relatively minor choices from a range of options within a fixed boundary or "horizon." Vertical liberty is the product of a much more radical choice, a leap of self-transcendence that expands or otherwise transforms one's horizon itself. Sometimes the new horizon, "though notably deeper and broader and richer" than the previous horizon, may still be "consonant with the old and a development out of its potentialities." However, sometimes a new horizon is "an about-face; it comes out of the old by repudiating characteristic features; it begins a new sequence that can keep revealing ever greater depth and breadth and wealth. Such an about-face and new beginning is what is meant by a conversion."[1]

Conversion is a positive change in the orientation of one's liberty toward better possible choices and terminal values. It causes a radical shift in one's fears and desires, satisfactions and values, beliefs and scales of preference. It frees one from inauthenticity for greater authenticity.

If conversion seems to function in a manner similar to grace,

1. Lonergan, *Method*, 237–38.

this is no accident. Conversion, particularly religious conversion, is the framework for Lonergan's discussion of what traditional theology calls "sanctifying grace"—that is, "an entitative habit, absolutely supernatural, infused into the essence of the soul."[2] Conversion is part of Lonergan's larger "transition from theoretical to methodical theology" that begins "not from a metaphysical psychology, but from intentionality analysis, and, indeed from transcendental method."[3] In terms of intentionality analysis and transcendental method, Lonergan identifies three conversions related to each other by self-transcendence: (1) intellectual conversion is the most basic, and it pertains to how we attain knowledge; (2) moral conversion expands on intellectual conversion into the human search for grasping the truly good and becoming principles of benevolence and beneficence; and (3) religious conversion transcends the prior two in its unrestricted falling in love with God and all things.[4]

Together they constitute the way divine grace works in the world to transform the orientation of human persons and thus to reverse decline and bring about redemption. Theoretically, intellectual conversion is the most basic of the three. In concrete reality, however, religious conversion tends to come first, for it is not until we fall in love unrestrictedly that moral action and unbiased knowing come easily and with joy. Consequently we begin with religious conversion.

Religious Conversion

Religious conversion is a type of "affective conversion."[5] Whereas affective conversion could occur in many relationships, with falling in love with one's family, one's community, *or* with God, reli-

---

2. *Method*, 120; cf. 288.   3. *Method*, 289.

4. Lonergan also acknowledges a fourth conversion developed by one of his best students, Robert Doran, S.J. In "Reality, Myth, Symbol," Lonergan calls it an advance and describes it: "It occurs when we uncover within ourselves the working of our own psyches, the *élan vital*."; Lonergan, "Reality, Myth, Symbol," in *Myth, Symbol, and Reality*, edited by Alan M. Olsen, 31–37 (Notre Dame, Ind.: University of Notre Dame Press, 1980). He refers the reader to Doran, "Psychic Conversion," *The Thomist* 41 (April 1977): 200–36, and Doran, *Subject and Psyche: Ricoeur, Jung, and the Search for Foundations* (Washington, D.C.: The Catholic University Press of America, 1977). Fr. Doran tells me its effect is to offset dramatic bias, since it is psychogenetic.

5. Lonergan mentions affective conversion in the trio intellectual, moral, and affective conversion in "Natural Right and Historical Mindedness," in *A Third Collection*, 179. Affective conver-

gious conversion includes all of these and is specified as falling
love with God *and thereby* with all things. Religious conversio
the culmination of affective conversion. It is "the deep-set joy u..
solid peace, the power and the vigor, of being in love with God."[6]
If one is in love with anything as a result of being in love with God,
then, according to the more classical "theoretical theology," one is
in a special state of being, the state of "sanctifying grace." "Being-
in-love" is the term Lonergan uses to translate the state of sanctifying grace into a methodological theology informed by intentionality analysis.[7] In a way, being-in-love is an end. But in a way, it is a
beginning, for even if one is already in love, one can fall more and
more deeply in love. And since any being in love is a continual becoming, Lonergan emphasizes that the being-in-love that is given
by God is a "dynamic state" that develops throughout the concrete,
ongoing experience that Lonergan calls "religious conversion."

More on "theoretical theology," "sanctifying grace," and the
"dynamic state of being-in-love" will be said as this chapter progresses. But first, what does Lonergan mean by the term "religious"
in religious conversion? Interestingly, he does not mean what commonly is meant by the word in the contemporary United States. He
does not mean what pertains to a particular, organized body of people who share beliefs and practices that relate them to a transcendent being or force. Nor does he exclude such groups, their systems
of belief, or their practices from the religious.

The religious, for Lonergan, is more than any one such organization or even all such organizations.[8] It pertains to "a reality that

---

sion is unpacked as "love in the family, loyalty in the community, and faith in God," and similarly
as "commitment to love in the home, loyalty in the community, faith in the destiny of man." Both
quotes seem to discuss an unrestricted love, one of which focuses on God and the other on humanity. Similarly, in "Religion," chapter 4 of *Method*, Lonergan discusses two exceptions to the
"normal" way by which knowing precedes loving. The first flows from God's love being poured into
our hearts, and the second arises when human persons fall in love with each other; *Method*, 122;
see also chapter 2 of this volume.

6. *Method*, 39. We will focus on being in love with God toward the end of this chapter.

7. *Method*, 105, 291.

8. Lonergan's view on the relation of Christianity to other religions is interesting and fertile.
A full treatment is beyond the scope of this book, but we may note that he rejects the thought that
other major world religions are evil or that their goodness is simply due to natural achievements.
He believes that all people are loved by God, can become conscious of this love, and are moved to
express this love. The major world religions are such expressions. But the fullest expression, the
one informed by the word of God made flesh, is Christianity. So Christianity has the fullness of

transcends the reality of this world,"[9] a being that is not virtually unconditioned but absolutely unconditioned, a value by which all values are measured, a love that knows no bounds. In our unrestricted desires to know and to choose, we seek the only thing that can fulfill our desire, namely a truly unrestricted, transcendent object. That being, value, love, and transcendent object is God, though it may be known by many names in many traditions.

Since the "religious" is what pertains to God, "religious experience" is the experience of God. Consequently it is unlike any other experience. It is not the product of our knowing and choosing as, say, the college experience or a night out at the opera is. Nor is it even technically an experience, because God is not merely one being among other beings, something that we can see, touch, taste, feel, or hear—at least, not in the usual way. Religious experience for Lonergan is more of a religious "consciousness." It occurs not on our first level of consciousness, as other experiences do, since it begins with God's gift of love, and "the gift of God's love occupies the fourth and highest level of human intentional consciousness. It takes over the peak of the soul, the *apex animae*."[10] But while religious experience begins at the peak of the soul, the fullness of religious conversion produces a being-in-love that affects the whole person on all levels of consciousness, starting at the fourth level and moving down to the others.[11]

Operating on all four levels, religious conversion fulfills the entire natural human thrust toward self-transcendence. Lonergan explains. "Being in love with God, as experienced, is being in love in an unrestricted fashion. All love is self-surrender, but being in love with God is being in love without limits or qualifications or conditions or reservations. Just as unrestricted questioning is our capacity for self-transcendence, so being in love in an unrestricted fashion is the proper fulfillment of that capacity."[12]

---

divine revelation. This is not to say that particular Christians are holier than particular members of other religions, for revelation must be accepted and lived out. For a brief but excellent treatment of Lonergan's scattered thoughts on the matter, see Frederick Crowe, *Appropriating the Lonergan Idea* (Washington, D.C.: The Catholic University of America Press, 1989), chaps. 17–19.

9. *Method*, 102.   10. *Method*, 107.

11. As mentioned in chapter 4 of this volume, "The Way From Above Downwards"; more to follow.

12. *Method*, 106; cf. 242: "Questions for intelligence, for reflection, for deliberation reveal the

Rudolf Otto describes being in love with God as an encounter with *mysterium fascinans et tremendum* [the mystery that both fascinates and terrifies]. Paul Tillich identifies it as "being grasped by ultimate concern." And for St. Ignatius of Loyola it is called "consolation with no cause."[13] All of these terms are a little strange. The experience of God's love is not "mysterious" in the sense of secretive, not "fascinating" like a car accident, or "terrifying" like a horror movie. It is these things because divine transcendence is so overwhelming in beauty, goodness, power, and love. We feel unworthy, but we are also lovingly drawn in. To be "grasped by ultimate concern" is not to be imagined as a giant hand reaching down to squeeze us and carry us off. It is more like relaxing into a warm, soothing river that unites us to all things in mutual love. It is "consolation with no cause" in the sense that the feeling seems to come out of the blue, while at other times when we feel happy or consoled ("with the sun," literally), we can easily identify the exact cause: a personal achievement, a friend's phone call, a mother's embrace.

Lonergan holds that since all people are loved by God and all people can become conscious of this love, such religious experience is common to some degree among the various major religious traditions. Nevertheless, there are important differences in the ways these traditions interpret and express their consciousness of being loved by God:[14]

For Christians it [religious conversion] is God's love flooding our hearts through the Holy Spirit given to us. It is the gift of grace, and since the days of Augustine, a distinction has been drawn between operative and cooperative grace. Operative grace is the replacement of the heart of stone by a heart of flesh, a replacement beyond the horizon of the heart of stone. Cooperative grace is the heart of flesh becoming effective in good works through human freedom. Operative grace is religious conversion. Cooperative grace is the

---

eros of the human spirit, its capacity and its desire for self-transcendence. But that capacity meets fulfillment, that desire turns to joy, when religious conversion transforms the existential subject into a subject in love, a subject held, grasped, possessed, owned through a total and so an otherworldly love."

13. *Method*, 106, referencing Rudolf Otto, *The Idea of the Holy* (London: Oxford, 1923), which notes that *tremendum* varies in meaning depending on one's religious development; D. M. Bron, *Ultimate Concern: Tillich in Dialogue* (New York: Harper and Row, 1965); and Karl Rahner, *The Dynamic Element in the Church: Quaestiones Disputatae 12* (Montreal: Palm, 1964), 131.

14. Cf. *Method*, 108–9.

effectiveness of conversion, the gradual movement towards a full and complete transformation of the whole of one's living and feeling, one's thoughts, words, deeds, and omissions."[15]

As this quote indicates, Lonergan connects religious conversion to some of the classical types of grace already discussed—namely, "operative" and "cooperative" grace. Religious conversion is operative grace in the sense that by it God "operates" directly on a person. Extending the metaphor of a surgical procedure, religious conversion is commonly thought of as God's replacing a cold, hard, unfeeling heart of stone with a living, loving heart of flesh.[16]

Religious conversion may begin with a change of heart, but it is a total transformation of one's entire life, such that all of one's inner and outer words and deeds are augmented by the power of grace. But while graced, such transformed words and deeds remain to some degree a product of the person's own conscious intentionality, his or her experience, understanding, judgment, and decision. Due to the fact that grace and human activity work together to achieve these further fruits of religious conversion, there is traditionally thought to be a "cooperative" type of grace.

Lonergan relates religious conversion not only to operative and cooperative grace, but also to sanctifying grace. In particular he identifies the operative element of religious conversion with sanctifying grace. But whereas the term "sanctifying grace" is preferred by theologians operating in the theoretical realm of meaning, those operating in the realm of interiority or method might prefer to speak of the same reality as a "dynamic state of being in love":

This gift [of religious conversion] we have been describing really is sanctifying grace but notionally differs from it. The notional difference arises from different stages of meaning. To speak of sanctifying grace pertains to the stage of meaning when the world of theory and the world of common sense are distinct but, as yet, have not been explicitly distinguished from and grounded in the world of interiority. To speak of the dynamic state of being in love with God pertains to the stage of meaning when the world of interiority

15. *Method*, 241. This paraphrases Rom. 5:5, Lonergan's most frequently cited passage of scripture; see also Andrew Tallon, "The Role of the Connaturalized Heart in Veritatis Splendor," in *Veritatis Splendor: American Responses*, edited by Michael Allsopp and John O'Keefe, 151 (Kansas City, Mo.: Sheed and Ward, 1995).

16. Ezekiel 11:19, 36:26.

has been made the explicit ground of the worlds of theory and of common sense. It follows that in this stage of meaning the gift of God's love first is described as an experience and only consequently is objectified in theoretical categories.[17]

Lonergan adds that whether called religious conversion, sanctifying grace, or the dynamic state of being-in-love, it is not simply a single moment, but a long process. If there is a particularly significant moment in the process of religious conversion, it is often preceded by instances of transformed feelings or "transient dispositions that also are both operative and cooperative. Again, once the dynamic state has been established, it is filled out and developed by still further additional graces."[18]

The mysterious workings of grace in effecting a religious conversion are indeed complicated, which is not too surprising, since ultimately sanctifying grace has a divinizing effect on human persons. It lifts up those religiously converted into the highest reality of love—namely, the triune God. Thus grace divinizes people in a trinitarian way, transforming them into "temples of Christ's Spirit, members of his body, adopted children of the Father."[19]

We will return to the divinizing aspect of religious conversion later, but let us look now at some of its more mundane effects. Religious conversion is manifested in everyday life in numerous ways, for being in love with God transforms one's whole way of being in the world. Many of these manifestations, expressions, or fruits have been discussed in part 1 under the general heading of love, and most of the particular ones will be considered in this chapter under the headings of charity, faith, and hope. For the remainder of this section I would like to focus on the fruit of religious conversion that Lonergan calls the "religious word."

In its most general definition the religious word is "any expression of religious meaning or of religious value. Its carrier may be intersubjectivity, or art, or symbol, or language, or the remem-

17. *Method*, 107. For more on Lonergan's realms of meaning, see chap. 4 of this volume, "Realms of Meaning."
18. *Method*, 107.
19. Lonergan, "*Existenz and Aggiornamento*," in *Collection*, 249. For much more on his work on the Trinity, see Lonergan, *Collected Works*, vol. 12, *The Triune God: Systematics*, edited by Robert Doran and H. D. Monsour (Toronto: University of Toronto, 2007); and vol. 11, *The Triune God: Doctrines*, edited by Robert Doran, H. D. Monsour, and M. Shields (Toronto: University of Toronto, 2009).

bered and portrayed lives or deeds or achievements of individuals or classes or groups."[20] Religious conversion is mediated to human beings by both religious experience and the religious word. By the religious word divine grace enters into the world mediated by meaning and regulated by value. For human communities there is a mutually beneficial relationship between the religious word and the common language and culture: On the one hand the religious word endows a culture with "its deepest meaning and its highest values."[21] On the other hand it is only in the context of a culture's meanings and values that human persons can come to understand the religious word and to relate it both to the object of ultimate concern and to more proximate objects of ordinary concerns.

Lonergan distinguishes between "the prior word that God speaks to us by flooding our hearts with his love" and the outer word that is expressed in time and space.[22] The outer word is not separate from love or an incidental byproduct of love, such as a mere expression of love. Rather, the outer word is constitutive of love. Lonergan demonstrates this with the example of a marriage vow: "When a man and a woman love each other but do not avow their love, they are not yet in love. Their very silence means that their love has not reached the point of self-surrender and self-donation."[23] The expression of love is not just a product of love but actually constitutive of love, because the outer word realizes love, sustains it, and helps it to grow.

For a religion (in the organized, institutional sense), this is the role of "the word of *tradition* that has accumulated religious wisdom, the word of *fellowship* that unites those that share in the gift of God's love, the word of the *gospel* that announces that God has loved us first and, in the fullness of time, has revealed that love in Christ crucified, dead and risen."[24] So the outer word of divine love in the form of texts, community, and tradition are constitutive of God's love. These effects are in a sense mundane, insofar as they are the works of human persons operating in this world. But they also have an otherworldly quality to them, insofar as these human

---

20. *Method*, 112.   21. *Method*, 112.
22. *Method*, 112.   23. *Method*, 113.

24. *Method*, 113, emphasis added; cf., 283: "[T]he gift of God's love has its proper counterpart in the revelational events in which God discloses to a particular people or to all mankind the completeness of his love for them."

personas have been religiously converted through operative grace and their works augmented by cooperative grace.

As expressed in time, space, and culture, the outer word of a religious tradition is historically conditioned. Human beings too are historically conditioned. They are raised in particular societies and come to know meaning and value through the particular words of their particular cultures. This is true also for the meanings and values of a religious tradition and its doctrines. We come to understand and appreciate the outer word of God only in the context of our cultures. We interpret or misinterpret the outer word in the various languages of our cultures and thus in relation to other nonreligious words and traditions. As time goes on and the meanings of a culture's words change, the outer words of a religious tradition must be updated if the inner meanings of its doctrines are to remain understood as they were originally intended.

Furthermore, religious expression takes part in the development of the various realms of meaning: common sense, theory, interiority, and transcendence. Misunderstanding and other resultant tensions may occur when words conceived in a commonsense context are transposed into a theoretical context and vice versa, since the meaning of the same word is different in each context. For example, in commonsense contexts people use the words "never" and "always" loosely to make a point. In a theoretical context these words have precise meanings. Tensions are likely to arise when a speaker uses these words in a rhetorical, hyperbolic manner of common sense and a listener receives them with the precision of theory. The tension may be resolved by a movement into the higher realm of interiority, where the parties may recognize that the same words are being used in different ways, or by a movement to the forgiving love of the realm of transcendence. But either way, there must be a translation of the words into different contexts. The same is true for religious words. They must continually undergo a type of translation if they are to be properly communicated, understood, and appreciated in different contexts.[25]

Lonergan mentions a good example in which "the God of Abra-

---

25. *Method*, 113–14; *Method*, chap. 14, "Communication."

ham, Isaac and Jacob is set against the God of the philosophers and theologians." The "God of Abraham, Isaac and Jacob" is a way of talking about God on a commonsense level taken from scriptural language. It is a rich way of talking that comes from narratives and may move people to intense feeling. The "God of the philosophers and theologians" is the "Unmoved Mover," the "First Cause" and "Final End." It is a "theoretical apprehension devoid of feeling and bristling with definitions and theorems."[26] Conflicts may occur between people who champion one type to the exclusion of the other. Lonergan believes that both ways have their advantages, and that to know this, one must shift into the higher realms of interiority and transcendence, where one can identify "the God of Abraham, Isaac and Jacob" and "the God of the philosophers and theologians" with the love poured into heights of one's consciousness and depths of one's heart.

In all cultures and in all of these realms of meaning, a primary function of the outer religious word is to constitute, to express, and to otherwise work with God's inner gift of love to help people grow in religious conversion. Concretely, religious conversion is not simply a single moment; it is a lifelong, precarious process. In itself religious conversion is an end, the fulfillment of self-transcendence, but the human subject in this life, even those religiously converted, are always "pilgrims," ever "on the way." Although one may have already become in some measure a being-in-love, one can always discover further depths to love, and there remains the need to make one's knowing and doing conform to one's loving. Lonergan explains:

For that love is the utmost of self-transcendence, and man's self-transcendence is ever precarious. Of itself, self-transcendence involves tension between the self as transcending and the self as transcended. So human authenticity is never some pure and serene and secure possession. It is ever a withdrawal from unauthenticity and every successful withdrawal only brings to light the need for still further withdrawals.... Genuine religion is discovered and realized by redemption from the many traps of religious aberration. So we are bid to watch and pray, to make our way in fear and trembling. And it is the greatest saints that proclaim themselves the greatest sinners, though their sins seem slight indeed to holy folk that lack their discernment and love.[27]

---

26. *Method*, 114–15.   27. *Method*, 110; cf., 252.

Despite the impossibility of perfection, there can be great progress. Citing scripture, Lonergan reminds us that there are standards for recognizing whether or not we or others are authentically living out religious conversion: "[Y]ou will recognize them by their fruits" (Mt 7, 20).[28]

Perhaps most prominent among the fruits of religious conversion are (1) the charity that allows us to love our neighbors as ourselves, (2) the faith that enables us to "see with the eyes of love," and (3) the hope by which we measure our successes and problems by an expected ultimate fulfillment. Faith, hope, and charity are listed by Paul in 1 Corinthians 13:13 as particularly excellent gifts of the Holy Spirit. Thomas Aquinas sought to understand Paul's faith, hope, and charity in light of Aristotle's philosophical account of virtue. In his *Nicomachean Ethics* Aristotle explains that virtues are habits, or dispositions of the soul, that are good (as opposed to bad habits, or vices). Aristotle's virtues are *acquired* by practice, or repeated action. However, Thomas teaches that the Christian virtues of faith, hope, and charity are "infused" or given by God, have God as their object or goal, and unite us to God in some way. For these three reasons, Thomas calls them the "theological" virtues.[29]

As Thomas's theoretical interpretation of charity, faith, and hope sublates Aristotle's virtue theory, so Lonergan's methodological interpretation of these virtues sublates Thomas's metaphysical account. For Lonergan and Thomas the three theological virtues are not the products of human achievement, but the free gifts of God's unmerited grace.[30] Let us consider each virtue in turn.

Charity

Charity is a religious love central to the reversal of decline and the restoration of progress. Lonergan explains: "If passions are to quiet down, if wrongs are to be not exacerbated, not ignored, not

28. *Method,* 119; cf., 269, where Lonergan extends this to recognizing moral and intellectual conversion.

29. Aquinas, *Summa Theologiae* I-II, q. 62.

30. Thus Lonergan scholar John Haughey calls them a "receivement"; see Haughey, "The Primacy of Receivement," in *Business as Calling,* an e-book at http://www.stthomas.edu/cathstudies/cst/publications/businessasacalling.html.

merely palliated, but acknowledged and removed, then human possessiveness and human pride have to be replaced by religious charity, by the charity of the suffering servant, by self-sacrificing love."[31]

Religious charity is the highest love a human being can have. It is an infused, supernatural love with both healing and elevating effects. It is a radical, revolutionary love that reverses many common expectations, particularly those of men and women living in a world marked by the sinful biases of egoism and shortsightedness; for charity allows one to love one's neighbor as oneself (Mk 12:31), to love even one's enemy (Mt 5:44), and, if need be, to lay down one's life for a friend (Jn 15:13). It was taught by words and deeds of Jesus Christ and poured into our hearts by the Holy Spirit (Rom. 5:5).

We tend to think of "charity" as volunteering at a homeless shelter or making a monetary donation. These are some of the fruits of charity, but traditionally speaking, as Paul, Thomas, and Lonergan use the term, charity itself is the inner love that inspires such external acts. We also tend to think that love is a bias, something that blinds a person. Charity is not a bias. Rather, it heals a person of his or her biases, thereby liberating a person to follow freely the unrestricted, transcendental desire and move authentically from attentive experience to intelligent understanding to reasonable judgment to responsible decision.

Charity, in short, heals our nature of the effects of sin, bias, and decline. Because it "promotes self-transcendence to the point, not merely of justice, but of self-sacrificial love," it has "a redemptive role in society, inasmuch as such love can undo the mischief of decline and restore the cumulative process of progress."[32] "For it is only insomuch as men are willing to meet evil with good, to love their enemies, to pray for those that persecute and calumniate them, that the social surd is a potential good."[33]

Charity operates on the whole person and the entire society, but its primary activity is on the fourth level of human conscious-

---

31. *Method*, 117; cf. 55, 113, 242, 291, 342, 362. Self-sacrifice is a difficult concept. An important thing to remember is that it is not something that will earn us God's love, but rather something that, if we are already united to God in love, we may be called to live. More on self-sacrifice will be said in chapter 10 of this volume.

32. *Method*, 55.

33. Lonergan, *Insight*, 721.

ness, the level of decision and commitment. Charity creates a good will. It enables a person to make authentic, responsible decisions. Let us examine charity's effect on three things in particular: (1) the expansion of one's horizon of concern to love God, the world order, and all people, (2) the repentance for one's sin, and (3) a general attitude of joyfulness.

The first may be explained in love's relation to bias. The divine gift of charity is the ultimate cure for bias. While bias shrinks the horizon of one's concern, charity expands it. By charity we are united to God and we participate in God's love. This is why Thomas compared charity to friendship with God. Two friends are united by their mutual love, and when united, each person shares the other's loves and aversions, their joys and sorrows, as if they were the person's own.[34] Through charity we become friends with God, united by our mutual love. We love what God loves, as God loves them. And since God loves all things without conditions or restrictions, through charity we love all things without conditions or restrictions. Our love flows from God to God, to ourselves, and to our neighbors, including our enemies and indeed the whole order of the universe, for

the actual order of the universe is a good and value chosen by God.... Moreover, it grounds the emergence, and includes the excellence of every other good within the universe, so that to will any other good is to will the order of the universe.... [A]nd so, to will the order of the universe because of one's love of God is to love all persons in the universe because of one's love of God.[35]

This limitless love leads to a repentance for one's sins. Love's expansion of concern corrects for the shrunken horizons of the four biases. This correction brings to light one's many past mistakes, inasmuch as they are failures to love. In the light of religious love one grows to repent how one surrendered to particular sins, betrayed oneself and others, and contributed to a general decline. The charitable soul:

deplores and regrets the scotosis of its dramatic bias and its involvement in the individual, group, and general bias of common sense; it repents its flight

34. Aquinas, *Summa Theologiae* II-II, q. 23, a. 1.
35. *Insight*, 722.

from self-knowledge, its rationalization of wrong, its surrender to evil; it detests its commitment to counterpositions [inauthentic beliefs], its contribution to man's decline through the successive adjustments of theory to ever worse practice, its share in the genesis and the propagation of the myths that confer on appearance the strength and power and passion that are the due of reality.[36]

Repentance is not merely a feeling of guilt. It is a more conscious, intelligent, reasonable, and responsible act that acknowledges our sin. It is a feeling as well as a judgment and a decision. We are sorry for our past offenses; we detest the damage they have done; and we resolve to never repeat them. We repent not only our actions against our own natural thrust toward self-transcendence, not only our acts against other human persons, but also our sins against God, for sin conceals the goodness of God and the universe from oneself and from others.

Repentance involves sorrow, but sorrow is not the last word. One looks back to past failure, but also forward to a bright future. A person in repentance "is at one with the universe in being in love with God, and it shares its dynamic resilience and expectancy." He or she celebrates the creativity of a world governed by emergent probability. Charity thus causes a deep joy in all things of creation.[37]

In the love, repentance, and joy of charity "one's living is transformed into a personal relation to the one loved above all and in all."[38] Charity affects all of one's life, and the effect is that all of one's living becomes a living in dialogue with God. As Pedro Arrupe expressed so beautifully in the passage quoted in chapter 4, "Nothing is more practical than finding God, that is, than falling in love in a quite absolute, final way.... Fall in love, stay in love, and it will decide everything."[39]

Ignatius of Loyola, the founder of the Jesuits, provides a concrete example of how the falling in love with God that is charity can heal a person of bias and help her or him to joyfully find goodness in all things:

---

36. *Insight*, 722; cf. *Method*, 110, 117, 364.   37. *Insight*, 722.
38. *Insight*, 722.
39. The full quotation is in chapter 4 of this volume, at the end of section 1, "Love."

It should be presupposed that every good Christian ought to be more eager to put a good interpretation on a neighbor's statement than to condemn it. Further, if one cannot interpret it favorably, one should ask how the other means it. If that meaning is wrong, one should correct the person with love; and if this is not enough, one should search out every appropriate means through which, by understanding the statement in a good way, it may be saved.[40]

Faith

In addition to charity, being in love with God produces faith. Faith is a form of the aforementioned knowledge born of love. Moreover, it is an otherworldly, absolutely supernatural type of knowledge. Hence Lonergan calls it "the knowledge born of *religious* love."[41] Faith, like the knowledge born of a natural love, is the heart's reasons that reason does not know, as named by Pascal.[42] As mentioned in chapter 4, such knowledge for Lonergan is part of a reversal of the normal "from below upwards" vector of experience, understanding, judgment, and decision. In chapter 8 we explained how typically we know before we love, as indicated by the scholastic expression *Nihil amatum nisi praecognitum* (Nothing is loved unless it is first known), and we considered the "minor exception" to this rule, which occurs when we fall in love with other human beings.

Religious conversion and the gift of charity that causes us to fall in love with God produce the "major exception" to the way knowledge ordinarily precedes love. This major exception reverses the way we tend to proceed from experience to understanding, judgment, and decision in the following manner: First, being in unrestricted love with God calls forth commitments and decisions on the fourth level of consciousness. These commitments and decisions bear fruit on the third level as judgments of truth and value that are informed by unrestricted love. They may be as basic as that all things come from one loving source or as advanced as regarding the inner life of the Trinity. Such judgments are the content of one's faith. These judgments then form the cognitional background that conditions

40. Ignatius of Loyola, *Ignatius of Loyola: Spiritual Exercises and Selected Works*, edited by George E. Ganss (New York: Paulist Press, 1991), 129.
41. *Method*, 115, emphasis added.
42. See chapter 4 of this volume.

which ideas might occur to a person of faith on the second level of her or his consciousness. Finally, the judgments of value and truth received in faith shape the way a person experiences the world on his or her first level of conscious intentionality.[43]

Faith has a similar effect on the communal life of the church. Faith flows from the fundamental decisions and commitments of a community moved by charity. The community's faith becomes expressed through the judgments expressed in magisterial teachings or doctrine. Theologians, professional or otherwise, then come up with ideas that seek to understand better these doctrines and to relate them systematically. Pastors and other ministers mine these ideas for their practical application to the everyday experience of the members of the church.[44]

Replete with practical implications, faith is first the "experienced fulfillment" of the natural human desire to know and to value. For in faith we are granted knowledge of our ultimate end. But it is an experience and a knowledge that are clouded. Faith is an overwhelming consciousness of "absolute intelligence and intelligibility, absolute truth and reality, absolute goodness and holiness."[45] God becomes known most intimately and most profoundly, yet God remains essentially a mystery. While faith answers many questions we have about God, it renews and strengthens our desire to know God.

The primary question of faith is the existential question on the fourth level of consciousness: decision. It is a question of whether or not we will accept or reject God: "Will I love him in return, or will I refuse? Will I live out the gift of his love, or will I hold back, turn away, withdraw? Only secondarily do there arise the questions of God's existence and nature, and they are the questions either of the lover seeking to know him or of the unbeliever seeking to escape him. Such is the basic option of the existential subject

---

43. Again, for more on "the way from above downward," see chapter 4.

44. *Method*, 336; see esp. chaps. 11, "Foundations"; 12, "Doctrines"; 13, "Systematics"; and 14, "Communications." Such pastoral work, systematic theology, and official teachings are helpful, in part because besides *fides ex infusione* (infused faith, from the way down), there is *fides ex auditu* (a faith that comes from hearing on the way up; see Lonergan, "Mission and the Spirit," *in A Third Collection*, 32; citing Aquinas, *Summa Theologiae* II-II, q.6, a.1.

45. *Method*, 116.

once called by God."[46] The option is not an easy one, for, as mentioned, love changes everything.

Faith is an "apprehension of transcendent value." It is an "actuated orientation towards the mystery of love and awe."[47] This apprehension and orientation provide a reorientation of one's entire world and thus a reapprehension of all one's vital, social, cultural, and personal values:[48]

Without faith the originating value is man and the terminal value is the human good man brings about. But in the light of faith, originating value is divine light and love, while terminal value is the whole universe. So the human good becomes absorbed in an all-encompassing good. Where before an account of the human good related men to one another and to nature, now human concern reaches beyond man's world to God and to God's world. Men meet not only to be together and to settle human affairs but also to worship. Human development is not only in skills and virtues but also in holiness. The power of God's love brings forth a new energy and efficacy in all goodness, and the limit of human expectation ceases to be the grave.[49]

In the classical terms of faculty psychology, faith provides the "will's hope with its object and assurance and the will's charity with its motives."[50] In the language of transcendental method, faith "places human efforts in a friendly universe; it reveals an ultimate significance in human achievement; it strengthens new undertakings with confidence."[51] Thus faith has the irreplaceable power of undoing decline, particularly the longer cycle of decline that is perpetuated by ideology: "Decline disrupts a culture with conflicting ideologies. It inflicts on individuals the social, economic, and psychological pressures that for human frailty amount to determinism. It multiplies and heaps up the abuses and absurdities that breed resentment, hatred, anger, violence. It is not propaganda, and it is not argument, but religious faith that will liberate human minds from its ideological prisons.[52]

To free human minds from the prisons of ideology, faith "reestablishes truth as a meaningful category." Lonergan reminds us of the critical link between truth and resistance to sin by calling to

46. *Method,* 116.
48. *Method,* 115.
50. *Insight,* 724.
52. *Method,* 117.

47. *Method,* 115.
49. *Method,* 116.
51. *Method,* 117.

mind Pilate's (in)action when others were calling for Jesus's death and he felt the man did not deserve to die. Pilate was able to succumb to the will of the crowd and do what he thought was wrong, because he had distanced himself from the truth, as revealed by his question, "What is truth?"[53]

Furthermore, on cognitive levels faith promotes a new order of meaning and values, one that flows from knowing that the universe is grounded in and moving toward unconditional love. "Without faith, without the eye of love, the world is too evil for God to be good, for a good God to exist. But faith recognizes that God grants men their freedom, that he wills them to be persons and not just his automata, that he calls them to the higher authenticity that overcomes evil with good."[54] To overcome evil with good, we need not only charity and faith, but also hope.

Hope

Hope flows from the commitments of love and the judgments of faith. Hope gives those caught in the downward spiral of decline the courage to resist personal and social tendencies to behave sinfully. It frees people from drudgery, "liberates the pilgrim in us," and "enables us to resist the pressures and the determinisms that are, as it were, the necessity of sinning further."[55] Hope gives ordinary people the "heroism" needed to resist negative situations that increase the probabilities of sin. Only a hero can overcome the various "peer pressures" of a community and a culture marred by the many aspects of social or original sin.

It can be very difficult to think and to act in opposition to others. We may think it is easy, and we may even think we do it all the time, but this is probably because we have been brainwashed by our culture to think we are free thinkers. In America, in particular, we are all raised to think we need to be self-made individuals, restless rebels, "cool" or indifferent to the opinion of others. So we pose and we pout, pretending not to care what others think, but we are desperate that they will notice us and want us. We flock to

---

53. Lonergan, *Topics in Education*, 67, with reference to Jn 18:38.
54. *Method*, 117.
55. *Topics in Education*, 67.

stores or websites to buy the latest trends that we hope will separate us from the crowds, but we do not realize that we are buying into whatever the trendsetters want us to think or do. And these trendsetters are sometimes the worst, hiding the sources of their inspiration, perhaps even from their own conscious minds. This is but one mundane, even petty example of a sinful social situation in which heroism from hope and other graces is required. Still, "without that heroism there is no victory over the cumulative effects of sin as a component in social process."[56]

According to faculty psychology, hope is a perfection of the will, a moral confidence that strengthens the intellect. This is important for Lonergan because the intellect functions properly, inasmuch as the detached and disinterested desire to know is allowed to direct one's cognitional operations. According to intentionality analysis this desire is the spontaneous, prior foundation for intelligent, rational, and responsible self-consciousness. It is detached, but not disembodied. Consequently it must compete on the one hand in an ultimately cooperative way with the natural attachments of sensitivity and spontaneous intersubjectivity, and on the other hand in an ultimately oppositional way with the disordered attachments of bias. In this dialectic hope reinforces the rational, unrestricted desire with a responsible commitment to discovering and acting according to transcendent truth and goodness.[57] Without hope one cannot commit to such a seemingly impractical goal.

This is particularly true in situations marked by sin, but it is also true simply because the unrestricted nature of human desire may tempt one to despair at ever fulfilling it. One may wish to rest in some partial, inadequate fulfillment—that is, an idol. This could be anything from the latest cell phone to discovering the cure for cancer. No matter how wonderful a thing, it will not fully satisfy our infinite desire unless it is an infinite good. This lesson is driven home again and again with each dissatisfaction we feel after the initial high of any acquisition or achievement wears off.

Through hope one avoids the temptation to despair or to settle. Through hope one knows that the objective of unrestricted desire

56. *Topics in Education*, 67; cf. *Method*, 117.
57. *Insight*, 723.

exists and is promised, but that it lies beyond the reach of empirical science, common sense, their unification in metaphysics, and even the transcendent knowledge by which we know *that* God exists. Hope is confident that, despite the transcendent nature of our fulfillment, it is promised. This confidence is a mean that excludes the extremes of "both despair and presumption." Lonergan summarizes: "the conjugate form of willingness that aids and supports and reinforces the pure desire is a confident hope that God will bring man's intellect to a knowledge, participation, possession of the unrestricted act of understanding."[58]

This is true for the desire we feel on the other levels of consciousness as well, for we desire not simply understanding, nor is God simply unrestricted intelligibility and truth. So as we desire unrestricted being, beauty, meaning, value, goodness, justice, and love, hope tells us that there exists an unrestricted being, beauty, meaning, value, goodness, justice, and love that will fulfill us. And as this desire is a single eros of the human spirit, so this fulfillment is a single God. It is the same God of Abraham, Isaac, and Jacob, the same God of the philosophers and theologians, the same God of Father, Son, and Spirit who generates the eternal Word and breathes unrestricted love into our world and into our hearts.

There are many other aspects and effects of faith, hope, and charity. But we leave them to be covered in part under moral and intellectual conversion. This is appropriate, since the effects of religious conversion flow "from above downwards," from the peak of the human person to the moral and cognitive aspects of human living. Intellectual conversion focuses on the truth grasped in cognitive self-transcendence; moral conversion pertains to values affirmed and realized in moral or "real" self-transcendence; and religious conversion brings one to a "total being-in-love as the efficacious ground of all self-transcendence, whether in the pursuit of truth, or in the realization of human values, or in the orientation man adopts to the universe, its ground, and its goal."[59]

58. *Insight*, 723–24.
59. *Method*, 241.

Moral Conversion

Moral conversion is typically the fruit of religious conversion. It is also very similar to religious conversion, with often overlapping effects. But it can occur in a person independently of religious conversion. Like religious conversion, moral conversion operates mainly on the level of choice and decision, but its effects are less pervasive and less expansive than those of religious conversion. The results particular to a graced moral conversion include decisions that, compared to sinful or even natural decisions, are more consistently responsible and thus produce better consequences for oneself and the community in the short term and the long run.

A key to the development of moral conversion is the discovery that one's choice for a particular good selects and influences not merely a single object, but a whole range and system of objects that go into the production, distribution, maintenance, and disposal of the object (that is, a good of order). Furthermore, one recognizes that along with choosing a particular object and a good of order, one is choosing oneself and who one is to become. Modern culture tends to identify freedom with the ability to choose from a range of objects. But Lonergan emphasizes that a person's decisions and actions usually affect him or her "more deeply" than they affect the objects chosen and acted upon. The cause of this is that when a person makes a choice and follows through with an action, it forms the "dispositions and habits" that "determine" a person, since one's dispositions and habits form one's character or essence. Lonergan calls the moment someone recognizes that his or her actions shape his or her character a "critical point" in the development of that person's growing autonomy. It occurs "when the subject finds out for himself that it is up to himself to decide what he is to make of himself."[60] At this point a person enters a second stage of personal responsibility that is concerned with both the objects of one's actions and the way one is forming one's self as a subject.

60. "Existenz and Aggiornamento," 242; cf. *Method*, 240. More classically trained readers will recognize important elements of Aristotle's and Thomas's virtue ethics in this aspect of moral conversion; those well-versed in modern or postmodern thought will notice its affinity with existentialism.

A further aspect of moral conversion is a shift in the criteria of one's decisions from satisfactions to values, from the apparent good to what is truly good, from a calculus of "pleasures and pains" to what truly is the right thing to do. Ideally this shift is produced by the natural human development by which a child reaches maturity: "As children or minors we are persuaded, cajoled, ordered, compelled to do what is right. As our knowledge of human reality increases, as our responses to human values are strengthened and refined, our mentors more and more leave us to ourselves so that our freedom may exercise its ever advancing thrust toward authenticity."[61]

Lonergan's name for one who has not yet begun the process of moral conversion is the "drifter." "The drifter has not yet found himself; he has not yet discovered his own deed and so is content to do whatever everyone else is doing."[62] In other words the drifter simply follows peer pressure and chooses, with little reflection or deliberation, to think, say, and do whatever others are choosing, thinking, saying, and doing.

By the measure in which one abandons being a slave to the whims of others as well as one's own superficial, selfish, short-term whims, one grows in vertical liberty and autonomy. Truly free, responsible, and moral actions are chosen (1) deliberately rather than by drifting, (2) out of knowledge of and concern for oneself, others, the whole of creation, and the long-term good, and (3) in preference to values over satisfactions. Or they may be chosen out of a good habit formed by many previous deliberate moral acts. With each moral act a person takes a step in the right direction, but authentic autonomy, indeed moral conversion itself, is a lifelong struggle that requires multiple repetitions of such moral acts. To advance in moral conversion one must discover and resist one's biases; one must grow in knowledge of one's community and one's world; one must keep scrutinizing one's motives and scales of value; and one must remain open to the criticism and the wisdom of one's community.[63] For no matter how many good acts one has

61. *Method*, 240.
62. "Existenz and Aggiornamento," 242; Lonergan, "Self-Transcendence," in *Philosophical and Theological Papers, 1965–1980*, 315.
63. *Method*, 240.

performed and how many good habits one has formed, there still remains room to grow.

Thus genuine liberty or autonomy should not be confused with an egotistical disregard for others and their perspectives. It is quite the opposite. Due to the shift from satisfactions to values, from being concerned with what is good merely for oneself to what is good for the whole community across time and space, the authentic, morally converted, autonomous subject is "armed against bias," egotistical and otherwise.[64] In fact moral conversion is the proximate means for people "to keep themselves free of individual, group and general bias."[65]

Finally, despite the significant measure we may grow in autonomy or in "open-eyed, deliberate self-control," Lonergan warns with haunting beauty that due to our limitations, we will never reach complete autonomy or self-control, at least not in this life: "We do not know ourselves very well; we cannot chart the future; we cannot control our environment completely or the influences that work on us; we cannot explore our unconscious and preconscious mechanisms. Our course is the night; our control is only rough and approximate; we have to believe and trust, to risk and dare."[66]

Intellectual Conversion

Intellectual conversion operates on the cognitive levels of understanding and judgment. It is a transformation of convictions about what is real and how we come to know the real. Typically we believe that the real is whatever we can experience, by which we mean whatever we can see, touch, taste, hear, or smell: How do you know that happened? I was there. I saw it.

The real, according to this view, is what Lonergan calls "really out there," or "the already-out-there-now-real."[67] He explains:

"Already" refers to the orientation and dynamic anticipation of biological consciousness; such consciousness does not create but finds its environment.... "Out" refers to the extroversion of a consciousness that is aware,

64. *Method*, 242.
65. *Method*, 270.
66. "Existenz and Aggiornamento," 242; "Self-Transcendence," 315.
67. *Insight*, 178, 181, 184, 449; cf. *Method*, 238.

not of its own ground, but of objects distinct from itself. "There" and "now" indicate the spatial and temporal determinations of extroverted consciousness. "Real," finally, is a subdivision within the field of the "already out there now": part of that is mere appearance; but part is real; and its reality consists in its relevance to biological success or failure, pleasure or pain.[68]

To Lonergan the persistent belief in the already-out-there-now-real is a damaging myth with fundamental implications for philosophy and indeed for all of human living:

The consequences of the myth are various. The naive realist knows the world mediated by meaning but thinks he knows it by looking. The empiricist restricts objective knowing to sense experience; for him, understanding and conceiving, judging and believing are merely subjective activities. The idealist insists that human knowing always includes understanding as well as sense; but he retains the empiricist's notion of reality, and so he thinks of the world mediated by meaning as not real but ideal.[69]

A major problem with thinking that reality is simply what can be sensed is that one cannot then account for the existence of such nonphysical realities as love and friendship, God and sin, to say nothing of simple causality.[70] Nor can one understand the world as conceived according to modern science, because quantum mechanics has

removed from science the relevance of any image of particles, or waves, or continuous process. No less than his predecessors, the contemporary scientist can observe and experiment, inquire and understand, form hypotheses and verify them. But unlike his predecessors, he has to think of knowledge, not as taking a look, but as experiencing, understanding and judging; he has to think of objectivity, not as mere extroversion, but as experiential, normative, and tending towards an absolute; he has to think of the real, not as a part of the "already out there now," but as the verifiable.[71]

Intellectual conversion is from these false views about reality and human knowing to the position Lonergan calls "critical real-

68. *Insight,* 276–77; cf. *Method,* 263–64.

69. *Method,* 238–39; cf. 76, 206, 213. Lonergan criticizes the immediacy of naive realism as "animal knowing"; however, he sometimes uses this term to indicate a limited but legitimate "immediate" human knowing that is transcended by a fuller human knowing that is enriched and "mediated by meaning"; *Insight,* 22, 439, 448; *Method,* 76–77.

70. In his *A Treatise of Human Nature,* Hume argued famously that we cannot see causality and so we cannot know it with certainty. Lonergan refers to this in *Insight,* 414, 438, 448, and in *Method,* 16, 239.

71. *Insight,* 449–50.

ism."[72] The critical realist knows that reality is a world of meaning and value, of things that both can and cannot be sensibly experienced. She or he knows that knowing is by self-transcendence, and this self-transcendence is attained by authentic experiencing, understanding, and judging. Reality is the set of actual, intelligible relations known to exist through judgment's process of verifying one's understanding by comparing it to the data gained by experience. One who is intellectually converted has judged this to be true. He or she has undertaken the difficult, introspective tasks of attending to his or her experience of coming to know, of understanding this process, and of making the existential self-judgment that one can and does know the truth by a compound of actions involving sensing, imagining, questioning, understanding, conceiving, verifying, and judging.

By opening one's mind to the existence of nonphysical realities, intellectual conversion can open the door to faith and other aspects of religious conversion. However, this typically works the other way, with religious conversion leading to intellectual and moral conversions. Faith usually comes before intellectual conversion, for "among the values discerned by the eye of love is the value of believing the truths taught by the religious tradition, and in such tradition and belief are the seeds of intellectual conversion."[73] Moreover, faith, "the eye of this [religious] love reveals values in their splendor, while the strength of this love brings about their realization, and that is moral conversion."[74]

A person may attain one of the three conversions separately or a combination of any two of them together. If all three are found in a person, the relation is of moral conversion sublating intellectual conversion and religious conversion sublating intellectual and moral conversions.

Marked by "high seriousness and a mature wisdom," as well as by responsible dedication to the welfare of all humanity and indeed all creation, converted individuals are a "foundational real-

72. *Method*, 239. For a related discussion on objectivity, see *Method*, 263–64; *Insight*, 399–400, 404–9; and Lonergan, "The Subject," in *A Second Collection*, 69–86.

73. *Method*, 243.

74. *Method*.

ity." They are the standards of authentic humanity, the principles for the reversal of decline, for the healing and elevation of human progress. Converted persons are the foundation for an authentic community and, as community, they are fundamental for the ongoing emergence of conversion.[75] Again, even among the converted, authenticity remains a dialectical development, for "the task of repentance and conversion is life-long."[76]

Fortunately, one is not responsible alone for even one's own conversion. "Though conversion is intensely personal, utterly intimate, still it is not so private as to be solitary. It can happen to many and they can form a community to sustain one another in their self-transformation, and to help one another in working out the implications, and in fulfilling the promise of their new life."[77] Such community is the topic of our final chapter.

Reflection Questions for Chapter 9

- Australian feminist and libertarian Germaine Greer once said, "You're only young once, but you can be immature forever." This statement is usually repeated with tongue in cheek, for there are two ways of interpreting it, one positive and one negative. The difference lies in the meaning one gives to the term "immature." If it means child*like*, as in spontaneous, joyful, optimistic, prone to wonder, ready to laugh and play, then it is something positive. If it means child*ish*, as in, whiny, selfish, impatient, and superficial, then it is something negative. In either case, the statement is true; a person can be childish or childlike forever.
- The hope is that as one grows old one remains or even grows more childlike, while losing one's childish ways. This is a big part of what conversion is all about. We have reflected upon how children provide clear examples of spontaneous wonder and endless questioning. Their wonder is a type of desire, a natural desire to know. It is also a kind of love, an eros for understanding the world. Children tend just as spontaneously to embody

---

75. *Method*, 267–70.   76. *Method*, 118.
77. The Subject," 66; cf. *Method*, 118, 130–31.

another kind of love: benevolence, willing the good for others. At some point, however, we tend to lose these loves, or we limit them to a small corner of the world. We say, "I couldn't care less!" about whatever or whoever falls outside of our shrunken horizon of concern.

- Some would call this maturity. But Lonergan believes that if we have lost these natural, childlike loves, whether due to our culture's sins or our own, we can still get them back. It just takes a long process of conversion, of transforming one's loves, one's beliefs, and one's actions.

- Whom do you consider to be a model of maturity? Whom do you want to become more like? Is this person fully alive and deeply curious about the world? Does she or he care about others? Does this person act with integrity, doing what's right and not just what's easy? Is he or she concerned only with accumulating honor and possessions, or does the person also attend to higher, "intangible" goods like love and friendship?

- Who do you want to be? What will it take to get there?

10 | A Redemptive Community

Cosmopolis

Typically, in *Insight* Lonergan credits progress to human intelligence as driven by the "detached and disinterested desire to know." Surprisingly, however, he sometimes in this same work credits liberty. Rather than view this as an irreconcilable inconsistency, I would argue that liberty and intelligence are complementary. They work hand in hand. And both are necessary for progress.[1] Good ideas can improve the situation, but there must be liberty in the community if the ideas are to be reflected on, communicated, tested, implemented, allowed to change the social situation, and eventually to be reevaluated and corrected by new ideas.

None of this movement is possible without both liberty and insight. Lonergan calls this process the "wheel of progress," and he believes it must be allowed to spin with a great deal of freedom. If it is artificially halted or forced to spin more quickly, it can quickly turn into a "wheel of decline."[2] This is because new ideas cannot be forced and should not be suppressed. They are best allowed to arise unpredictably and under conditions of genuine liberty on personal and local levels. Thus "one might as well declare openly

1. Lonergan, *Insight*, 1992, 261. This interpretation is supported by *Method*'s higher synthesis of insight and liberty in the four levels of conscious intentionality or transcendental method: experience, understanding, judgment, and decision.
2. The terms "wheel of progress" and "wheel of decline" are found in Lonergan, "Healing and Creating in History," in *A Third Collection*, 105.

that all new ideas were taboo, as require that they be examined, evaluated, and approved by some hierarchy of officials and bureaucrats."[3] This, of course, is not to say that liberty is license—in other words, that there are no ways of judging and deciding which ideas and courses of action are reasonable and responsible, virtuous or vicious, authentic or inauthentic. As we have seen in the chapters on authenticity and sin, Lonergan believes firmly that freedom must be taken seriously, that there are good and bad decisions, and that some are justly treated as crimes.

In the language of politics one might say that Lonergan advocates neither a very conservative approach to new ideas nor a strictly liberal one. He finds good on both sides and thus counsels moderation:

There is bound to be formed a solid right that is determined to live in a world that no longer exists. There is bound to be formed a scattered left, captivated by now this, now that new development, exploring now this and now that new possibility. But what will count is a perhaps not numerous center, big enough to be at home in both the old and the new, painstaking enough to work out one by one the transitions to be made, strong enough to refuse half-measures and insist on complete solutions even though it has to wait.[4]

What exactly might such a "not numerous center" look like? What kind of a community would allow the wheel of progress to spin freely and not force it to slow down or to speed up? How would they make prudent, unbiased judgments and decisions about which ideas should be tested and implemented and which should not? How should their authority be exercised? Lonergan calls for a moderate, critical synthesis of the predominant models of unregulated liberalism ("liberal" in the classical sense that favors free-market capitalism) and bureaucratic Marxism,[5] but he does not champion any particular type of political or economic organization.[6] Rather, he focuses on a redemptive community that would motivate people

3. *Insight*, 259.
4. Lonergan, "Dimensions of Meaning," in *Collection*, 266–67.
5. For more on the changing meaning of the term "liberal" see this book's introduction, note 5, and chap. 5, note 3.
6. *Insight*, 266. Lonergan did, however, write two books on economics as an exploration into a third way between liberal capitalism and bureaucratic communism: *For a New Political Economy*, edited by Philip McShane (Toronto: University of Toronto Press, 1998), and *Macroeconomic Dynamics: An Essay in Circulation Analysis*, edited by Patrick H. Byrne and Frederick G. Lawrence (Toronto: University of Toronto Press, 1999).

on a *cultural* level instead of attempting through economics or politics to impose new social structures.

As mentioned in chapter 5's discussion of sin, Lonergan believes that "the social surd resides least of all in outer things and most of all in the minds and wills of men."[7] Thus the problem of decline is first of all a challenge to transform human hearts and minds. Because of his conviction that human beings have a natural desire for God, Lonergan argues that the best way to transform hearts and minds is not through control and ideology, but by promoting liberty and thought.[8] A liberated and liberating culture provides a collaborative communal context for its people to wonder, to reflect, to critique, and to deliberate in a way that at once satisfies their minds and speaks to their hearts. Consequently, if we are to meet the challenge of the longer cycle of decline with wisdom, then our best option is not to turn to social structures "with their teeth in them" so much as to the persuasive meanings and values of culture.[9]

"Cosmopolis" is Lonergan's term, within *Insight*'s philosophical context, for the social unit that works on the level of culture to reverse the cycles of decline. Standing against the shorter cycle caused by group bias, cosmopolis "is neither class nor state." It is "too universal to be bribed, too impalpable to be forced, too effective to be ignored." Cosmopolis is also not a police force. It works mainly through ideas and symbols. Force is instrumental at best, and then no more than "residual and incidental."[10] Cosmopolis is not one group that defines itself in opposition to other groups, nor is it a formal institution with enrolled members, a superstate ruling states, an academy endorsing ideas, or a court enforcing a legal code.

Cosmopolis is not an organized body, but the cultural embodiment of the unrestricted eros of the human spirit. It is similar to

---

7. *Insight*, 712.

8. Of course, as mentioned in chapter 3 of this volume, liberty for Lonergan is not "anything goes," but something that is realized the more one knows and chooses the true and the good, and thus grows in an authenticity that finds its fulfillment in being in love with God and all that God loves.

9. Frederick Lawrence, "Expanding Challenge to Authenticity in Insight: Lonergan's Hermeneutics of Facticity (1953–1964)," *Divyadaan* 15, no. 3 (2004): 449; cf. *Insight*, 261.

10. *Insight*, 263.

what contemporary thinkers sometimes refer to as "the creative class" and what Lonergan, following Toynbee, called "creative personalities." It is men and women in different parts of the world, engaged in various types of work, but united in their attempt to promote social change through culture. Its membership might include the people we tend to think of as "creative types": poets and playwrights, actors and actresses, artists and musicians. But it may just as well include scientists and athletes, mothers and fathers, plumbers and electricians, reporters and religious leaders—anyone who is attempting through word and deed, idea and affect to transform people's hearts and minds, to change what they hold to be true and good, what they believe and how they act.

In particular, Lonergan writes, cosmopolis should focus its endeavor on counteracting general bias in order to diminish, reverse, and prevent the longer cycle of decline that general bias can cause. If we recall, general bias is a negative temptation to which common sense is susceptible. Common sense is an indispensable specialization of consciousness that deals with everyday situations. But its focus on practicality can become dangerously narrow-minded when it judges the value of a thing, or even a person, based solely on its perceived immediate usefulness.[11] The members of a cosmopolis inhabit all the realms of meaning available to a culture: common sense, theory, interiority, and transcendence.[12] They are not against commonsense practicality, but in their words and deeds they teach and exemplify that "practicality is for man and not man for practicality,"[13] and that there is more to the value of a thing, a person, an environment, an artwork, or an academic endeavor than its perceived immediate usefulness.

"Delight and suffering, laughter and tears, joy and sorrow, aspiration and frustration, achievement and failure, wit and humor, stand not within practicality but above it."[14] To appeal to these areas of human life, cosmopolis enlists multiple means of communication: fine arts and literature, theater and journalism, schools and universities, public opinion and "personal depth."[15]

11. See chapter 6 of this volume.
12. See chapter 4 of this volume.
13. *Insight*, 267.
14. *Insight*, 261.
15. *Insight*, 264–66.

Lonergan believes that in particular, "education is the great means for transforming the human situation."[16] Education is key, because it can transform hearts and minds at a time when they are most open to change. Such education relies heavily on scholarly theoretical disciplines like natural science, history, and philosophy, because their focus on how things are related to themselves helps to free people from common sense's narrow focus on things as they are related to us. These disciplines have broad and long-term viewpoints that help balance out the short-term thinking of common sense, which can tend toward general bias. At the same time, human beings are not "pure intelligences," and education is not simply academic. So cosmopolis does not work merely through philosophy, science, or other forms of theory;[17] it uses all the realms of meaning, indeed every resource available within a culture.

"Culture," as Lonergan defines it, is "a set of meanings and values that informs a way of life." If cosmopolis is to transform a society through culture, it must change the meanings and values that inform its way of life. Lonergan lists several ways that meaning and value are conveyed from person to person. The first, most fundamental way is "intersubjective." This includes the many "natural and spontaneous" ways we communicate through bodily gestures, tones of voice, postures, all the things an actress in a silent film might use to convey her thoughts or feelings. "Art" is second. Here Lonergan borrows from the art theorist Susan Langer to define art as "the objectification of a purely experiential pattern." It combines "colors, tones, volumes, movements" in ways that invite us "to withdraw from practical living and to explore possibilities of fuller living in a richer world."[18]

The third carrier of meaning and value is "symbols," which are images of real or imaginary objects that evoke feelings. And feelings are "the mass and momentum and power of [a person's] conscious living, the actuation of his affective capacities, dispositions, habits, the effective orientation of his being."[19] By evoking feelings, symbols influence the thoughts in our minds, the desires of our hearts, and the actions of our bodies.

16. Lonergan, *Topics in Education*, 5.   17. *Insight*, 261–64.
18. *Method*, 61, 64.   19. *Method*, 64–65.

The words of a "language" are the fourth carrier. As mentioned in part 1, learning a language is a tremendous leap in a person's development, taking her or him from the infant's world of immediacy to a much larger world mediated by meaning and regulated by value, the world populated by the sayings and the writings of women and men, living and dead. Such language can be more or less logical or symbolic. It can describe or explain, praise or complain, inspire or depress, inform or exhort.[20]

Finally, Lonergan writes that there is an "incarnate" carrier. This is the way in which a whole person speaks to us. It is how the sum total of a person's character, words, deeds, and way of life teaches something. A person's life is a rich form of communication. It may combine all the other carriers of meaning and value: intersubjectively, artistically, symbolically, and linguistically. And it can be even more meaningful and valuable than these, for "*Cor ad cor loquitur* [Heart speaks to heart]."[21] In fact, as the communication of a whole person, incarnate meaning appeals to the whole person. It moves us physically, sensibly, in our deep desires and fears, our imaginations, our senses of wonder, our quests for understanding and truth, our capacities for feeling and commitment.

An important part of the reason incarnate meaning is so moving is our natural desire for truth, goodness, and love. This desire is not simply a desire to *know* and to *feel* truth, goodness, and love. It is also a desire to *embody* and to *create* truth, goodness, and love. Because this desire is unrestricted, we seek to know, feel, embody, and create unrestricted truth, unconditional goodness, and otherworldly love. Such is the natural human orientation toward self-transcendence on intellectual, moral, and religious levels. It is why the members of cosmopolis must be able to operate in the four realms of meaning (common sense, theory, interiority, and transcendence) and to point to these realms through multiple ways of communicating meaning and value (intersubjectivity, art, symbol, language, and incarnate living).

This is not an easy task. Furthermore, to counteract the general bias of a society and a culture in decline, the members of cosmopolis must protect themselves from general bias. To do this they

20. *Method*, 70–73.   21. *Method*, 73.

need to distance themselves in some ways from their own society and culture. At the same time they must reject the individual and group biases that tempt them either to retreat completely from society and found their own private utopias or to reject their culture wholesale and become bitter, self-superior critics. To be able to work within a society while not succumbing to all of its errors is difficult but important work. "It is by moving with that [general] bias than against it, by differing from it slightly rather than opposing it thoroughly, that one has the best prospect of selling books and newspapers, entertainment and education."[22]

Though the work is difficult, it is a task for all of us, no matter one's occupation, age, sex, race, nationality, or religion. What is important is that we do it not through force or fraud, but by peace and persuasion, through edifying instruction and attractive inspiration. For people are free. And violence and lies tend to breed more violence and lies. Our best method makes use of culture—with all its realms and carriers of meaning and value—to appeal to people's natural, transcendent cores in the hopes of inspiring them toward the transformation of their hearts, minds, and actions. When sin, bias, and decline have damaged a person and a community, such transformation becomes a matter of conversion.

Technically or theoretically, cosmopolis is not part of the absolutely supernatural order of grace, which promotes conversion, particularly religious conversion. But in its actual, concrete realization, cosmopolis will in all probability be made possible by the three conversions, for its members must be guarded against bias, and this is made possible by the expansive concern of religious conversion and charity. Members of cosmopolis should be converted so that they may be free from their own bias, and ultimately because their goal of freeing others from bias is really the goal of converting hearts and minds, and thus spreading redemption throughout the world.

The Body of Christ

Cosmopolis is a philosophical term for a community that operates on the level of culture. Its task is to combat decline and to liberate

22. *Method,* 266.

the natural creativity of the pure, unrestricted human desire for a transcendent fulfillment. Only implicitly, by its *de facto* role of reversing decline, may cosmopolis be categorized as redemptive. The body of Christ, however, is explicitly a religious, redemptive community, since by definition it operates on the supernatural level of grace, to heal and to elevate human nature.

The body of Christ could mean literally the physical body of Jesus of Nazareth, the Christ, the incarnation of the Son of God, who was born, lived, suffered, died, was buried, and rose again. It could also mean the real presence of Christ in the Eucharist, as proclaimed by Jesus at the Last Supper (Mt 26:26; Lk 22:19). The third meaning is of all the members of the church, living and dead, united in one body with Christ as its head. Colossians 1:17–20 explains this briefly:

He is before all things and in him all things hold together. He is the head of the body, the church. He is the beginning, the firstborn from that dead, that in all things he himself might be preeminent. For in him all the fullness was pleased to dwell, and through him to reconcile all things for him, making peace by the blood of his cross, whether those on earth or those in heaven.

Of course, Lonergan holds that the body of Christ is redemptive in all three senses. Here, to culminate our consideration of Lonergan's theological anthropology, we will focus on the third sense, the human community united in Christ to cooperate in the redemption of the world. According to Christian faith, the body of Christ is not simply *a* redemptive community, as cosmopolis may be, but *the* redemptive community. For Lonergan it is "a concrete union of the divine Persons with one another and with man"[23] or, more specifically, "a new society in Father, Son, and Holy Ghost, in which there is communicated to us personally, through the person of the Son and through the person of the Spirit, a participation of divine perfection, a participation of the order of truth and love that binds the three persons of the Blessed Trinity."[24]

23. Lonergan, "The Mystical Body of Christ," in *Collected Works*, vol. 20, *Shorter Papers* (Toronto: University of Toronto Press, 2008), 106.
24. *Topics in Education*, 68. For more on Lonergan's Trinitarian theology, see his *Collected Works*, vol. 11, *The Triune God: Doctrines*, edited by Robert Doran, H.D. Monsour, and M. Shields (Toronto: University of Toronto), 2009; and vol. 12, *The Triune God: Systematics*, edited by Robert Doran and H.D. Monsour (Toronto: University of Toronto, 2007).

The term "participation" is very important for understanding the body of Christ, as it is for redemption in general. Earlier we discussed how the theological virtues allow us to participate in the divine life. By charity we are able to take part in God's love; faith provides us with a share in God's knowledge, and hope in the expectation of the "kingdom of heaven" or "reign of God"—when all of humanity will be united with each other and God in harmonious, peaceful, loving relationships. First Corinthians 12:12–26 expresses this well:

As a body is one though it has many parts, and all the parts of the body, though many, are one body, so also Christ. For in one Spirit we were all baptized into one body, whether Jews or Greeks, slaves or free persons, and we were all given to drink of one Spirit.

Now the body is not a single part, but many. If a foot should say, "Because I am not a hand I do not belong to the body," it does not for this reason belong any less to the body. Or if an ear should say, "Because I am not an eye I do not belong to the body," it does not for this reason belong any less to the body.

If the whole body were an eye, where would the hearing be? If the whole body were hearing, where would the sense of smell be? But as it is, God placed the parts, each one of them, in the body as he intended. If they were all one part, where would the body be? But as it is, there are many parts, yet one body. The eye cannot say to the hand, "I do not need you," nor again the head to the feet, "I do not need you."

Indeed, the parts of the body that seem to be weaker are all the more necessary, and those parts of the body that we consider less honorable we surround with greater honor, and our less presentable parts are treated with greater propriety, whereas our more presentable parts do not need this. But God has so constructed the body as to give greater honor to a part that is without it, so that there may be no division in the body, but that the parts may have the same concern for one another.

If [one] part suffers, all the parts suffer with it; if one part is honored, all the parts share its joy. Now you are Christ's body, and individually parts of it.[25]

This passage makes a few points: (1) all people, regardless of their differences, are united into the body of Christ by the Holy Spirit; (2) as parts of one body, all people need each other; (3) each person has unique gifts to contribute to the whole; (4) the people we think are weakest or most embarrassing are the most necessary

25. This translation is from *The New American Bible*.

and deserve special treatment; (5) if one person is hurt, everyone suffers, just as everyone is able to share each other's joy.

As we discussed in chapter 4, human beings are social by nature. Our operations of knowing, valuing, choosing, loving, and acting are, for the most part, *co*operations. When we make progress, just one person's insights and innovations can set the conditions for the emergence of many more insights and innovations by that person and other people. This is true in a negative manner for a state of decline: one person's sins set negative conditions that increase the likelihood that others will sin. Given the social nature of human progress and decline, it is fitting that redemption be achieved not simply through isolated conversions, but in community. Thus, Lonergan affirms, "just as there is human solidarity in sin with a dialectical descent deforming knowledge and perverting will, so there is a divine solidarity in grace which is the mystical body of Christ."[26]

Lonergan devoted a paper to the subject of the body of Christ.[27] In it he states that because the body of Christ is a community with God, and because God is a mystery, the body too is a mystery and thus is not *fully* comprehensible to finite human minds. However, to explore the mystery of the body of Christ and to gain some fruitful understanding of it, he selects as "a guiding thread through the labyrinth of wealth, the single but basic and familiar theme of *love*."[28]

In the mysterious or "mystical" body of Christ, divine and human persons are bound by a manifold love. First there is the love of the eternal Father for the eternal Son. Both are God, so this love is of God for God. Because this love is an infinite love for an infinite lovableness, this love is God too: God the Holy Ghost or Holy Spirit.

Second, there is the love of God the Father for the Son as human. The second person of the trinity possesses two natures, divine and human. But since he is one person, and love is for a person, the Father has a single love, and God's love for the Son as man is the same love as the Father's love for the Son as divine: it

---

26. Lonergan, "Finality, Love, Marriage," in *Collection*, 26; cf. 27.
27. See note 23.
28. Lonergan, "The Mystical Body of Christ," 106, emphasis added.

is an infinite love, the Holy Spirit. Furthermore, because the Son adopted a human nature, the infinite love of the Father for the Son, the same Holy Spirit, is extended to human nature and thus to all human persons. "Such is the stupendous corollary of the Incarnation. Because God became man, the love of God for God became the love of God for man. Because love is for a person, when God became man, when the Word was made flesh, divine love broke the confines of divinity to love a created humanity in the way that God the Father loves God the Son."[29]

This extension of divine love through Christ is expressed in the theological doctrine that Christ mediates a sanctifying grace that is infinite. This is how divine love confers divine, infinite lovableness on finite creatures.

The third love comprising the mystical body of Christ is the love Christ as human has for humanity. Lonergan writes movingly of this love. Here is just a taste:

It is the love of the Sacred Heart of Jesus, the love of a human will, motivated by a human mind, operating through human senses, resonating through human emotions and feelings and sentiments, implemented by a human body with its structure of bones and muscles, flesh, its mobile features, its terrible capacities for pleasure and pain, for joy and sorrow, for rapture and agony. It is the love of the Good Shepherd, knowing his own, known by his own, and ready to lose his life for them. (Jn 10:14–15)[30]

Jesus' love is not calculating. It gives without measure and without hope for personal gain. "What is the use of living and dying for men who will not believe, or if they believe, do not love, or if they love only half-heartedly. Can love be love and not give all? Can Christ's love give all and be happy about it, when not met by the same total self-surrender in the beloved? But do men? Do we?"[31] Christ lived and died to communicate God's love to us, to unite us to God in love. But this requires that we accept God's love and reciprocate it, which we certainly do not always do.

As discussed, the Incarnation itself occasioned the extension of the Father's infinite love for the Son to all of humanity. To emphasize this effect, Lonergan devotes a distinct, fourth category to

29. "The Mystical Body of Christ," 107.   30. "The Mystical Body of Christ," 107–8.
31. "The Mystical Body of Christ," 108.

the Father's love for humanity. Christ prays for it when asking that all who believe in him may be *one*, as the Father and he are one, that all may be one *in* the Father and the Son, and that we may *know* the Father has loved us *as* the Father has loved the Son.[32] The Father's love for humanity is the infinite love of the Holy Spirit. It is the occasion for its recipient to be "born again," to receive many graces and gifts, and to become an adopted daughter or son of God, a full heir to the reign of God.[33]

One of the gifts "diffused in our hearts by the Holy Ghost" is charity, the fifth and final love Lonergan examines in this context of the body of Christ.[34] Already we have identified charity as the love of God with one's whole heart, soul, mind, and strength, which leads to love of oneself and love of one's neighbor. We have presented charity's role in undoing decline by promoting repentance of one's own sins and self-sacrificial love of neighbor that can undo decline.[35] But in this essay Lonergan adds that the love of the Father, Son, and Spirit that is received and made one's own in charity is mediated through the fellowship and sacraments of the church, such as baptism, reconciliation, and the Eucharist.[36]

Joined by this fivefold love, we are made members of the body of Christ and begin "a new and higher life [that] is not lived in isolation."[37] Human beings flourish to the extent that we are united with Christ. "He is the vine and we are the branches. As branches wither and die, when separated from the vine, so are we without the life of grace, when separated from Christ. As branches flower and fructify when united fully with the vine, so too, do we, when united fully with Christ."[38]

There is a limit to the analogy: to some measure each human person has an existence, a freedom, and an accountability of her or his own. But the merits of the analogy remain, for our roots and stem are in one God. The body of Christ is first and foremost a di-

---

32. "The Mystical Body of Christ," 107, paraphrasing Jn 17:11, 22–23.
33. "The Mystical Body of Christ," 109; cf. Eph 1:5.
34. "The Mystical Body of Christ," 110.
35. In chapters 2 and 9 of this volume.
36. "The Mystical Body of Christ," 109, 111. Sadly, Lonergan wrote very little on ecclesiology and sacramental theology.
37. "The Mystical Body of Christ," 109.
38. "The Mystical Body of Christ," 109.

vine initiative, particularly through the two missions of God to the world—the sending of the Spirit and the sending of the Son. Their works communicate to us as, respectively, the "inner word" and the "outer word." The Holy Spirit pours forth charity and other gifts that consist in the "inner word of grace." The Son is the principle for the outer word—that is, the incarnation, life, death, and, resurrection of Jesus Christ; his being, words, and deeds that expressed divine wisdom and love on human terms and were passed down in the narratives of the gospels through the ongoing fellowship of the church and by the authority of tradition and doctrine.[39]

These missions are not merely the effects of God on the world, but rather "a personal entrance of God himself into history, a communication of God to his people, the advent of God's word into the world of religious expression. Such was the religion of Israel. Such has been Christianity. Then not only the inner word that is God's gift of his love but also the outer word of the religious tradition comes from God."[40]

Due to its reception of the inner and the outer words of God there is a unique kind of authority, authenticity, and saving power that belongs to the church. However, Lonergan reminds us that Christians must be overwhelmingly humble, for that all we have, we have been given. And we are far from perfect, still distant from our goal. We are "pilgrims," ever on the way. Not only are we not complete in the good; we have some admixture of evil. The church is a concrete group of human persons who have accepted and rejected the gift of grace in different degrees at different times, so even the church is not entirely free from sin. "Not only is there the progress of mankind but also there is development and progress within Christianity itself; and as there is development, so too there is decline; and as there is decline, there is also the problem of undoing it, of overcoming evil with the good not only in the world but also in the church."[41]

In addition, there are elements of redemption found within secular society. "Being in Christ Jesus is not tied down to place or

39. See chapter 9, in the section "Religious Conversion," where the inner and outer words are discussed, as well as *Method*, 112–19, 298.
40. *Method*, 119.
41. *Method*, 291.

time, culture or epoch. It is catholic with the catholicity of the Spirit of the Lord. Neither is it an abstraction that dwells apart from every place and time, every culture and epoch. It is identical with personal living, and personal living is always here and now."[42]

What matters is that members of the body of Christ receive and accept the sanctifying gifts of God's love and God's word given to all. What matters is that each person grows in religious conversion, in otherworldly being-in-love, and that this love is shared and developed in a community with common meanings and values. The body of Christ is about personal growth and growth in relationships, and these growths are not opposed, since "we grow into who we are through our relationships with others."[43]

The doctrine of the mystical body of Christ teaches us that we are blessed to grow in relationship, indeed in friendship, not only with each other, but also and most importantly with God the Father, Son, and Holy Spirit. It teaches us that through these friendships a human person is blessed to cooperate in the salvation of her or his own soul as well as to collaborate in God's redemption of all creation. Such growth, friendship, and collaboration are received and achieved not only through the gifts of God's healing and elevating grace, not only in threefold conversion, and not only in communion with a redemptive community that includes the holy Trinity, but in particular in imitation of Christ, in following the head of the body. As members of the body of Christ we are called to incarnate the divine healing presence, to preach the coming kingdom or reign of God, to pray and to work for increased knowledge and love of goodness and truth.

We are even called at times, like Christ, to overcome evil with good through self-sacrificial love. In such love, Christ led by word and deed. He exhorted us to love one's neighbor as oneself (Mk 12:31), to love even one's enemy (Mt 5:44), and, if need be, to lay down one's life for a friend (Jn 15:13). He practiced what he preached, while on the cross forgiving even those who crucified him (Lk 23:34). And he called us to imitate him in this love, saying,

42. Lonergan, "Existenz and Aggiornamento," in *Collection*, 250; see also *Topics in Education*, 69. The term "catholic" literally means "universal" or "of the whole."

43. Lonergan, "The Mediation of Christ in Prayer," in *Philosophical and Theological Papers*, *1958–1964*, 174; cf. 180.

"Love one another. As I have loved you, so you should love one another" (Jn 13:34), and "If anyone wishes to come after me, he must deny himself and take up his cross daily and follow me" (Lk 9:23).

Situating self-sacrificial love within the overarching categories of progress, decline, and redemption, Lonergan affirms that, "As human authenticity promotes progress, and human unauthenticity generates decline, so Christian authenticity—which is a love of others that does not shrink from self-sacrifice and suffering—is the sovereign means for overcoming evil. Christians bring about the kingdom of God in the world not only by doing good but also by overcoming evil with good (Rom 12:21)."[44]

This "overcoming evil with good" is at the heart of redemption. It is the culmination of Christ's entire being and doing, as well as what human beings are called to do as members of the body of Christ. God could have chosen any possible way of solving the problems of sin and evil. God could have destroyed humanity completely and remade us from scratch. God might have made us perfect, unable to make mistakes, unfailing in our choosing good and avoiding evil. According to Lonergan, however, this would not have been "fitting" with God's original plan, the plan God chose from the beginning for humankind.[45] That plan is for us to love, and to love freely. In creating the world God wills only the good and in no way wills sin (as mentioned in chapter 5). However, in willing the good of freedom, God does *permit* sin. And in willing the goodness of a world order in which our freedom is real and can affect that world order, God also allowed for there to be real consequences to our choices: good consequences for good choices and evil ones for sins. God gives us a natural orientation toward choosing goodness, but again we are created free to reject this orientation. Ultimately God wills for us to choose the goods of knowing and loving and thus to unite with God and all things.

Given this plan, if God had chosen to solve the problem of sin by some power play that instantaneously took away our sins and their consequences, this also would have destroyed our freedom and with it the possibility of the supreme good, the union of all

44. *Method*, 291.
45. Lonergan, "The Redemption," in *Philosophical and Theological Papers, 1958–1964*, 24–28.

things in love, which God intended from the beginning. Because God is wise and loving, God chose instead to cooperate with our freedom in a way that allows sins to remain, but transforms their evil consequences into the opportunity for good. Lonergan affirms this poetically in one of his earliest writings:

This is why the Son of God became man, suffered, died, and was raised again: because divine wisdom has ordained and divine goodness has willed, not to do away with the evils of the human race through power, but to convert those evils into a supreme good according to the just and mysterious Law of the Cross.[46]

Lonergan believes that the ability to overcome evil through self-sacrificial love is a fruit of our participation in the friendships of the Trinity as members of the mystical body of Christ. It is the peak of the charity given to us by the Holy Spirit and the word of God as communicated to us in the person of Jesus Christ, in the scriptures, and in the tradition of the church.

By becoming charitable members of the body of Christ, we can and should take up our own "daily crosses."[47] What this means exactly is much debated, and the debate is of tremendous significance, because proper imitation of Christ depends in part on proper understanding of what he did. This is particularly true of his work on the cross. It is easily misunderstood, and such misunderstanding can lead to terrible consequences. So we should keep in mind from the start that proper imitation of Christ's work requires the unrestricted love given to us in Christ's Spirit. It is not a human achievement. Similarly, proper understanding of the cross requires grace. The way it functions is ultimately a divine mystery that finite human intellects cannot comprehend perfectly.

Nevertheless, if we are to follow Christ on the cross and thus participate in his work of redemption, we can and should seek to gain some measure of fruitful understanding of this and other mysteries, as Vatican I affirmed in chapter 4 of the *Dogmatic Constitution Concerning the Catholic Faith*:

---

46. Lonergan, *De Verbo Incarnato*, 3rd ed. (Rome: Pontifical Gregorian University, 1964), 552; unpublished translation by Charles Hefling.

47. Lonergan, "The Mediation of Christ in Prayer," in *Philosophical and Theological Papers, 1958–1964*, 181, with an uncited quotation of Lk 9:23.

[R]eason illustrated by faith, when it zealously, piously, and soberly seeks, attains with the help of God some understanding of the mysteries, and that a most profitable one, not only from the analogy of those things which it knows naturally, but also from the connection of the mysteries among themselves and with the last end of man; nevertheless it is never capable of perceiving those mysteries in the way it does the truths which constitute its own proper object.[48]

First, a note must be made to help safeguard against perhaps the most common misunderstanding of the cross. All too often Christian culture interprets Christ's death through the analogy of paying a "debt": Human sin, the thought goes, creates a debt that someone must pay in order for God to forgive us and continue to love us. Jesus Christ pays for this debt by taking on a punishment that outweighs the countless sins of innumerable sinners.[49] Christians who buy into this misunderstanding think they are imitating Jesus by passively allowing others to sin, no matter what the consequences to themselves or others.

Lonergan's primary analogy for understanding the crucifixion is not the payment of debt but that of "communication."[50] This analogy lifts up the debt analogies of satisfaction and punishment from the cold, calculating context of payments and exchange into a higher, richer context of interpersonal relationships. Redemption, as conceived according to the analogy of communication, is not simply restoring a zero sum balance; it is the restoration of friendship or mutual love. It is reconciliation.

Understanding Christ's work as a communication that promotes reconciliation rescues us from misunderstanding God as, at best, having conditional love and, at worst, being wrathful or sadistic. God's forgiveness is not contingent on our actions. We do not earn love through self-sacrifice or any other "work." God already created us good and thus made us lovable by nature. Moreover, God makes us infinitely lovable through the grace of the Son's incarnation that united human nature to divine nature, as well as

48. Henry Denzinger, *The Sources of Catholic Dogma,* translated by Roy Deferrari (St. Louis: Herde, 1957), 1796; see *Method,* 132, 321; Lonergan quotes part of this on 321.

49. Anselm of Canterbury is generally credited (or blamed) with coming up with the debt analogy, while Calvin is usually, again, credited or blamed with first saying that God's wrath required Christ to pay the debt with his death.

50. "The Redemption," 6–7.

through the gift of the Holy Spirit that divinizes us with the ability to love unrestrictedly. Sin damages our relationship with God, and it may make us less lovable, but it does not make us unlovable. Perhaps nothing can.[51] Sin is the rejection of divine love, and it makes the sinner enter a state of being more or less separated from God,[52] but even sinners are loved by God's unrestricted love. This is why Jesus spent so much time among sinners (Mk 2:17: "Those who are well do not need a physician, but the sick do. I did not come to call the righteous but sinners") and died for them: (Rom 5:6: "God proves his love for us in that while we were still sinners Christ died for us").

The cross thus does not earn God's love. It is the expression of divine love. It is what happens when a truly loving person enters into a world marked by sin and its violent consequences.

Lonergan's explanation of how the cross redeems by a communication that promotes reconciliation is tremendously complicated. An adequate treatment of it is beyond the scope of this book, for it exceeds the bounds of Lonergan's theological anthropology and enters his systematic soteriology. However, we must explain it briefly, because it is so central to Christ's work of redemption in which we participate as members of his body.

The key to understanding this work is grasping how it operates, not through power, but through conversion or transformation. God did not instantaneously or magically make us perfect by removing our freedom, our ability to sin, and the evil consequences of sin. God chose instead to work with our freedom and the rest of the natural gifts God gave us: our natural desire for perfect truth, goodness, justice, love, and beauty, as well as our human abilities to experience, understand, judge, decide, love, operate, and cooperate in the building of a better world.

God works with us in Jesus Christ by transforming the evil effects of sin into a good that shifts the probabilities in human history toward the emergence of further goods. The first good created by Christ's work on the cross is the transformation of the evil conse-

51. "For I am convinced that neither life nor angels nor principalities, nor present things, nor future things, nor powers nor height nor depth, nor an other creature will be able to separate us from the love of God in Christ Jesus our Lord"; Rom. 8:38–39.

52. See chapter 5 of this volume for a discussion of venial and mortal sin.

quences of human sin into a divine communication. On the cross Christ did not respond to sin with sin, to evil with evil, or to violence with violence. That would merely have continued the downward spiral of decline. Instead, he responded to pride and hatred with humility and love, to violence and coercion with peace and persuasion. He forgave our sins, and he accepted their evil consequences. Moreover, he did so in an infinitely wise way, a way that transformed the evil consequences of sin—his horrific suffering and death—into a twofold human communication of divine meaning and value. Raised up on the cross, Christ reveals for all to see (1) the goodness of God's love for us, a love that is with us no matter what we do, and (2) the evils of human sin, the terrible results of our biased, selfish, shortsighted choices.

From all possible ways of effecting our redemption, this is the way God chose. And the way is infinitely wise and loving, because it does not destroy us, our freedom, or our choices. Rather, it works with them. It transforms the evils of our sin into a moving incarnation of meaning and value. To this divine communication of infinite, unmerited love, we are inspired to return our own love. And to the divine communication of the evils of our sin, we are inspired to respond with repentance of our sins and the resolve never to sin again. For if such suffering is the result of our choices, and if we are naturally oriented to the good (in both our spontaneous intersubjectivity and our deep desires to discover truth, to choose good, and to live with integrity), then when we are lovingly confronted with the consequences of our sins, we are moved to condemn them with sorrow and disgust. The more we grow in love, the stronger is our repentance, and vice versa, until we have felt a just measure of sorrow and our love is made full in the union of God and, we hope, all of humanity.[53]

Christ lived but one life among us on earth. He is with us still as the head of the community of his followers. His Spirit remains as well, flooding our hearts and minds with truth and love. Until the reign of God has come to completion, our incorporation into the body of Christ and our reception of the gifts of the Holy Spirit continues. Conversion, as Lonergan reminds us, is an ongoing pro-

53. "The Redemption," 9–10, cf. 19–23.

cess, even a lifelong one. And conversion is not a private matter, worked out by isolated individuals. It is the work of a community of human persons united in God so that they may cooperate with God and each other. God's inner gift of love requires a corresponding outer word to express and embody it, to make it fully realized in our world. This is why each generation is called to "complete what is lacking in the afflictions of Christ on behalf of his body, which is the church" (1 Col 1:24).[54]

This does not necessarily mean that when we participate in Christ's self-sacrificial work of overcoming evil with good we are called literally to die on a cross—or any other sort of martyr's death. Such may be the very rare case, but as Jesus says in the gospel of Luke, we are all to follow him in taking up our crosses "daily."[55] The good news is that by following Jesus, taking up our cross, and losing our lives (whether literally or not), we will gain them through the gift of the resurrection and eternal life.[56]

Lonergan enumerates four ways we can join Christ in his suffering, death, and resurrection: sacramental, moral, ascetical, and physical. A sacramental death buries us in the waters of baptism so that we may to rise again to a new, Christian life. Morally, we are told, "You also must consider yourself dead to sin, but alive to God in Christ Jesus our Lord" (Rom 6:11). Ascetically we should, through fasting and other forms of self-discipline, put to death our self-indulgent, licentious cravings for lower goods and short-term satisfactions so that we will be reborn to the greater freedom or liberty that comes from genuine self-control. Eventually we all will die physically, whether by accident, violence, or old age, but we have hope and faith in the resurrection of the body and a new, glorious life united in love with God and all of humankind.[57]

Christ's death and resurrection prefigure our resurrections and the coming kingdom or reign of God. With his work on the cross, Christ does save the world, but as the Bible says, the reign of God is paradoxically both here "already" and "not yet."[58]

---

54. See *De Verbo Incarnato*, 556, 572, 582.

55. Lk 9:23–24. Corresponding passages in Mark 9:34–35 and Matthew 12:24–25 omit the modifier "daily," lending the possibility, along with the example of many apostles, to actual martyrdom.

56. "*De Verbo Incarnato*, 557, 571–73.   57. "*De Verbo Incarnato*, 109.

58. See for example, Mt 3:2: "Repent, for the kingdom of heaven is at hand."

It is not yet in that "redemption in Christ Jesus does not change the fundamental fact that sin continues to head for suffering and death. However, the suffering and death that follow from sin attain a new significance in Christ Jesus. They are no longer the sad, disastrous end to the differential of sin, but also the means towards transfiguration and resurrection. Beyond death on the cross, there is the risen Savior."[59]

The kingdom of God is already here in its beginnings, like a seed recently sown.[60] Its flowers and its fruit, the full flourishing of the divine order, are yet to come. So sin and bias, suffering and death remain in our world, but they are no longer merely the road to total destruction. If we accept them with love and wisdom, they can be transformed into a blessed opportunity for new life, for loving friendship with God and with each other. This is "the Law of the Cross." This is the way God has chosen to heal the world from sin, suffering, and death—not by destroying our freedom and our capacity for true love, but by working with our freedom, by inviting us to convert from sin to love, and by inviting us to invite others as members of the body of Christ.

The full conversion of our own minds, hearts, and souls, let alone the redemption of the world, has not yet happened. Still, it is absolutely essential that our participation in God's redemptive work be motivated, like Christ's, by a divine, unrestricted, unconditional love and wisdom. Throughout his life, but most visibly in his death, Christ absorbed the evil consequences of sin in order to transform them into the good of an inviting and inspiring communication of love. Moved by Christ's example and the Spirit of love he has given us, we too can absorb the evil consequences of others' sins. We can accept unjust suffering in order to manifest the evils of sin and the goodness of love in a way that invites and inspires others to repent of their sins and return love for love.

These notions are neither impossible nor impractical. The nonviolent movements led by Mohandas Gandhi, Martin Luther King,

---

59. *Topics in Education*, 66–67.
60. "The kingdom of heaven is like a mustard seed that a person took and sowed in a field. It is the smallest of all the seeds, yet when full-grown it is the largest of plants"; Mt 13:31–32; cf. Mk 4:30–32; Lk 13:18–19.

Jr., Corazon Aquino, and others provide clear and recent examples of how self-sacrificial love is redeeming the world. These leaders and their supporters were not perfect, and neither are we. But they were moved by the gift of unrestricted love to accept the evil consequences of colonialism, racism, and tyranny. Their choice to respond to bias and violence with nonviolence and love communicated to their oppressors the evils of their oppression and the goodness of their victims' love. Their communication inspired a response of love and repentance and thus promoted the reconciliation that is redemption.

But again, while self-sacrificial love is an option, it is not the only legitimate option. To be a legitimate option, however, it must be for us, as it was for Jesus, an expression of a concord of wills with God; it must be a communication of divine wisdom and love. It can never be an effort to earn God's love. We can choose to accept suffering if we are moved by the divine charity that is communicated by Christ and poured into our hearts by the Spirit. A choice to accept suffering is not necessary, and it is not the only way of imitating Christ (Christ also responded to evil with words of correction, with avoidance, and with other, more controversial action).[61] But it can be wise and fitting *if* it will communicate both detestation of sin and love for persons in a way that would invite sinners to repent of their sins and to love God, people, and all things.

As members of the body of Christ we may each be given different roles and talents, but all of us are valuable, and each of us is called to follow Christ our head and to work together for the redemption of the world.

Conclusion

In this chapter we considered a community dedicated to healing the world from sin and bias, liberating its natural potencies, and elevating them into a divine, supernatural realm.

We studied this community philosophically as a cosmopolis that neither shuns tradition nor scorns innovation, that feels at home in multiple cultures and makes use of the meanings and val-

61. See for example, Mt 12:22–37, 16:21–23, 25:31–46; Lk 11:37–52; Jn 2:13–16, 10:22–39.

ues of culture to educate hearts and minds, and thus to promote positive social change.

We examined this community theologically as "the body of Christ," a union of God and humanity, an interdependent whole in which each person participates through her or his own unique gifts. We reflected on how human participation in the body of Christ is created by the infinite love of God extended to us through the divine incarnation. We discovered that the inner word of the Holy Spirit affects us on the way from above downwards and the outer word of the Son influences us on the way from below upwards. Finally, we have seen that through these gifts we grow in conversion so that we may imitate Christ in his redemptive work of overcoming evil in an inspiring, self-sacrificial communication of love.

In the book as a whole we have examined Bernard Lonergan's theological anthropology in three parts: progress, decline, and redemption. Within each part, the movement was from basic to complex, from fundamental metaphysical generalities to the operations of individual persons, the cooperation within human communities, and eventually the historical development of those communities. Progress, decline, and redemption transpose the traditional Christian categories of nature, sin, and grace into a contemporary context rich with the insights of modern and postmodern developments in natural science, history, and psychology. Progress, decline, and redemption are theoretical categories that help us to understand intelligently, to explain reasonably, and to direct responsibly the lives we lead in common. All three aspects affect us at all times. But it is helpful to consider them individually. First and most fundamentally our existence is comprised of a good nature, one that orients human persons toward truth and goodness, makes us capable of authentic self-transcendence, and impels us continually to craft a progressive human good. However, our lives are also affected by an evil vector of sin and bias that causes the worsening situations and downward cycles of decline. Finally, there is a corrective vector caused by the absolutely supernatural, the grace of God that converts human persons, healing and elevating our nature so that we might participate in the divine life and love of the Trinity.

God created humanity with freedom. We are granted by nature

the ability to affirm or deny truth and value, to choose or reject goodness and love. While freedom and such natural capabilities are good in themselves and are creative of many additional goods, they also constitute a potential for sin and evil so apparent in our world damaged by cycles of hatred and violence. To solve the problem of sin, God is working in history in a wise and loving way, a way that destroys neither human freedom in particular nor the integrity of the whole world order. The world order God has made and that we live in is a product of infinite wisdom and love. It is the best of all possible world orders.

So instead of annihilating creation and starting anew, God is working in a way that is consonant with its original, good, existing order. The divine solution to the problem of evil is the introduction of a higher, transcendent scheme of recurrence, one that shifts probabilities from an inclination toward evil to a tendency toward the good. This solution fittingly does not destroy human freedom but works with it. It is an incarnate communication of divine love that invites and inspires human hearts, minds, and senses. It works to transform those very human hearts, minds, and senses and thus to convert human persons. And it is not only an incarnate communication that inspires conversion. The divine solution to the problem of evil is a supernatural friendship with God that lifts our lives into the trinitarian life, reinforces the trickle of our love into the unrestricted river of divine love, and divinizes our very being so that all our operations may be a cooperation in God's work of redemption.

This concludes my attempt to write, as mentioned in the introduction of this work, "a clear and basic, yet broad and solid" introduction to the theological anthropology of Bernard Lonergan. It is not a comprehensive summary of Lonergan's entire, formidable body of work; thus I have left much unwritten on his economics, cognitive theory, metaphysics, trinitarian theology, Christology, pneumatology, ecclesiology, and soteriology. But I hope that by working through this introduction, the reader will have developed the fundamental theoretical tools required for deeper engagement with Lonergan's own writing, as well as the work of the many scholars he has influenced. I hope too that—as is often the case with human achievement—the reader's completion of this little work is just another promising beginning in a lifelong journey of coming to know, to love, and to serve God in all things. The future of the world is in our hands. Let us be attentive to all that is, so that we might be intelligent in our ideas, reasonable in our conclusions, and responsible in the way we cooperate to shape our common destiny.

Reflection Questions for Chapter 10

- Living with other people can be a pain. Too often life seems like one big competition. This can be true at home, in romantic relationships, and among friends, no less than in sports, school, or the workplace. The experience of sin and its consequences can cause us to wonder: Are people mostly selfish and competitive, or loving and cooperative? If we tend to be the former, can we become more of the latter? If so, how?

- Lonergan believes that while people are good by nature, we often choose to sin and become biased. Thankfully, divine grace can cause conversion. Moreover, human beings may participate in God's redemptive activity, working together, sometimes even self-sacrificially, to change each other's minds, hearts, and actions. Do you think such work is possible? Can we cooperate with each other to convert each other?

- Much of what I have learned in theology I learned first by practicing martial arts. A common saying among martial artists is that the better one becomes at the art, the less one has to use it. Beginners tend to have fragile egos that fixate on the ability to beat people up. They seek constantly to prove their toughness, but they often end up hurting themselves and others. No less than anyone else, martial artists can remain immature, in the sense of childish, forever. But if they do mature, they learn to avoid harming people as much as possible. So good martial artists do not pick fights, and they end confrontations as quickly as possible. Instead of wildly brawling, they end a fight with a single punch or a kick. Better still, they avoid striking altogether by blocking attacks in a way that impresses the opponent enough to halt aggression. Very advanced practitioners of a martial art are able to prevent conflicts with a look or a smile. Finally, the greatest of martial artists follow Abraham Lincoln's wise dictate, "The best way to destroy an enemy is to make him a friend."

- Transforming an enemy into a friend takes not only a tremendous amount of skill, but also genuine self-mastery—far more than what is required to "beat people up." This is because true strength includes the ability to let oneself appear weak. It involves a patient, self-sacrificial love that sometimes places the needs of another above one's own. Such is the achievement of Christ on the cross. And such is the task to which all of us are called daily if we are to promote progress and reverse decline in our personal relationships, throughout the world, and across history.

- How can we prepare ourselves for such a difficult project? Do we know anyone already working to heal hearts and educate minds? What can we learn from them? What should we do differently in our own local communities? What am I called to do that no one else can do? How can I cooperate with others for the sake of the whole? How might I gain the mental and physical fortitude required to give my time, energy, material resources, and indeed my very self to the redemption of the world?

BIBLIOGRAPHY

Aquinas, Thomas. *Summa contra Gentiles*. Translated by Charles J. O'Neil. Garden City, N.Y.: Image Books, 1957.

———. *Summa Theologiae*. Translated by the Fathers of the English Dominican Province. Westminster, Md.: Christian Classics, 1981.

———. *De Caritate*. Translated by Lottie H. Kendzierski. Milwaukee, Wisc.: Marquette University Press, 1984.

Aristotle. *Nicomachean Ethics*. Translated by Martin Oswald. Upper Saddle, N.J.: Prentice Hall, 1999.

Augustine. *Confessions*. Translated by Henry Chadwick. Oxford: Oxford University Press, 1991.

Barron, Robert. "Why Bernard Lonergan Matters for Pastoral People." *Chicago Studies* 43, no. 3 (Fall/Winter 2004): 240–51.

Beshear, Beth. "The Problem of Desire in Human Knowing and Loving." *Method: Journal of Lonergan Studies* 20 (Fall 2002): 155–74.

Bosco, Mark, and David Stagman, eds. *Finding God in All Things: Celebrating Bernard Lonergan, John Courtney Murray, and Karl Rahner*. New York: Fordham University Press, 2007.

Bron, D. M. *Ultimate Concern: Tillich in Dialogue*. New York: Harper and Row, 1965.

Brown, Patrick. "'Aiming Excessively High and Far': The Early Lonergan and the Challenge of Theory in Catholic Social Thought." *Theological Studies* 72 (September 2011): 620–44.

Byrne, Patrick. "The Thomist Sources of Lonergan's Dynamic Worldview." *The Thomist* 46 (1982): 108–45.

Conn, Walter. *Christian Conversion: A Developmental Interpretation of Autonomy and Surrender*. New York: Paulist Press, 1986.

———. ed. *Conversion: Perspectives on Personal and Social Transformation*. New York: Alba House, 1978.

Connor, James, L., ed. *The Dynamism of Desire: Bernard J. F. Lonergan, S.J., on the Spiritual Exercises of Ignatius of Loyola*. St. Louis: The Institute of Jesuit Sources, 2006.

Copeland, M. Shawn. "A Genetic Study of the Idea of the Human Good in the

Thought of Bernard Lonergan." Ph.D. diss., Boston College, 1991.

———. "A Theologian in the Factory: Toward a Theology of Social Transformation in the United States." In *Spirit in the Cities: Searching for Soul in the Urban Landscape,* edited by Kathryn Tanner, 20–46, 126–31. Minneapolis, Minn.: Fortress, 2004.

———. *Enfleshing Freedom: Body, Race, and Being.* Fortress Press, 2010.

Cronin, Brian. *Value Ethics: A Lonergan Perspective.* Nairobi: Consolatia Institute of Philosophy, 2006.

Crowe, Frederick E. "An Exploration of Lonergan's New Notion of Value." *Lonergan Workshop* 3 (1982): 1–24.

———. "The Transcendental Deduction: A Lonerganian Meaning and Use." *Method: Journal of Lonergan Studies* 2 (March 1984): 21–39.

———. *Old Things and New: A Strategy for Education.* Atlanta: Scholars Press, 1985.

———. *Appropriating the Lonergan Idea.* Washington, D.C.: The Catholic University of America Press, 1989.

———. *Lonergan.* Outstanding Christian Thinkers Series. Series edited by Brian Davies. London: Geoffrey Chapman, 1992.

———. "All My Work Has Been Introducing History into Catholic Theology." In *Lonergan Workshop: The Legacy of Lonergan* 10 (1994): 49–81.

———. *Developing the Lonergan Legacy: Historical, Theoretical, and Existential Themes.* Edited by Michael Vertin. Toronto: University of Toronto Press, 2004.

———. *Christ and History: The Christology of Bernard Lonergan from 1935–1982.* Ottawa: Novalis, 2005.

Crysdale, Cynthia S. W. *Lonergan and Feminism.* Toronto: University of Toronto Press, 1994.

———. "Revisioning Natural Law: From the Classicist Paradigm to Emergent Probability." *Theological Studies* 56 (Spring 1995): 464–84.

———. *Embracing Travail: Retrieving the Cross Today.* New York: Continuum, 2001.

Dalton, Anne Marie. *A Theology for the Earth: The Contributions of Thomas Berry and Bernard Lonergan.* Ottawa: University of Ottawa Press, 1999.

De Finance, Joseph. *Essai sur l'agir humain.* Rome: Presses de l'Université Grégorienne, 1962.

Denzinger, Henry. *The Sources of Catholic Dogma.* Translated by Roy Deferrari. St. Louis: Herder, 1957.

Doorley, Mark. "Nonviolence, Creation, Healing." *Method: Journal of Lonergan Studies* 17, no. 2 (Fall 1999): 97–110.

Doran, Robert. "Psychic Conversion." *The Thomist* 41 (April 1977): 200–36.

———. *Subject and Psyche: Ricoeur, Jung, and the Search for Foundations.* Washington, D.C.: The Catholic University Press of America, 1977.

————. "Christ and the Psyche." In *Trinification of the Word: A Festschrift in Honor of Frederick E. Crowe*, edited by T. A. Dunne and J. M. Laporte, 112–43. Toronto: Regis College, 1978.

————. *Psychic Conversion and Theological Foundations: Towards a Reorientation of the Human Sciences*. Chico, Calif.: Scholars Press, 1981.

————. "Education for Cosmopolis." *Method: Journal of Lonergan Studies* 1, no. 2 (1983): 134–57.

————. "Duality and Dialectic." *Lonergan Workshop* 7 (1988): 59–84.

————. "Psychic Conversion and Lonergan's Hermeneutics." In *Lonergan's Hermeneutics: Its Development and Application*, edited by Sean E. McEvenue and Ben F. Meyer, 161–208. Washington, D.C.: The Catholic University of America Press, 1989.

————. *Theology and the Dialectics of History*. Toronto: University of Toronto Press, 1990.

Dunne, Tad. "Lonergan on Social Process and Community." Ph.D. diss., University of St. Michael's, Toronto, 1975.

————. "Faith, Charity and Hope." In *Lonergan Workshop* 5 (1985) 49–70.

————. *Lonergan and Spirituality: Towards a Spiritual Integration*. Chicago: Loyola University Press, 1985.

Fiorenza, Francis Schüssler, and John P. Galvin. *Systematic Theology: Roman Catholic Perspectives*. 2 vols. Minneapolis, Minn.: Augsburg Fortress, 1991.

Flanagan, Joseph. *Quest for Self-Knowledge: An Essay in Lonergan's Philosophy*. Toronto: University of Toronto Press, 1997.

Frankl, Victor. *Man's Search for Meaning*. New York: Washington Square Press, 1985.

Frings, Manfred. *Max Scheler*. Pittsburgh: Duquesne University Press; Luvain: Nauwelaerts, 1965.

Gregson, Vernon, ed. *Desires of the Human Heart*. New York: Paulist Press, 1988.

Haughey, John. "The Primacy of Receivement." In *Business as Calling*, an e-book at http://www.stthomas.edu/cathstudies/cst/publications/businessasacalling.html.

Hefling, Charles. *Why Doctrines?* Cambridge, Mass.: Crowleys, 1984.

————. "Redemption and Intellectual Conversion: Notes on Lonergan's 'Christology Today.'" *Lonergan Workshop* 5 (1985): 219–61.

————. "On Understanding Salvation History." In *Lonergan's Hermeneutics: Its Development and Application*, edited by Sean E. McEvenue and Ben F. Meyer, 221–75. Washington, D.C.: The Catholic University of America Press, 1989.

————. "A Perhaps Permanently Valid Achievement: Lonergan on Christ's Satisfaction." *Method: Journal of Lonergan Studies* (1992): 51–76.

Humphrey, John. *The Law of the Cross in Bernard Lonergan's Redemption Theory*.

Dissertation for STL at Pontifical Gregorian University, Rome, 1976.

Hume, David. *A Treatise of Human Nature.* New York: Oxford University Press, 2000.

Ignatius of Loyola. *Ignatius of Loyola: Spiritual Exercises and Selected Works.* Edited by George E. Ganss. New York: Paulist Press, 1991.

Kant, Immanuel. *Groundwork for the Metaphysics of Morals.* Translated by James W. Ellington. Indianapolis: Hackett, 1993.

Komonchak, Joseph. "Lonergan's Early Essays on the Redemption of History." *Lonergan Workshop* 10 (1990): 159–78.

Lawrence, Frederick. "Expanding Challenge to Authenticity in Insight: Lonergan's Hermeneutics of Facticity (1953–1964)." *Divyadaan* 15, no. 3 (2004): 427–56.

———. "The Horizon of Political Theology." In *Trinification of the World,* 46–70. Toronto: Regis College Press, 1978.

———. "Political Theology and the Longer Cycle of Decline." *Lonergan Workshop* 1 (1981): 223–55.

———. "Transcendence as Interruption: Theology in a Political Mode." In *Transcendence and the Sacred,* 208–25. Notre Dame, Ind.: University of Notre Dame Press (1981).

———. "The Human Good and Christian Conversation." In *Searching for Cultural Foundations,* edited by Philip McShane, 86–112. Lanham, Md.: University Press of America, 1984.

———. "Lonergan, the Integral Postmodern?" *Method: Journal of Lonergan Studies* (Fall 2000): 95–123.

———. "Grace and Friendship." *Gregorianum* 85, no. 4 (2004): 795–820.

———. "The Ethics of Authenticity and the Human Good, in Honour of Michael Vertin, an Authentic Colleague." In *The Importance of Insight: Essays in Honour of Michael Vertin,* edited by Michael Vertin, John J. Liptay, and David S. Liptay, 127–50. Toronto: University of Toronto Press, 2007.

Liddy, Richard M. *Transforming Light: Intellectual Conversion in the Early Lonergan.* Collegeville, Minn.: The Liturgical Press, 1993.

———. *Startling Strangeness: Reading Lonergan's Insight.* Lantham, Md.: University Press of America, 2007.

Lonergan, Bernard. *De Verbo Incarnato.* 3rd edition. Pontifical Gregorian University, 1964. Translated by Charles Hefling as *The Incarnate Word* (unpublished).

———. *Collection: Papers by Bernard J. F. Lonergan, S.J.* Edited by Frederick Crowe. New York: Herder and Herder (1967).

———. *The Way to Nicea.* Philadelphia: Westminster Press, 1976.

———. "Reality, Myth, and Symbol." In *Myth, Symbol, and Reality,* edited by Alan M. Olsen, 31–37. Notre Dame: University of Notre Dame Press (1980).

———. *Curiosity at the Center of One's Life: Statements and Questions of R. Eric*

O'Connor. Edited by J. Martin O'Hara. Montreal: Thomas More Institute, 1984.

———. "Mediation of Christ in Prayer." *Method: Journal of Lonergan Studies* 2, no. 1 (1984): 1–35.

———. "Questionnaire on Philosophy." In *Method: Journal of Lonergan Studies* 2, no. 2 (1984): 1–35.

———. *A Third Collection: Papers by Bernard J. F. Lonergan, S.J.* New York: Paulist Press, 1985.

———. *Insight: A Study of Human Understanding.* Edited by Frederick Crowe and Robert Doran. Toronto: University of Toronto Press, 1992.

———. *Topics in Education.* Toronto: University of Toronto Press, 1993.

———. *Method in Theology.* Toronto: University of Toronto Press, 1994.

———. *Collected Works of Bernard Lonergan.* 25 vols. Toronto: University of Toronto Press, 1990–.

———. *A Second Collection: Papers by Bernard J. F. Lonergan.* Edited by William Ryan and Bernard Tyrrell. Toronto: University of Toronto Press, 1996.

———. *For a New Political Economy.* Edited by Philip McShane. Toronto: University of Toronto Press, 1998.

———. *Macroeconomic Dynamics: An Essay in Circulation Analysis.* Edited by Patrick H. Byrne and Frederick G. Lawrence. Toronto: University of Toronto Press, 1999.

———. *Grace and Freedom: Operative Grace in the Thought of St. Thomas Aquinas.* Vol. 1 of *Collected Works of Bernard Lonergan.* Toronto: University of Toronto Press, 2000.

———. "Appendix: Three Drafts on the Idea of Sacrifice. *Method: Journal of Lonergan Studies* 19, no. 1 (Spring 2001): 29–34.

———. "The Notion of Sacrifice." *Method: Journal of Lonergan Studies* 19, no. 1 (Spring 2001): 3–28.

———. *Philosophical and Theological Papers, 1965–1980.* Edited by Robert C. Croken, Frederick E. Crowe, and Robert M. Doran. Vol. 17 of *Collected Works of Bernard Lonergan.* Toronto: University of Toronto Press, 2004.

———. *Verbum: Word and Idea in Aquinas.* Edited by Robert C. Croken, Frederick E. Crowe, and Robert M. Doran. Vol. 2 of *Collected Works of Bernard Lonergan.* Toronto: University of Toronto Press, 2004.

———. *The Triune God: Systematics.* Edited by R. Doran and H. D. Monsour. Vol. 12 of *Collected Works of Bernard Lonergan.* Toronto: University of Toronto, 2007.

———. *Shorter Papers.* Vol. 20 of *Collected Works of Bernard Lonergan.* Toronto: University of Toronto Press, 2008.

———. *The Triune God: Doctrines.* Edited by Robert Doran, H. D. Monsour, and M. Shields. Vol. 11 of Collected Works of Bernard Lonergan. Toronto: University of Toronto, 2009.

Lowe, William. "Towards a Responsible Contemporary Soteriology." In *Creativity and Method: Essays in Honor of Bernard Lonergan*, edited by Matthew L. Lamb, 213–27. Milwaukee, Wisc.: Marquette University Press, 1981.

———. *The College Student's Introduction to Christology*. Collegeville, Minn.: The Liturgical Press, 1996.

Luther, Martin. *On Christian Liberty*. Translated by W. A. Lambert. Minneapolis, Minn.: Fortress Press, 2003.

Mathews, William A. *Lonergan's Quest: A Study of Desire in the Authoring of Insight*. Toronto: University of Toronto Press, 2005.

McPartland, Thomas J. *Lonergan and the Philosophy of Historical Existence*. Columbia: University of Missouri Press, 2001.

Melchin, Kenneth. *History, Ethics, and Emergent Probability: Ethics, Society and History in the Work of Bernard Lonergan*. Lanham, Md.: University Press of America, 1987.

———. *Living With Other People*. Collegeville, Md. The Liturgical Press, 1998.

Meynell, Hugo. *The Theology of Bernard Lonergan*. Atlanta, Ga.: Scholars Press, 1986.

Miller, Jerome A. *The Way of Suffering: A Geography of Suffering*. Washington, D.C.: Georgetown University Press, 1988.

———. *In the Throe of Wonder*. Albany: State University of New York Press, 1992.

Mitchel, Alan C. "Greet the Friends by Name": New Testament Evidence for the Greco-Roman *Topos* on Friendship." In *Greco-Roman Perspectives on Friendship*, edited by John T. Fitzgerald, 225–62. Atlanta, Ga.: Scholars Press, 1997.

Moore, Sebastian. "For a Soteriology of the Existential Subject." In *Creativity and Method: Essays in Honor of Bernard Lonergan*, edited by Matthew L. Lamb, 229–47. Milwaukee, Wisc.: Marquette University Press, 1981.

Morelli, Mark D. *At the Threshold of the Halfway House: A Study of Bernard Lonergan's Encounter with John Alexander Stewart*. Boston: The Lonergan Institute, 2007.

Muck, Otto. *The Transcendental Method*. New York: Herder and Herder, 1968.

The New Oxford Annotated Bible, NRSV. Edited by Bruce Metzger and Roland Murphy. New York: Oxford University Press, 1994.

Newman, John Henry Cardinal. *An Essay in Aid of a Grammar of Ascent*. Oxford: Clarendon Press, 1992.

Nudas, Alfeo G. *Was Rizal Happy?* Quezon City, Philippines: Cardinal Bea Institute, 1993.

Ormerod, Neil. *Creation, Grace, and Redemption*. Maryknoll, N.Y.: Orbis Press, 2007.

O'Hara, J. Martin, ed. *Curiosity at the Center of One's Life: Statements and questions of R. Eric O'Connor*. Montreal: Thomas More institute, 1984.

Otto, Rudolf. *The Idea of the Holy.* London: Oxford, 1923.

Pascal, Blaise. *Pensées.* Translated by A. J. Krailsheimer. London: Penguin, 1995.

Plato. *Five Dialogues* Translated by G. M. A. Grube. Edited by John Cooper. Indianapolis: Hackett, 2002.

Rahner, Karl. *The Dynamic Element in the Church: Quaestiones disputate 12.* Montreal: Palm, 1964.

Ranieri, John. "Girard, Lonergan, and the Limits of Common Sense." Paper presented at the Second International Lonergan Workshop, Toronto, August 2004.

Ring, Nancy. "Alienation and Reconciliation." In *Creativity and Method: Essays in Honor of Bernard Lonergan,* edited by Matthew L. Lamb, 249–62. Milwaukee, Wisc: Marquette University Press, 1981.

Rixon, Gordon. "Bernard Lonergan's Notion of Vertical Finality in His Early Writings." Ph.D. dissertation, Boston College, 1995.

Rosenberg, Randall S. "Christ's Human Knowledge: A Conversation with Lonergan and Balthasar." *Theological Studies* 71 (December 2011): 817–45.

Ross, W. David. *Aristotle's Prior and Posterior Analytics.* Oxford: Clarendon Press, 1949.

Shute, Michael. *The Origins of Lonergan's Notion of the Dialectic of History.* Lanham, Md.: University Press of America, 1993.

Snell, Bruno. *The Discovery of the Mind.* New York: Harper Torchbook, 1960.

Stebbins, Michael. *The Divine Initiative Grace, World-Order, and Human Freedom in the Early Writings of Bernard Lonergan.* Toronto: University of Toronto Press, 1995.

Tallon, Andrew. "The Role of the Connaturalized Heart in Veritatis Splendor." In *Veritatis Splendor: American Responses,* edited by Michael Allsopp and John O'Keefe, 137–56. Kansas City, Mo.: Sheed and Ward, 1995.

Toynbee, Arnold J. *A Study of History.* Vol. 3, *The Growth of Civilizations.* London: Oxford University Press, 1934.

Von Hildebrand, Dietrich. *Christian Ethics.* New York: David McKay, 1953.

Webb, Eugene. *Philosophers of Consciousness: Polyani, Lonergan, Voegelin, Ricoeur, Girard, Kierkegaard.* Seattle: University of Washington Press, 1998.

Wiley, Tatha. *Original Sin: Origins, Development, Contemporary Meanings.* New York: Paulist Press, 2002.

Wilkins, Jeremy. "Grace and Growth: Aquinas, Lonergan, and the Problematic of Habitual Grace. *Theological Studies* 72, no. 4 (December 2011): 723–49.

———. "Trinity and Divine Economy: The Development of a Tradition in Augustine, Thomas Aquinas, and Lonergan." Essay forthcoming.

Wright, N. T. *The Challenge of Jesus: Rediscovering Who Jesus Was and Is.* Downers Grove, Ill.: IVP Academic, 1999.

Ysaac, Walter L. *The Third World and Bernard Lonergan: A Tribute to a Concerned Thinker.* Manila, Philippines: Lonergan Centre, 1986.

INDEX

Aberration, 130. *See also* bias

Above downwards. *See* way, from above downwards

Absolutely supernatural. *See* supernatural

Abstractions: nature and progress as, 63

Action, in transcendental method, 10, 31–32, 41, 47, 58, 64, 86, 116, 127, 150, 169–75

Aeterni Patris, 4

Affective conversion. *See* conversion

Alienation, 114; as caused by sin, 138–39; as disregard of transcendental precepts, 135. *See also* sin

Already-out-there-now-real, 171–72

Altruism, 120–21

Analogy, xiii, 41, 70, 146, 187; of communication, 192

Anselm of Canterbury, 192n49

Aquino, Corazon, 197

Archaism, 111

Aristotle: xii, xiii, 4–9, 11, 49n13, 53, 59n44, 61n51, 75–76, 85, 109n16; final cause, 65n64; on self-love, 120–21; treatment of pleasure 57n40; on vices, 116; on virtue, 121, 159, 169

Arrupe, Pedro, 80, 162

Art, 35, 48, 66, 134; as carrier of meaning and value, 82, 155, 180–81; as pattern of experience, 117, 180; as realm of meaning, 93n71; artists, 96, 98, 179; God as Artisan, 22

Asceticism, 195

Augustine, St., 75; on original sin, 105–106

Authenticity, xiii, xv, 22, 30, 41, 51n18, 52, 54, 59, 62–72, 79, 84, 90, 97 100, 137,

141, 198; and love 73–80, 159–162, 190; and inauthenticity, 108, 114, 116–118, 149, 158, 162, 166, 170–74, 177–78, 188, 190; Christian, 190

Autonomy, 92, 97, 98, 166, 169–71

Baptism, 105–106, 187, 195

Basic sin. *See* sin

Beatific vision, 70. *See also* fulfillment; heaven; joy; love; mystic; religious conversion; satisfaction; reign of God; union with God

Being-in-love, 77, 151–52, 158

Belief, xiiin6, 52, 56n34, 74, 82–84, 90, 98, 149, 151, 162, 172–73, 175

Berkeley, George, 11

Bernard of Chartres, 23

Bias, 51n18, 101, 110, 116–28; cumulative effects of group bias, 132; dramatic bias, 117–20; dramatic bias as offset by Doran's psychic conversion, 150n4; effect of general bias on self-transcendence, 134; general bias, 125–28, 179; general bias and cosmopolis, 181–82; group bias, 123–25, 179; healed by charity, 160; individual bias, 120–22

Bible, 100n7, 103–104, 146, 184, 195; not always literal, 104; citations or quotations: Acts, 4; Corinthians, 158, 184; Genesis, 103–105; John's gospel, 160, 166, 186, 187, 189, 190, 197; John's letters, 183, 189, 190, 191, 195, 196, 197; Luke, 75; Mark, 75, 160, 193, 195, 196; Matthew, 146, 159, 160, 183, 189, 195-7; Romans, 100, 108, 109, 136, 154, 193. *See also* Gospel; Revelation; Scripture

Body of Christ, xvi, 142, 182–91, 194; as a redemptive community, 183, 184, 189–91, 196, 197; three meanings of, 183

Buber, Martin, 40n41

Calvin, John, 192n49

Categorical imperative, 7

Censor, 117–19; for Freud, 117

Challenge-and-response, 91

Charity, 75, 159–62; as cure for bias, 161; effects of charity, 161; as healing the effects of sin, 160; as love in the context of the body of Christ, 187; as transcending justice, 145–46. *See also* love

Child/children, x, xiin10, xivn10, 74–75, 82, 88, 106 106n6, 117, 148, 179; of God, 155, 187; and wonder, 33, 43–44; childish/childlike, 174, 200

Choice: consequences of, 190, 194; as determining one's character, 169; and effective freedom, 60–61, 90; egotistical choices, 122; minor choices, 149; radical choice, 149; and responsibility, 65–66; in relation to human progress, 26n3; in relation to shorter cycle of decline, 132. *See also* decision; existential

Christ, 121m16, 155–56, 160. *See also* body of Christ; cross; Jesus; Incarnation; Son; Trinity

Christian/Christianity xiii, 19, 85, 94n77, 96, 100, 103, 107, 141, 144, 148, 153, 159 and other religions, 151–52n8

Christology, xii, 199

Church: as the body of Christ, 183, 195; as a graced community, xv; faith and the communal life of, 164; as mediator of charity, 187–88, 191; and the outer word 156–58. *See also* body of Christ

Classical: laws, 11, 14–16, 23, 25, 94; liberalism, 177; science, 21; theological theory, 151; worldview, 5–9, 14; types of grace, 151, 154; view of nature, 7–9, 99. *See also* faculty psychology; determinism; necessity; universality

Classicism, 5–7, 11, 13, 95; need for change within the context of the church,

92n66. *See also* faculty psychology, determinism; necessity; universality

Cognitive theory, xii, 46, 199; and transcendence, 8n20

Common good, 3, 77. *See also* good; human good

Common meaning: as constituting community, 80–87, 189; and the human good, 85

Common sense, 31–43, 82, 105, 168; and bias, 123–28, 130, 161; compared to science, 36; and cosmopolis, 179–181; and decline, 134–37, 140; and egoism, 121–25; general bias of, 125–28, 134; and group bias, 123–25; and individual bias, 121–23; as logical, 35–36; main role, 127; as realm of meaning, 93–96, 154–55, 157, 179–81; and theory, 105n4

Communication, 26, 84 157, 164; and common sense, 35; and cosmopolis, 179; crucifixion as, 192–99; as incarnate carrier of meaning and value, 181; as recurrent scheme, 27. *See also* cross; self-communication

Communion: of saints, vii, 189. *See also* church; Eucharist; saints

Community, xv, 8, 10, 45, 58, 62, 116, 117n3, 123–25, 136–38, 150, 151n5, 156, 164, 166, 169–71, 174; constituted by meaning, 84; human, 10, 26, 32–39, 72–98; redemptive, 176–201. *See also* cosmopolis

Competition, xiii, 16, 39, 59n44, 69, 99, 104, 134, 139, 148, 200

Concrete: xiii; and common sense, 34–38, 126; and conscious intentionality, 47; effects of grace, 142; and human good, 85–86; and insight, 31–32; and intelligence, 26–27; reality, 8–11, 18n45, 26, 62–63, 72, 74n3, 97, 147, 150; situations, xv, 10, 97, 122; transcendental notions as intending, 65; and vertical finality, 22

Conscience, 66–68; driven by notion of transcendent value, 66; and egoism, 123–25; guilty, 68, 118, 123, 125, 139; social, 135–36

Conscious intentionality, 46–73, 77–79, 113–14, 116, 164, 176n1; in cooperative grace, 154; and the eros of the human spirit, 67–68; failure of, 108, 114; four levels of, 46–62; operations of, 46–62, 66–67, 71; standard for correct judgment, 52. *See also* consciousness; decision; experience; intentionality analysis; judgment; operations; transcendental method; understanding

Consciousness, 28, 42, 47–49, 58, 62–67, 93, 101, 117–19, 171–72; aberration of, 111; becoming conscience, 66, 123; contraction of, 108, 111, 119; common sense as a specialization of, 179; in contrast with nature or substance, 28; data of, 29n12, 49, 134; differentiation of, 93–96, 125; extroverted, 171; levels of, 46–47, 66, 79, 118, 123, 137, 163–68; raising one's, 53, 58; religious, 96, 152–58, 164; repressing one's, 119; significance in human living, 62; and transcendental precepts, 64–66; undifferentiated, 96. *See also* decision; differentiation; experience; judgment; realms of meaning; subjectivity; understanding

Consolation, as being in love with God, 153. *See also* love; mystic

Contingency, 6, 13, 14, 22; God's forgiveness as not, 192; laws, 11. *See also* emergent probability; fittingness; interdependence; necessity; probability; statistical laws; universality.

Conversion, xv, 71, 74n4, 89–90, 142, 149–75, 182, 185–89, 198–200; affective, 75n4, 150–51; converted individuals, 173–74; and cosmopolis, 182; and the cross, 193–94; divinizing aspect of religious conversion, 155; fruits of religious conversion, 154–59, 168–69; intellectual, 150, 168, 171–173; moral, 150, 168–171, 173; as ongoing process, 155, 158, 170, 174, 194–96; psychic, 74n4, 150n4; religious, 69n77, 74n4, 150–68, 163, 168–69, 173, 182, 189; as operative grace, 153–54; and trans-

formation of culture, 182. *See also* authenticity; religious word

Cooperating human community, 10, 26, 72–98, 183, 198

Cooperation, 185; with common sense for human progress, 34–35; with God, 113, 144, 189–200; in evil, 112; social, xv, 10, 100, 183, 198–201. *See also* cooperating human community; grace

Copernican revolution in theory, 145

Cosmology, 10–11, 22–23; cosmological context, 10, 45. *See also* emergent probability

Cosmos, 22–23, 25, 45. *See also* creation; environment; universe; world order

Creation, xv, 11–24, 57, 85, 103–105, 108, 143, 148, 162, 170, 173, 189, 199; conflicting accounts of, 103–104; as good, 104; humanity's role in, 26; as virtually unconditioned, 54. *See also* cosmos; environment; universe; world order

Creativity, 58, 81, 98, 183, 199; of genius, 30; of the world process, *see* emergent probability; creative class, 179; creative personalities, 92, 110, 179; creative tension, 41–43, 46, 134

Crime. *See* sin

Critical realism. *See* realism

Cronin, Brian, 56n34

Cross, 183, 189–201; as communication, 192–99; goods created by, 193; Law of the Cross, 191, 196; as satisfaction, 192. *See also* crucifixion; sacrifice

Crowe, Frederick, 7n19, 81n29; on the relation of Christianity to other religions, 151n8

Crucifixion, 156, 189, 192. *See also* cross; sacrifice

Cultural values. *See* values

Culture, x, 3–4, 6, 14, 19, 26, 87, 92–92, 115, 144, 156–58, 166, 169, 178; affected by sin, 111–12; as a carrier of meaning and value, 180; and common sense, 34, 39, 128, 134; cosmopolis and, 178–98; and decline, 106, 134–38; driven by values, 91; and the human good, 87, 91; and realms of meaning, 93–98

Cycles of decline, 112, 130–39, 198–99; shorter, 125, 131–33, 178; longer, 133–138, 165, 178–79; perpetuated by ideology, 165. *See also* bias; decline

Cyclical and cumulative process, 10, 46n4, 86, 160; decline as a, 130

Darwin, 12–13, 16; Darwinian worldview, 16

Data, 29n12, 31, 49–53, 64, 87, 173; of consciousness, 49. *See also* experience

Dawson, Christopher, 8n21

De Finance, Joseph, 61n50

Debt, and crucifixion, 192

Decision, 27, 38–39, 65, 73–74, 77–81, 89–90, 96, 103, 116–19, 124–29, 137, 154, 160–64, 169–70, 177; as level of conscious intentionality, 46–48, 58–62, 66, 176n1; as the primary question of faith, 164; and responsibility, 47, 60, 64–65, 169. *See also* choice; existential

Decline, ix, xv–xvi, 27, 42, 46, 62–63, 71, 97, 99–140, 174, 187–88, 194, 198, 201; biblical roots of, 103–105; as category of Lonergan's theological anthropology, xii, xiv, 190; caused by sin, xv, 25–26, 100, 109, 114, 130; challenge of, 178; and cosmopolis, 178–85; cycles of, 125, 130–38; caused by unauthenticity, 63, 71; healed by charity, 159–62; healed by faith, 165; healed by hope, 166; historical dimensions of, 131–140; psychological aspects of, 116–29; and redemption, 141–50; as a vector, xiv; wheel of decline, 176. *See also* bias; cycles of decline

Deconstruction, 51n18; *See also* hermeneutics of suspicion; indeterminism; relativism; postmodernity

Dependence: between schemes of recurrence, 18–20, 23–24; on belief, 83; on community, 80–93, 98; on environment, 12, 27; on God. *See also* grace; hierarchy; interdependence; intersubjectivity; world order

Descartes, Rene, 11, 95, 96

Desire, 62, 66–67, 71, 77, 88–90, 97, 118,

127, 135, 149; desire to know, 30–33, 36–37, 49, 54, 59, 66–71, 108, 174; desire to understand, 28–30, 33, 49; disinterested, 58–59, 176; as a good, 85, 88; insight as fulfillment of, 29; natural desire, xi, xv, 49, 72, 112–14, 118, 137; natural desire for God, xv, 69–70, 145, 178; natural desire for God in Augustine, 70; perversion of, 100, 121–23, 128, 138–39; spontaneous desire, 38–43, 45, 57–58, 61, 120; transcendental, 160; unrestricted, 73, 76, 78, 181; unrestricted desire to know, 54, 67, 69–70; unrestricted desire for ultimate fulfillment, 69–70. *See also* eros; orientation; wonder

Determinism, 22–23, 106, 108, 165–66; mechanistic, 7n17, 11–13, 23; self-, 90. *See also* classicism

Dialectic, 41–42, 46, 51n18, 109, 121, 136, 167, 174, 185; tripolar dialectic of history, xii, xiv, 142n4, 147

Differentiation, 22, 120; of consciousness, 93–96, 125. *See also* realms of meaning

Disinterested desire to know. *See* desire

Divinization, 142, 155, 193, 199. *See also* grace; conversion, religious

Dogmatic Constitution Concerning the Catholic Faith, 105n5, 191–192

Doran, Robert 74n4, 150n4

Dostoyevski, 13n38

Drifter, 59n45, 112–13, 170

Dynamism, 76–77, 162; of conscious intentionality, 65–67; dynamic community, 73; dynamic process, xiii, 34, 99; dynamic state of being-in-love, 151–55; dynamic world order, xi, xiv, 10–17, 22–23. *See also* being-in-love; conversion; emergent probability; hierarchy

Education: and common sense, 127; in a tradition, 81n29, 82; and social transformation, 180–82, 198

Effective freedom. *See* freedom; liberty

Egoism, xiii, 99, 120–25, 128, 132, 139, 160; for Hobbes, 122; in Aristotle, 120; and obscurantism, 121–22. *See also* bias

Einstein, Albert, 13

Emergent probability, 10–23, 25–26, 43, 45, 58, 91, 97, 108, 127, 137; and common sense, 127; and interdependence of the human good, 91; world of, 47, 162; affected by grace, 144, 147. *See also* contingent; hierarchy; world order

Empirical. *See* conscious intentionality

Empiricism, 51, 172. *See also* materialism; naïve realism

Enlightenment, 7, 95–96; intellectual.

Environment, 12, 16, 26, 28, 42, 104, 108, 115, 127, 138, 171, 179. *See also* cosmos; creation; universe; world order

Epistemology, 46. *See also* cognitive theory; transcendental method

Eros, 174; cultural embodiment of, 178; of the human spirit, 67–69, 135, 153n12, 168, 178; of the mind, 123. *See also* cosmopolis; desire; questions; wonder

Error, 51n18, 72, 84, 126, 136, 182; in self-correcting process of learning, 32, 35

Essential freedom. *See* freedom; liberty; license

Ethics, xii, 46, 92; virtue ethics in Aristotle and Thomas, 169n60

Eucharist, 183, 187

Events, in schemes of recurrence, 15–16

Evidence: and bias, 133; and judgment, 46n4, 47, 52–54, 64, 66; sense evidence, 94

Evil, ix, xiin3, 85n41, 107, 116, 132, 138–39, 141–42, 188; divine solution to, 199; human nature, xv; moral evil, 107–109, 114; organized evils, 112; other religions as not, 151n8; overcoming with good, 160, 162, 166, 188–99; particular evils, 112; physical evil, 107–109; and sin, 99–101, 103–115, 193–99. *See also* crime; negation of value; schemes of recurrence; sin

Existential, 58–61, 65, 69n77, 153n12, 164n60, 169, 173

Experience, xi, xv, 10, 15n39, 28–31, 34, 43, 64–68, 72, 73, 78–84, 86–87, 90, 108, 111, 116–19, 125, 137, 148, 160, 163–64, 193, 200; as a form of know-

ing, 5; as level of conscious intentionality, 46–59, 154, 176n1; of God, 151–53, 155–56; and the real, 171–72

Faculty psychology, 59n44, 95 ; on faith, 165; on hope, 167; on sin, 107

Faith, 3–4, 70, 143n2, 145, 163–66, 168, 183–84, 192, 195; in Aristotle, 145; as form of knowing, 5; as given by grace 145; and conversion, 151n5, 155, 159, 173; as supernatural virtue, xv, 145, 147; in Thomas, 159; as transcending reason 145; as undoing decline, 165. *See also* metaphysics

Fall, the, 100, 103–105, 106n6. *See also* sin

Feelings, 26, 39–41, 50, 52, 61, 70, 78–79, 90, 111, 123–125, 148, 153–55, 158, 162, 180–81, 186; and the censor, 118–19; in *Method* and *Insight*, 56–57, 74n4; an intentional response to value, 56, 76; non-intentional, 56. *See also* resentment

Fellow-feeling, 81, 123. *See also* interdependence; love; prior we

Final End. *See* God of the philosophers and theologians

Finality, 19–22

Finding goodness in all things, 80, 162. *See also* way, from above downwards; faith; love

First Cause. *See* God of the philosophers and theologians

Fittingness, 23, 185, 190, 197, 199

Flanagan, Joseph, 15n41

Flight from understanding, 118, 139, 161–62. *See also* bias; rationalization

Forgiveness, 148, 192. *See also* charity; love; reconciliation; sacrifice

Frankl, Victor, 120n14

Freedom, 26, 46, 58–60, 71, 105, 109, 132, 153, 166, 169–70, 176–77, 193–99; effective, 60–61, 123n22, 131; essential, 60, 112; as a good, 190–91. *See also* liberty

Freud, Sigmund, 13, 117

Friendship, x, 8–9, 75–76, 78, 120–21, 172, 175, 189, 191–92; with God, 161, 189, 196, 199

Fruit, 24, 154–55, 159–60

Fulfillment, xi, 7, 19, 21, 29, 33–34, 38–40, 45–47, 54, 58, 69–70, 76, 78, 89, 114, 117, 147, 152–53, 158–59, 164, 167–68, 174, 178n8, 183. *See also* satisfaction

Fundamental option, 113, 164; against God. *See also* sin

Futurism, 111

Gandhi, Mohandas, 196

General bias. *See* bias

Genesis, book of, 103–105

God, 69, 104–107, 145–46, 156–66, 168, 172, 184–200: of Abraham, Isaac, and Jacob, 157–58, 168; as creator, 104–105; as absolutely supernatural, 143; as transcendent, 46, 152; as unconditioned, 54; missions of, 144, 188; names for God, 69; natural desire for, 178; and redemption, 141–42; and sin, 107–108, 113–14, 193; Son of, 183; of the philosophers and theologians, 158; triune, 155, 189; as willing the good, 107, 166, 190; union with, 183, 190, 194, 197–198. *See also* being in love; grace; Holy Spirit; kingdom of God; love; Son; Trinity

Good life, ix, 8

Good(s), ix, xii, 5, 9n27, 22, 27, 37, 41–42, 57–77, 98, 105–115, 124, 126–27, 132, 138–42, 150, 159–75, 178n8, 195–200: coordinated human operations, 87; creation as, 103–104, 143, 199; God willing the, 107, 190; human good, 73, 84–91, 97, 109, 112, 121, 135, 149, 165, 198; human nature as, xv, 3–24, 192, 198; natural desire for, 41n43, 135, 190, 193–94; overcoming evil with, 188–90, 195; particular, 38–39, 60, 86–89, 93, 109, 112; of order, 86–93, 109–110, 112, 169, 190; of order, in moral conversion, 169; as transcendental notion, 66; personal status, 88; supreme good, 190–91. *See also* common good; nature

Goodness, 14, 22, 61, 68–70, 73, 100–101, 112–13, 118; of religions, 151n8, 153, 181, 189, 194, 199

Gospel, 146, 156, 188, 195. *See also* Bible; revelation; Scripture

Grace, xi–xvi, 63, 77, 100n7, 105–106, 143–57, 167, 185–92, 198, 200; and conversion, 142, 149–50, 153–55, 169; cooperative, 153–57; effects of, 97, 142–47, 155; elevating, 145, 147, 150–55, 186; as gift, 71, 138, 143, 146, 159, 188; healing, 145–47; and nature, 142–47, 189; operative, 153–57; and redemption, 77, 139; as requirement for understanding the cross, 191; sanctifying, 147, 150 151, 154, 155, 186, 189; supernatural aspect of, xiin3, 142–44, 182

Gratia elevans. See grace

Gratia sanans. See grace

Greer, Germaine, 174.

Haughey, John, 159n30

Heart, 75, 77n17, 80, 88, 98, 111, 151n5, 153–54, 156, 158, 160, 168, 181, 187, 197; and mind, xi, 59n44, 116, 178–80, 182, 187, 194, 196, 198–201; reasons of, 78, 163; restless, 70; sacred, 186; of stone/ of flesh, 147, 153–54

Heaven(s), 11, 84, 104, 146, 183–84, 195n58, 196n60. See also beatific vision; God, union with; reign of God

Hefling, Charles, 191n46

Hegel, xiin3, 19n48, 95

Heremeneutics of suspicion, 51n18. *See also* deconstruction; postmodernity; relativism

Heroism of hope, 166–67

Heuristic structure, 15, 46n2

Hierarchy: dynamic, interdependent, 17–20, 45, 58; of essential and excellent goods, 45. *See also* values, scale of

Higher viewpoint, 133, 137, 180

History, x, xii–xvi, 5, 7, 37, 57, 86–88, 105, 111, 116, 128, 131, 180, 188, 198–201; human, 3, 8, 10, 26, 62, 71, 99–101, 138, 144, 193; philosophy of, xiii. *See also* dialectic

Hobbes, Thomas, 11, 39–40, 122

Holy Spirit. 144, 153, 155, 159–60, 168,

Judgment, xv, 27, 30, 39, 51–58, 62, 64, 86–89, 115, 147, 160, 162, 176n1, 177, 193; as distinct from understanding, 50; of fact, 53–56; and faith, 163–66; and intellectual conversion, 171–73; as a level of conscious intentionality, 46–48, 51–62, 65, 68, 72–73, 78–84; and the real, 84–86; and sin, 108, 114, 116–119, 122n18, 138; of value 56–59

Justice, xiii, 76, 115, 118, 138, 139, 160, 168, 193; as transcended by charity, 145–47

Kant, Immanuel, 7, 95, 96
Kemp, Raymond, xi
King, Jr., Martin Luther, 196–97
Kingdom of God, 146, 184, 189–90, 195–96. *See also* reign of God
Knowing, 29–30, 36, 37n34, 46n1, 49, 54, 65, 67–70, 83–84, 96, 116n2, 150, 152, 158, 166, 172, 185, 190; different forms of, 5–6, 105, 126; as distinct from understanding, 50; false views of 171–172; major and minor ways of, 78–79, 151n5; and self-transcendence, 55, 58–59, 173; in Thomas, 145n6. *See also* judgment; knowledge
Knowledge, 10, 29, 31, 36, 44, 50–51, 64–65, 72, 73, 83–85, 93–94, 118, 126–27, 136, 140, 145, 150, 162–64, 168–72, 184–85, 189; common fund of, 34, 83; and experience, 48–49; four levels of knowing, 48–62; of good and evil, 106, 109; human desire for, 69; in relation to love, 78, 163; religious, 46n2; understandings of, 5–6. *See also* judgment; knowing
Known unknown, 65

Langer, Susan, 180
Language, x, 31, 33, 35, 40n41, 48, 50, 69, 82, 98, 108, 165, 177; as a carrier of meaning and value, 155–58, 181; as entry into the world mediated by meaning, 93–94
Last Supper, 183. *See also* Eucharist
Law of the Cross, 191, 196
Lawrence, Frederick, 178n9

Levels of conscious intentionality. *See* conscious intentionality
Lewis, C. S., 148
Liberalism, xiii, 132, 177; modern vs. contemporary, 99
Liberty, 58, 89–90, 112, 171, 176–78, 195; and conversion, 149; horizontal, 60–61, 149; liberation of, 147; license, 177; vertical, 60–61, 79, 149, 170. *See also* freedom
License. *See* liberty
Liddy, Richard, xivn12, 8n21
Lincoln, Abraham, 201
Locke, John, 11
Logic, 94–95, 181; and common sense, 35–36; as distinct from reason, 46n4, 64; logical animal, 8
Love, xi, xv, 6, 18–19, 26n3, 38, 40, 61–62, 64n57, 73–81, 85, 87, 96–98, 117n3, 145–46, 150–75, 181, 183–201; as concrete or abstract, xiiin10; and decline, 100–101, 113–15, 118, 135–39; falling in love, 46; fivefold, in the mystical body of Christ, 185–88; self-love, 120–21; self-sacrificial, 160, 189–91, 196–97, 201; unrestricted, xi, xv, 68–70, 72, 114, 150–53, 161, 163, 191, 193, 196–97, 199. *See also* authenticity; being-in-love; charity; conversion, religious; sacrifice; way, from above downwards
Luther, Martin, 100n7

Machiavelli, Niccolo, 13n38
Marx, Karl, xiin3, 92, 95
Marxism, xiii, 136, 177
Materialism, 7, 51, 84. *See also* empiricism; naïve realism
Mathews, William, xiiin4, xivn12, 8n21
Mechanistic determinism. *See* determinism
Metaphysics, xii, xvi, 8; 46, 48, 150, 158, 168, 198–99
Method. *See* transcendental method
Mimesis, 92
Missions, Trinitarian. *See* Trinity
Modern, 4, 7, 13–14, 26, 39, 50, 59n44, 83, 99, 122, 129, 144, 269, 172, 198

Modernity, 3, 13, 99
Moral conversion. *See* conversion
Moral evil. *See* evil
Moral self-transcendence. *See* self-transcendence
Mystery, 33, 153, 164–65, 185, 191; *Mysterium fascinans et tremendum*, 153
Mystic(s), 36, 96; mystical pattern of experience, 117n5
Mystical body of Christ. *See* body of Christ
Mysticism. *See* love; mystic; religious conversion; word, inner; way, from above downwards

Naïve realism. *See* realism
Natural desire. *See* desire
Natural evil. *See* evil
Nature, xii, xiv–xvi, 5–14, 50–51, 62–63, 71, 76n12, 77, 81, 84, 97, 99–100, 106, 138–39, 143–47, 164–65, 167–68, 185, 192, 198, 200; human, 28, 33, 39, 49, 62, 67–68, 112, 114, 118, 122, 135, 138, 160, 183–86; goodness of, xiin3, xv, 103; as fallen, 142; as orientated toward goodness, xv, 19–21, 40, 41n42, 67, 101, 106, 118, 136 145, 181, 19
Necessity, 6–8, 11–17, 22–23, 35, 48, 51n18, 59–60, 96–97, 106, 121, 137, 166. *See also* classical laws; classicism; contingency; fittingness; universality
Negation of value. *See* evil
Newton, Isaac, xiii–xiv, 7
Nicomachean Ethics, 6, 8–9, 57n40, 61n51, 75n6, 76n9, 85n43, 116n2, 120–21, 159
Nietzsche, Friedrich, 13n38, 95, 125n27
Nihil amatum nisi praecognitum, 78, 163. *See also* love
Nihilism, 14, 136
Nonviolence, xiii, 196–97
Not numerous center, 177

Obscurantism, 121–22. *See also* bias; decline
Operation(s), xv–xvi, 10–11, 16, 18–19, 73, 85–89, 100, 112, 143–44, 198; of conscious intentionality, 30, 46–62, 66–67,

71, 73, 78, 83, 117, 147, 167, 185; human, 85–87. *See also* conscious intentionality; invariant structure of the human good; transcendental method
Orientation, xv, 19–21, 40, 67, 72, 89–90, 106, 136, 149–50, 165, 168, 171, 180–81; and bias, 116; toward the good by nature, xv, 19–21, 40, 41n42, 67, 101, 106, 118, 136 145, 181, 190
Original sin. *See* sin
Otto, Rudolf, 153
Outer word. *See* word
Oversight, 71, 130–32

Parmenides, 94
Participation, 85; in the Body of Christ, 184, 191, 193, 198; in God, 70, 161, 168, 183; in redemption, 3, 191, 195–96, 200; in world mediated by meaning, 82
Particular goods, 38, 60, 86–91, 93, 109, 112, 169
Pascal, Blaise, 78, 100, 163
Pattern of experience, dramatic, 117
Paul, St., 4, 109, 159–60. *See also* Bible; Corinthians; Romans
Peace, x, xiii, 78, 114, 182–84, 194; in relation to conscience, 66, 71, 151
Pelagius, 105–106
Penance, 187. *See also* repentance
Personal sin. *See* sin
Philip the Chancellor, 145
Philosophy, x–xiv 4, 13, 29, 37, 51, 69, 95, 105, 111, 134, 180; of history, xiii–xiv
Physical evil. *See* evil
Pilgrim(s), 158, 166, 188
Plato, xiin3, 12, 13n38, 41, 76, 84, 126
Pleasure/pain machine, 61
Pope Leo XIII, 4, 7
Postmodernity, 13–14, 169n60, 198. *See also* deconstruction; hermeneutics of suspicion; indeterminism; relativism
Practicality, 15, 27, 31–37, 41, 44, 59, 63–64, 67, 94–96, 179–180; and bias, 37, 125–128, 130, 133–37, 139–140, 179; and faith, 164; and hope, 167; and love with God, 80, 162; and nonviolence, 196

Restriction of further questions, 36–37. *See also* common sense; obscurantism

Revelation, divine, xi, 3–4, 151n8, 156n24. *See also* Bible; self-communication

Sacrament(s), 105–106, 183, 187, 195

Sacramentality, 3, 22, 192. *See also* nature

Sacrifice, 30; self-sacrifice, 160, 187, 189–192, 195–98, 200. *See also* cross; crucifixion; love

Saint(s), vii, 9, 82, 96, 100n8, 158

Sanctifying grace. *See* grace

Sartre, Jean-Paul, 13n28

Satisfaction, 32, 38, 43, 66. 71–72, 82, 86, 120, 138, 167, 178, 195. *See also* crucifixion; fulfillment and the cross; sacrifice; values

Scale of values. *See* values, scale of

Scheler, Max, 125n27

Schemes of recurrence, 16–19, 21–23, 27, 45, 86, 112–13, 117, 124, 127, 130, 143–44, 199

Scholasticism, 19, 22, 85, 163; decadent, 7

Science, x–xi, 4–7, 12–13, 21–23, 31–41, 48, 63, 83, 94–95, 99, 104–105, 128, 134, 137, 144, 168, 172, 180, 198; Aristotle's definition of, 5- 6

Scotosis, 119, 128, 161

Scripture, 3, 52, 77, 94, 105, 108, 154, 159, 161. *See also* Bible; gospel; revelation

Self-communication, divine, 3, 71, 156n24, 188; through crucifixion, 192–99. *See also* grace; revelation; word

Self-correcting process of learning, 10, 25, 32–34, 38–39, 47, 67, 91

Self-love, 120–21

Self-transcendence, 10, 25, 46, 55–78, 85, 90, 97, 108, 137, 149–52, 158, 160, 162, 168, 173, 181, 198; affective, 73–78, 85; in faculty psychology, 59n44; as fulfilled by religious conversion, 152; intellectual, 55–56, 59, 64, 73, 78, 85, 107; moral, 55–59, 61–62, 64, 73–75, 78, 85, 107; religious, 55n32, 75n4; and sin, 108, 114, 134–35. *See also* conscious intentionality; conversion

Sensitivity, 39–43, 56, 74n4, 76–77, 82, 121, 167. *See also* intersubjectivity

Sexism, x, 106–107

Shortsightedness. *See* bias

Shute, Michael, xiin4, 142n4

Sin, xii–xvi, 25, 63, 84n36, 86, 97, 99–101, 103–118, 120, 123, 128, 130–32, 135–40, 146–47, 161–62, 165–67, 169, 172, 175, 177–78, 182, 185, 187–88, 190–200; as alienation, 114; and authenticity, 71; crime, 109–110; in faculty psychology, 107; as failure of conscious intentionality, 114; God permitting, 107, 190; original sin, 100, 103, 105–106, 110; personal sin, 106–110, 114, 135; as social process, 109–111. *See also* evil

Snell, Bruno, 94

Social surd. *See* surd

Socrates, 94, 126

Son, 144, 168, 183–89, 191–92, 98. *See also* Christ; Jesus; God; Incarnation; Trinity

Spirit, human, 67–71, 98, 111, 135–36, 168, 178; Holy. *See* Holy Spirit

Spiritual/ity, 22, 96, 108, 136, 138, 163n43

Spontaneous intersubjectivity. *See* intersubjectivity

Statistical laws, 14–16, 21, 23, 25

Struggle: class, xii; and creativity, 92; Darwinian, 16n42; moral, 170; and transcendence, xi. *See also* suffering

Subject, 9, 28–29, 52, 62, 64–65, 69n77, 73, 75, 92, 125, 128, 153n12, 158, 164, 169, 171–72

Subjectivity, 28, 51n18, 52, 62

Sublation, 7n20, 17–19, 45–47, 144, 159, 173

Substance, human as, 9, 28

Suffering, ix, 108–109, 112, 119–20, 125, 138, 140, 160, 179, 183–85, 190–91, 194–97. *See also* struggle

Supernatural, 143–47, 199; absolutely, 142–44, 150, 163, 182, 198; fulfillment, 70; gifts, xv, 77; knowledge, 145; relatively, 143, vector in human history, 138; 143. *See also* virtues

Superstructure, 95

Surd, 135–36, 160, 178
Symbols, as carriers of meaning and
value, 30, 82n30, 93, 100n8, 150n4,
155, 178, 180–81

Tallon, Andrew, 154n15
Teresa of Avila, 196
Theological anthropology, xii–xvi, 5–9,
183, 193, 198–99
Theology, 7, 29, 48n10, 69–70, 77n16,
94, 105, 107, 116, 143, 150–51, 183n24,
164n44, 200; of grace, 143–44, 150;
scholastic, 19; task of, 3–5; as theoretical discipline, 105
Theory: and common sense, 105; as a
realm of meaning, 94–96, 157, 179–81.
See also cognitive theory; realms of
meaning; science
Thomas Aquinas, St., 3–7, 19n50, 49n13,
53n22, 59n44, 69n79, 70, 75, 77n17,
107n8, 116n2, 169n60; on God's existence and faith, 145n6; on theological
virtues, 159–61
Tillich, Paul 153
Totalitarianism, 113, 136–37, 139
Toynbee, Arnold, 8n21, 91–92, 179
Transcendence, v, xi, 7–10, 16–18, 32,
47, 73, 153; as a realm of meaning,
96, 157–58, 179, 181. See also self-
transcendence
Transcendent viewpoint, 137–38
Transcendental method, xi, 10, 26, 45–73,
78, 91, 109n16, 114, 137, 141, 150, 165,
176n1; and conversion, 150; reason,
46n4; on sin, 107; virtually unconditioned, 54, 57. See also conscious
intentionality; decision; experience;
judgment; operations; understanding
Transcendental notions, 65–71, 77, 85, 118
Transcendental operations, 71–72, 185
Transcendental precepts, 62–65, 71, 100,
114, 137
Trinity, 155, 163, 183–91, 198; missions
(inner and outer word), 144, 188. See
also God; word
Tripolar dialectic. See dialectic
Truth: and the transcendental notions,

65–71, 77, 85, 118; in resistance to sin,
165–66

Ultimate questions. See questions
Unauthenticity, 63, 71, 158, 190
Unconditioned. See God
Understanding, ix, xiv–xv, 8, 14–15,
25–30, 80–81, 86–87, 154, 160, 163,
168, 174, 181, 184–85; Christ's work,
191–93; and conscious intentionality,
46–59, 63–73, 84, 147, 171–73, 176n2;
and love, 78–80; and sin, 110, 114,
116–20, 122, 129, 139; unrestricted act
of, 168. See also insight; transcendental method
Unintelligibility, 135; of sin, 107
Union with God. See God, union with
Universality, 6, 13–14, 35, 100n6. See also
classical laws; classicism; contingency; fittingness; necessity; relativism
Universe, 3, 8, 17, 22–23, 43, 62, 77, 108,
113, 141–42, 144, 161–2, 165–66, 168.
See also cosmos; creation; environment; world order
Unmoved mover. See God
Unrestricted desire. See desire; love

Value(s), 5, 26, 40, 42, 57, 59–61, 64, 67–
69, 74n4, 75–81, 83, 86–100, 109, 112,
116, 123, 125, 134–40, 149, 155–57, 161,
163–66, 168, 170–73, 178–82, 189, 194,
199; approaches to, 88–90; as level of
human good, 86–93, 109; negation of,
112–13; and satisfaction, 61, 90, 134,
149, 170–1; scale of, 58, 90, 149, 170;
as a transcendental notion, 66–67, 69.
See also feelings; good; judgment
Vectors, 71, 99, 138–39, 163, 198; Newtonian, xiv
Vertical. See finality; liberty
Virtually unconditioned, 54–55, 57, 59,
152
Virtue(s), 9, 61n51, 75–76, 111, 121, 136,
147, 165; in Aquinas, 59n44, 159,
169n60; in Aristotle, 9n27, 59n44,
121, 159, 169n60; in Paul, 159; supernatural, xv, 147, 159, 184. See also

authenticity; charity; faith; hope; integrity

Von Hildebrand, Dietrich, 56n35

Way, from above downwards, 78–84, 116n3, 163, 164n43, 168, 198. *See also* from below upwards; love; mystic; religious conversion; self-correcting process of learning; transcendental method

Wheel, of decline, 176; of progress, 176–77

Withdrawal: from inauthenticity, 71, 158; for the sake of return, 92, 180

Wonder, 32–33, 43–44, 49, 53–55, 59, 64, 71, 174, 178, 181. *See also* desire; eros; questions

Word: inner and outer, 188–89, 195, 198; prior, 156; religious, 154–59

World mediated by meaning, 80–84, 93–96, 156, 172, 181

World of immediacy, 82, 181

World order, 6, 10–23, 91, 97, 108, 127, 144, 161, 190, 199. *See also* emergent probability

CPSIA information can be obtained
at www.ICGtesting.com
Printed in the USA
FFHW020740271118
49652500-54015FF